# Rolling Thunder

## THE SPIRIT OF KAREKARE

### BOB HARVEY

**EXISLE**

ISBN 0-908988-17-6

Exisle Publishing Limited

PO Box 8077, Auckland 1035, New Zealand.

Ph: 64-9-520 1162. Fax: 64-9-520 1146.

email: mail@exisle.co.nz

www.exisle.co.nz

Design and cover by Heather Ball.

Typeset in Adobe Garamond, Bank Gothic and Helvetica.

Artwork by Streamline Creative Ltd, Auckland.

Map by Raymond Salisbury.

Printed by Tien Wah Press (Pte) Ltd, Singapore.

This book is published with the generous assistance of the Auckland Regional Council
and Watercare Services Ltd. We gratefully acknowledge their support and their
continued commitment to the preservation of the Waitakere Ranges
and coastline and the regional parks of Auckland.

This book is respectfully dedicated to

Hariata Arapo Ewe (née Taua)

Hariata is the hereditary rangatira of Te Kawerau ā Maki tribe of Waitakere, Kaipara and other areas. Hariata descends from the senior line of Te Kawerau ā Maki. From the time of Te Au o Te Whenua, the ancestor whose *mana* presided over the whole of the Waitakeres, the title of head of the iwi has been maintained by the first born. Hariata was born in 1920 and has dedicated her life to working for her people. As a child, she lived between Te Henga at the northern end of the Waitakeres, and Pukaki Pa on the shores of the Manukau Harbour. In those days, their transport was horse and buggy. Hariata attended Mangere Central Primary and Kurahuna Maori Girls School in Onehunga. As a child, she was prepared for her responsibilities by her mother's sister Kahupaake Rongonui (see Vol. 3 of the *Dictionary of New Zealand Biography* 1996). Hariata would accompany Kahupaake and other rangatira, sometimes including Princess Te Puea, to hui and to Maori Land Court sittings, often acting as their scribe.

# ACKNOWLEDGEMENTS

THE IDEA for this book was born in the early 1970s as a dream shared with the photographer Phil Morton, whose work graces these pages. Phil spent weekends and holidays throughout the 1970s and 80s at Karekare. He began taking photographs and I drafted some text. Our lives took different paths but we never gave up the idea. I am delighted that his work is featured here alongside other fine work by supporting photographers including my friends Ted Scott, Ian Anderson, Jocelyn Carlin, CPL (Craig Levers), Marti Friedlander, Miles Hargest, Martin Hill, Chris Hoult, Glen Jowett, Arne Loot, Antoine Millett, Rachel Mooney, Becky Nunes, Kirsty Russell, Bernard Schofield, Jenny Scown, Julien Senamaud and Jane Ussher, and the known and unknown photographers whose historic black and white work adds another dimension to the illustrations. I thank them all.

I feel privileged that so many people have given me access to their lives and family histories. Everyone I talked to was adamant that Karekare is a place of special

(PREVIOUS PAGE AND FOLLOWING) *WESTERN WALK*, A SERIES OF FIVE PAINTINGS BY PETER SIDDELL, 1990. EACH PAINTING OIL ON CANVAS; 505x1220MM. KAREKARE; ZION RIDGE; PARARAHA; OHAKA; WHATIPU.

significance. The sentiment was almost invariably the same: their belief was that the beach and its surrounding area should be nurtured and carefully managed. Here, nature should be allowed to call the tune.

I would like to thank Te Kawerau ā Maki for their unfailing support in allowing their history at Karekare to be told by me in this form. With special thanks and deep appreciation to Hariata Arapo Ewe (Auntie Sally) and Te Warena Taua for making the pathway accessible.

I would also like to acknowledge Graeme Murdoch, Historian of the Auckland Regional Council, for his research on the iwi of the ranges.

Margaret Clarke grew up and was schooled for a while at Karekare. Over the years she has provided a wealth of information on the years and times of Brownes' Boarding House. She has been exceedingly helpful and supportive in providing contacts and talking about her memories of Karekare.

At 87, Wally Badham has his own storehouse of memories which he kindly allowed me to access. We started exploring this in 1985 and his unpublished manuscript 'The Iron Bound Coast' is an invaluable resource. Wally's nephew John Eden Badham also generously assisted with the family history as it related to Karekare.

Family histories have been told through the generosity of descendants, whom I gratefully acknowledge for their interest in this book and for allowing me to reproduce images from their treasured albums: Daphne Coleman (Shaw family), Lindsay Darrow (the Odlin family), Howard Foote (Foote collection), Alan Gribble and his sister Robyn Agnew (the Gribble family), Warren and Caroline Grove (Lone Kauri Farm history and Trevor Lloyd etching); Gwen Harvey (the Murdoch collection), Jeff Murray and his mother Cherie (the Liddle years), Karel, Kubi and Alex Witten-Hannah (family and school),

Thanks to Con Anderson and James Northcote-Bade from the West Auckland Historical Society for use of photographs and contacts. Susan Smith for permission

to reproduce the paintings of Ellen La Trobe. June Fletcher for the Farley years. Lisa Fallow for her invaluable help in sourcing historical family photographs. Dorothy and Roy Butler for their Winchelsea House photographs. Kerry Littlewood for the Walker years. The Casey family for the Manukau Cycling Club history.

Ian Rockel, Historian at Waitakere City Libraries, has over many years assisted with information and rare photographs, as did Dave Pearson, Gordon Maitland, Pastor Bruce Patrick of the Baptist Tabernacle and the late Peter Buffett. John Gow, Bill Haigh, Robert Newton, Bruce Mai and Pat Murphy for paintings, etchings, glass slides, medals and maps. Anna Dunsheath for road maps, postcards and memorabilia. Peter and Sophie Webb for sourcing Blomfield paintings and Lloyd etchings. Dennis and Shirley May for the Whatipu glass slide collection. David Beatson of Air New Zealand, Dale Spencer of The Media Edge and Chris Burke for videos, advertising and film material. Author Euan McQueen and Graham Stewart for his father W.W. Stewart's bush tram painting. A special thank you to Bernard McDonald, Derek Henderson and the team at *Pavement* magazine and to Capitol Records for the artwork from the Crowded House CD *Together Alone*.

Don Selwyn of He Taonga films for the *Kahu & Maia* and *Feathers of Peace* stills by John Miller, Robin Scholes of Communicado for the *Greenstone* stills by Chris Bayley, and Grant Matthews for the *Piano* stills.

I would like to record my thanks to the staff of the Auckland City Art Gallery, the Alexander Turnbull Library, the National Library, the Auckland City Library, the Auckland Museum, and the archive researchers at the Edinburgh, London, Nova Scotia and the Sydney Central Library for their helpful assistance. Staff of Purewa Cemetary and Waikaraka Cemetery for their help in locating graves.

Artists who kindly consented to allow their work to be reproduced include Gretchen Albrecht, Don Binney, Dean Buchanan, Justin Burroughs, Ruth Cole, John Edgar, Martin Hill, Paul Jackson, Virginia King, John Madden, Richard

McWhannell, Barry Miller, Tony Ogle, Stanley Palmer, Ann Robinson, Peter Siddell and Justin Summerton.

The doyen of New Zealand poets, Karekare aficionado Allen Curnow, generously allowed *Lone Kauri Road* to be included and I thank him for such a pleasure. My thanks too, to longtime Lone Kauri Road weekender C.K. Stead for his poem *A Coastline and Two Facts*. Poet Sam Sampson has also kindly allowed me to use his Karekare work to enhance this book.

Tui Eaves and Barney White helped with the surfing terms. Mark Thomson loaned his invaluable collection of surfing memorabilia and allowed me to select some items for reproduction in the book. Karel and Shalema Witten-Hannah and Shawn Wanden advised on the tracks and walks. To my Surf Club friends of 45 seasons, a family that continues to renew itself, I will always be grateful for the good times you have given me and for what I have learned from you about life.

Thanks to Susie Blowers who typed my manuscript, and Craig Levers, Stuart Hammond, Tony Reid and Graeme Leitch for editing assistance. Diane Dorrans Saeks and Warwick Roger kindly read the text and both offered invaluable advice.

I would like to acknowledge my two mentors whose lives are linked with my own Karekare years. Geoff Fairburn, who taught me to question the accepted order of things, and Des Dubbelt, who opened my eyes and mind to the possibilities of the written word.

To Barbara and our children Celia, Fraser, Rupert, Tessa and Claris, who share my obsession with this beach, thank you for always being there for me.

And finally to the people of Karekare, a small coastal community I feel so privileged to belong to, thank you for supporting me in the making of this book.

*Karekare, 2001*

# CONTENTS

*Standing on the beach at sunset,
reflecting on eternal contradictions...*

*Wedded to this place,
as a sailor to the sea...*

# Approaching
# Karekare

*...Karekare, the centre of my world.*

# KINDRED SPIRITS

(ABOVE) "...ISHMAEL ADVENTURING ON THAT GREAT 'WATERY PART OF THE WORLD.'" (OPPOSITE) PARA-TAHI ISLAND GUARDS THE SOUTH END OF KAREKARE BEACH.

THIS BOOK is about a beach and a passion. The beach is Karekare, Aotearoa New Zealand, and the passion is mine. It's my love affair with a special place, whose sense of mystery continually unfolds for me. It draws to itself individuals who seek to look beyond the surface features of a landscape in the here and now.

Until the release of Jane Campion's film *The Piano* in 1993, Karekare was probably better known internationally, at least to the surfing fraternity, than it was to New Zealanders outside of Auckland. This beach has since become a backdrop for other feature films, as well as for television series and commercials, fashion shoots and musical works, so images of Karekare have become familiar to almost everyone in this country, even if they have yet to visit. *Condé Nast* named Karekare one of the 10 great beaches of the world, as if you could rank such places.

When New Zealanders think about their favourite places, the odds are that most would nominate a beach. Beaches seem to encapsulate our golden moments, especially our rites of passage, and are often the setting for some of our happiest memories. Every beach in Aotearoa contains a long and rich history. Yet if we think we know these places well, our own knowledge and experience can be compared with the size of a grain of sand in relation to the entire beach.

So, a whole book about a single beach? Why not? The stories and histories and people and landscapes described here are a mere scratching on the sands of time of this place we know as Karekare. Above all, I wanted to write a book about the people who came to this dramatic setting, where the western edge of the Auckland isthmus ends in a series of cliffs and steep-sided, narrow valleys. Karekare attracts a certain kind of individual – artists, writers and craftspeople for sure, but if you could identify a single characteristic of the people who call this place home, it would be originality. Not for them a one-room city apartment where your domestic arrangements are not too far removed from those of battery hens.

In the spring of 1961, I was given an old brass bed that had rested under a barn in Oratia for 50 years. Peeling enamel and pearl shell inlays suggested a more

(ABOVE) **SNAPSHOTS FROM AUTHOR'S BACK PAGES.**

romantic past. I brought it out to Karekare and placed it on the beach in a nikau shelter close to the high tide mark, near the dunes, and I lay on that bed on those summer nights watching the stars slide slowly overhead, absorbed by the surf flashing in the moonlight and the sonic boom of the waves echoing around the hills.

On the high tides, the phosphorescent surf would swirl under the legs and the bed would dip precariously. I didn't give a damn. Each night as the sun set, I would read Melville's classic *Moby Dick* and think of myself as Ishmael adventuring on that great "watery part of the world". If it rained – which it seldom did in those days, at least in my memory – I would retreat to the Surf Club, a small, one-room building under the mantle of the Watchman rock. There was no electric power at the beach. We made do with old Coleman kerosene lamps that, when lit and pumped vigorously, burned with a bright intensity, hissing away with an acrid smell that filled the room. The lamps had a tendency to send jets of flame to the ceiling, before blasting to eternity the gauze filament, returning my world to darkness.

I wanted to be a poet, or a writer like Herman Melville. His narrative influenced my thoughts and shaped my life. I scribbled furiously into the night, my own flame burning with a fire that lit up my soul. Ghostly echoes off the cliffs, choruses from the underworld, joined the discordant thrum of the surf, at times making the hair on the back of my neck stand on end. Finally, towards morning, dream-filled sleep would come to me on that brass bed at Karekare.

As summer turned to autumn, a waterspout rose slowly but menacingly out of the Manukau Bar, moving down the coast as dawn broke. I took it as an omen. Later that day, when I walked along the beach towards the Pararaha Valley where the stream fans out into the Tasman surf, I came upon the decaying carcass of a large blue whale. These signs told me that it was now time for me to cast *Moby Dick* aside and move on. So I caught the Wednesday bus up the dusty unsealed road to Auckland and got myself a job at the *New Zealand Herald*, selling classified advertising in what is now called Waitakere City. I called on the vineyards and orchardists to help them market their apples, pears and terrible wine. As the wheel turned, the orchards would improve and so would the wine, and one day in the distant future I would become mayor of the vineyards, the ranges and the beach.

Advertising became my life's work, or at least it did for the next 30 years, while I founded and then developed a major agency. The work was good. I got to wear a suit, drive expensive cars and make some money, yet I always allowed myself the freedom to return to Karekare. It wasn't poetry, but it was a job. Every Friday evening I would go out there, intending to stay the weekend, living in the Surf Club and being in a surf patrol, watching for helpless and hopeless swimmers, who at any moment could be swept toward their deaths. Some were lost in the waves but many were saved. Witnessing the ebb and flow of life on this beach captured me emotionally. I found I was woven into the invisible web of this place.

Karekare has absorbed a huge part of my life. I always want to be there, to savour its sensations of smell, sound and texture; its freshness bites into me. I am never bored there. At moments when my life is on a down, I will go out and sleep with a blanket in the sand dunes or walk at night under the rolling canopy of stars, and wake refreshed, to return to whatever challenge awaits me. Because Karekare is so much a part of me now, I never want to leave, and if there were so much as a choice of another life, I would simply choose this one, at this place.

This story is my journey, and that of others, to this place. I believe all of us need such a destination, a beach in time where our world finishes and the great ocean begins. Something happens to sharpen your sense of self on a beach, when you are alone with the elements.

This book is also about the past, a time when other people came to this spot and probably felt the same way. They journeyed here for their own reasons; some fled here to hide in the hills, to find peace in the valleys and later, others came from far shores to fell the forest, to clear the land, to farm and to fish. They stayed on for other reasons, raising families and eventually realising they never wanted to leave.

Places like Karekare allow you to believe that there are other worlds and kindred spirits moving through aeons of time and cheering you on. Suspend disbelief: come with me and walk, drift like the sand moving over the dunes and believe that these places do exist, not only in our imaginations but in our senses. My destiny has been to discover for myself this place called Karekare. I'd like to share it with you.

# UNEXPECTED GIFTS

KAREKARE BEACH is not for those who prefer safe landscapes. There's an over-powering sense of place here. The moment you arrive, you know this is a special place. You either like it instantly, or you're out of here fast, never to return. Stay, and your senses start picking up a myriad of sensations.

At the carpark, you can hear the booming surf. It comes at you like rolling thunder, echoing off the valley walls and pushing into your ears. The great, gnarled face of the Watchman keens the sound and sends it hurling towards you as you jump the creek before heading towards the beach. Do this at night, and the beach amplifies pure sound, picking up bass chords from the collision of waves against Paratahi Island and sampling the shoreline surf action on the way in.

The Karekare sound is different from that of any beach I know. The surf does not 'crash' here; it rolls the sound waves and pops them onto the Zion Hill cliffs.

I've slept on this beach at night and never felt cold, drifting off for 20 minutes and waking up feeling like I've slept for days. When I was young, I had a favourite Surf Club blanket which I wore like a toga, and a moth-eaten sleeping bag, singed by the embers of beach bonfires. I still have a passion for fire on this beach.

In the 1960s, some Californians brought peyote to the coast. Through the dazzling haze, a profound experience of sound and night unfolded. In some strange way, it opened me up to another direction in my life; it made me believe that I had something to offer, and it gave me an acute sense of life and death. The experience wedded me to this place as a sailor to the sea.

One afternoon during my first year with the Surf Club, I was swept out to sea. In those distant days, surf rescue was not assured. No matter how hard I tried, I could not regain the beach. Strangely, there was no sense of panic. I felt a sense of safety in the midst of a growing awareness that my life might soon end. In this state of mind, I saved myself. I knew then that this was the doorway to my life. When I reached the sand, I felt a great mystery had unravelled. When I come to a crisis in my life, I will swim out to sea and return later with a sharper view of things.

This beach has changed as I have. When I first arrived, it was flat and strewn with logs, and always shimmering in summer. In the 1950s, we patrolled sitting on the gear shed roof. On the high tide, the waves would swirl around the rock and for a time it would be an island. As I got older, the sand dunes grew, engulfing both the rock and the shed. The sea retreated as the sand piled up.

There's no easy access to the beach now; you have to work for it. The direct route involves crossing the creek by the carpark, where you can take a flying leap, step over strategically-placed stones, or wade right in, washing the city from your feet. The water follows you down to the sea. Black ironsand attaches to your shoes and skin; you can't come to this place without taking some of it away with you.

There's a supercharged energy here from the surf, that's borne on the wind, and invigorates those who come here. It's a place where nature's moods change constantly; you can feel it all around you.

When I was a young lifeguard, I was in awe of the older club members. Men like Doug Monds, a top field events athlete. We used to spend all afternoon hurling the shot and throwing the javelin across the sands. I was taught to surf and understand the waves by Fred Neale, and learned to body-surf better than most, developing my own style of riding down a wave, even mastering a 360 turn. I thought I could be as good as any world champ. I coulda been a contender, or so it seemed to me then. When you're young and strong and confident, anything seems possible.

Understanding waves means everything to the surfer. When I'm approaching

(ABOVE AND BELOW) **KAREKARE DEMANDS YOUR ENERGY AND INVOLVEMENT. THERE'S NO EASY ROUTE TO THE BEACH HERE – DRIVING ENDS AT THE CAR-PARK.**

Karekare, I search for signals, looking for the way the waves are falling and forming, and where the rips and currents are today. My eyes map the sea, and my senses measure the direction and strength of even the slightest breeze. Why is it that people believe that the surf is moving? It isn't. It's only you, and trillions of rotating molecules of water energised from a thousand miles at sea, stirred by the wind and urged by the moon. The ocean attacks the shore at Karekare, its fury finally unleashed and spent on shallows of black sand.

If you stand on this beach at sunset, the red orb appears to sink into the surf. This is because we have been told as children that the sun goes down, and yet for centuries we have known that the earth rises. At Karekare, these two eternal contradictions never cease to amaze me. Up on the Ahu Ahu cliffs where I confront a huge horizon stretching from the Kaipara to Taranaki, I allow myself to believe that I can see the curvature of the earth, with Karekare at the centre of my world.

When each of our children was born, the weekend following their arrival became a family ritual, as we took the newborn out to Karekare and introduced him or her to the sea. As they were all born in winter, we baptised them with a generous sprinkling of chilly, foaming surf, amid much squealing. The boys have developed into excellent lifeguards and the girls are fine swimmers. The beach has always been an extension of home to all five children.

Walk south along the beach now. Behind the dunes is the secret, sensual side of Karekare. This is the place where lovers go. Here in a quiet glade you can be alone. The small stream from Zion Hill cools nikau palms and pohutukawa. The cliffs are human-scale here; it feels as though there are hidden caverns or entrances to another world waiting to be revealed, if only you knew which rock to lean against.

Beyond the headland, the wide, wild spaces of the coastline to the Manukau Heads open out before you. People become specks against the horizon along these reaches. Karekare and its stretch of coast offers up to me unexpected gifts. One day a seahorse skeleton, another, a lost doll. A lone leopard seal in winter, perhaps sick or old. And the tragic surprise of a beached whale. Here, I never feel like a visitor; I know that I belong to this place and time. Everything seems to fit here in my life, and probably it's the same for other Karekare people.

While writing this book, I have been astonished at the connections through personal experience of so many people of like mind and soul. We have unknowingly become another coastal tribe. In some respects, Karekare is a shared experience for this kin; it is also intensely personal. These days, I may have quietened down a little, but I refuse to snuff the spark this place has given me. It burns within me, part of the universe of fiery stars and comets.

I'm planning a beach symphony, a nighttime cacophony of gongs, sheets of corrugated iron and brass, driftwood sticks and kerosene tins, barking dogs and the rhythm of the surf, a mystic orchestra beating with a passion for life.

This place demands homage and participation. Karekare is not for the passive.

(TOP AND ABOVE) THE COAST OFFERS UP SURPRISES, LIKE A STRANDED WHALE OR A LOST TREASURE IN THE SAND. THE SPERM WHALE BEACHED AT A WHALE GRAVEYARD NEAR MOUTH OF PARARAHA STREAM. (OPPOSITE) THE WORLD TURNING, OVER ZION HILL.

## COAST OF PARADISE

I CAN RECALL vividly my first glimpse of Karekare on a crisp autumn morning in 1956 when I stopped on my way to Piha, astride my massive black Raleigh school bike. With my two mates and army canvas rucksacks on our backs, we wanted to get as far away from home as we could. I'd read about the west coast and wanted to discover it for myself, riding out from the heart of Auckland City where I grew up.

At the top of the Cutting high above Karekare, you look down to the south rocks and Paratahi Island. Beyond, the coast curves out towards the turbulent Manukau bar. Known by Māori as Te Kupenga o Taramainuku, or Taramainuku's Net, the bar is forever working, as dangerous as ever. It covers a treacherous shoaling sand mass that was once a peninsula. It is said that from the beginning of the first Maori arrivals, fishing settlements were built here on this land known as Paorae. All of this was washed away by the beginning of the 19th century.

From this magnificent vantage point, the sea seems to reach halfway into the sky. It is usually a dense, rich blue that almost makes your eyes ache, to stare at it for long. I have never seen this depth of blue anywhere else in my travels.

Long ago, long before the Dutchman navigator Abel Tasman passed along this coast, the sea was known as Nga Tai Whakatu a Kupe – the uprising seas of Kupe. The term comes from a karakia, a ritual chant made by Kupe to throw off a dangerous pursuer. Clearly it worked. The seas rose up and raged and have never ceased to do just that. This beach also gave its name to Waikarekere, which means boisterous or troubled waters, as do the shorter names Kakare, or Karekare. The name has also been simply translated as 'Surf'.

Although we had intended going on that day to Piha, where the road ends, some-how I found myself cycling down a precipitous incline, standing on my brakes, not knowing where this was leading, nor how I would ever get back up that hill. As a city boy whose beach experience was limited to the tame waters of the Waitemata Harbour where we'd picnic and make sandcastles, this was my first experience of the

New Zealand bush. It was exhilarating and terrifying at the same time. Exhausted from the long ride, I knew I'd never get home by sundown. I'd gone as far west as you can go on this margin of the land, and found myself confronted with my future. I was 15.

I had chosen a special day: the Surf Club was celebrating its 21st birthday on a grassy paddock under the pohutukawa opposite the carpark. It seemed to be a grand party and it had been going all weekend. I got talking to one of the club members who asked me if I could swim, and when I answered yes, he invited me to join. Fred Neale has remained a friend ever since. I thought it was such a good idea, and the beach looked so different from what I had known. The surf on that day was huge and thunderous, and the idea of being part of a group of men who actually ventured into these dangerous seas really thrilled me. They were fit, and for the conservative 1950s, they flouted convention with their public drinking and general hilarity, relaxing under the trees with an admiring throng of beautiful, tanned young women. On a makeshift table, gleaming trophies, prizes and medals suggested heroic deeds and added to the glamour in my eyes. In an instant, I realised that this was where I wanted to be.

From the age of five, I had learned to swim under the guidance of my mother at

(ABOVE) **FRANK WRIGHT, *THE MILL VALLEY, KARARE BAY;* 1899, OIL ON CANVAS. AUCKLAND ART GALLERY TOI O TAMAKI, PRESENTED ON BEHALF OF MR & MRS GEORGE HELEN BOYD, 1899. (OPPOSITE) RUTH COLE, *FROM THE DUNES, KAREKARE;* 1999, OIL ON LINEN ON BOARD; 250x800MM. COURTESY THE ARTIST.**

W. Menzies Gibb

(ABOVE) **FRANK WRIGHT,** *UNION BAY*; 1898; OIL ON CANVAS; 595x1060MM; SIGNED & DATED. COURTESY PAT MURPHY. (OPPOSITE) **WILLIAM MENZIES GIBB,** *MOUNTAINS AND STREAM, KAREKARE.* OIL ON CANVAS. AUCKLAND ART GALLERY TOI O TAMAKI, PRESENTED BY AUCKLAND SOCIETY OF ARTS, 1913.

the Tepid Baths. I'd grown up in a very sheltered, half-Catholic family, and my life had been centred around the Gully area of Newton and Symonds Street. My adventure world revolved around movie matinées at the Ponsonby and Karanga-hape Road cinemas. The Church played a central role in my childhood, and during those formative years I saw myself as a future priest, saving souls.

Signing up with the Karekare Surf Club took me into an alternative order, a tribal hierarchy with its own rituals, conventions and bonds. They had a different way of saving souls.

The west coast beaches in those days seemed a hundred miles from the dreary, treeless inner city. I noticed the enormous amount of booze that was being consumed at the club's birthday celebrations. In fact, it was 100 gallons, which was considerable even for that time, and donated by Dominion Breweries, the club's generous sponsors. The 10-gallon kegs had been transported to the coast on the club truck and were cooling off in the creek.

As the afternoon wore on, the trophies were presented while blue smoke from barbecued sausages and steak drifted through the ferns. When darkness fell, I was offered a ride home on the club truck, but not before the driver was woken up from his stupor. With our bikes rattling on the back, we got home to a terrible reception at the unheard-off hour, for a schoolboy, of 9 pm. But my life was changed from that day. I had glimpsed a new adult world that I wanted to be a part of. I had drunk my first beer and listened to the way men talk. It was my own rite of passage. Any remaining ambition for the priesthood vanished with the smoke on that memorable autumn afternoon.

I was told that the club truck left the Central Post Office every Sunday morning at 8 o'clock and that anyone who wanted a lift to the beach simply advised where they would be on the way west. The next Sunday at the appointed time, I turned up in white shorts and my school shirt, and a bag with togs and towel. I was a young man going west to learn to be a lifeguard.

A Coastline and Two Facts

...there we went four of us
walking down the coast where
the surf boom floats over the dunes

and up to those high-flying cliffs
a place of wild reaches and
eye illusions...

C.K. Stead

(LEFT) **STANLEY PALMER**, *ABOVE KAREKARE*, 1970-71,
ETCHING AND LITHOGRAPH ON PAPER. COURTESY
THE ARTIST.

# THE
# LIVING PAST

# THE
# BLOODSTAINED LAND

(ABOVE) TE KAWERAU A MAKI, WHOSE PRESENCE IN THE WAITAKERE RANGES EXTENDS BACK SEVERAL CENTURIES, IS RECOGNISED AS TANGATA WHENUA OF THE AREA. SENTINEL WARRIORS PERFORM A KARAKIA ON THE SITE OF AN ANCIENT WATCHTOWER.

AT ARATAKI Visitor Centre in the Waitakere Ranges in March 2000, Te Kawerau ā Maki presented their case for grievances against the Crown to the Waitangi Tribunal. They had been waiting over 150 years to be heard and to have their grief and anguish assuaged. I was proud to be one of the speakers in their favour, to ask that their voice be listened to and their mana restored.

My journey was made so much easier by the arrival of the rangatira, Te Warena Taua, and through him the tribal lineage opened and flowed around me. Te Warena is the custodian of the rich and ancient tribal history. Between the years 1992 and 2001, I have been able to support Te Warena and Auntie Hariata and the whanaunga (relatives), as they journeyed towards that moment when the Crown, in the form of the Waitangi Tribunal, called them forth to present their evidence. It was a moment of great significance, a time for healing, understanding and re-establishing a rightful inheritance.

These people, I believe, had suffered and grieved for so long, as much for their loss of land and life, as for the distortion of their history. When I first went to Karekare in the mid-1950s, around the campfires on the beach, when local Māori were talked about they were regarded as a vanquished, vanished people, lost in time and place. Their history was largely unknown, mostly ignored, and viewed from an uninformed perspective. To my Surf Club mates and the local bach owners and weekenders, they had simply disappeared. The legend of a lost tribe holds a certain fascination for Pakeha, but Karekare's story contained an extra twist to it.

According to the tale, the local tribe was besieged and wiped out entirely – except for one survivor who, escaping from the bloodbath, climbed down the northern

(BELOW) **TE KAWERAU PUTAANGA (SENTRY) AWAITS ENEMY ON A CLIFF-TOP OVERLOOKING UNION BAY,. WHILE HIS WARRIOR COMPANION WARNS THE IWI OF APPROACHING DANGER WITH AID OF A TRITON SHELL.**

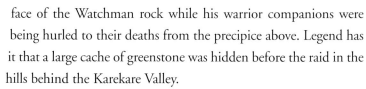face of the Watchman rock while his warrior companions were being hurled to their deaths from the precipice above. Legend has it that a large cache of greenstone was hidden before the raid in the hills behind the Karekare Valley.

Like many popular 'true' stories, this one was a mix of fact and fiction. In the oral and written histories of the European settlers in the valley, the same fiction is woven of a sole survivor who returns to Karekare and brings with him his tale of a lost treasure. At Karekare, the century-long treasure hunt was a frequent topic of conversation. In the 19th century, Māori artifacts were greatly prized. Burial caves were raided, greenstone heirlooms, whalebone pendants and taiaha were stolen for museums and private collections.

From time to time this account was repeated in print. The nearest anyone got to uncovering the hoard was when a flax kete of fishing hooks and sinkers was found on a ledge at the entrance of the Pararaha. Discovered by Ted Browne and the illustrator Trevor Lloyd in 1933, the remains of the basket held a fine collection of pre-European fishing gear crafted at least 200 years ago. It is now kept in the Auckland War Memorial Museum. What it reveals is superb craftsmanship, with an extraordinary attention to detail. Descendants of Te Kawerau ā Maki, appearing before the Tribunal, were wearing glorious taonga with the same distinctive style of carving. You can see examples of their traditional carving at the Arataki Visitor Centre and at the War Memorial in New Lynn. A massive carved gateway to the City of Waitakere is planned for the Te Atatu Interchange.

Media articles perpetuated a distorted version of Te Kawerau history. Often when Karekare was mentioned in any historical context, by such authors as George Graham, S. Percy Smith or in the late 1800s by George Grey's translator, the prolific author John White, it served to reinforce belief in the demise of Te Kawerau. In the 20th century, esteemed local historian the late Jack Diamond was also incorrect in his retelling of their history with his popular *Once The Wilderness*. Jack, whom I admired enormously for his energy and commitment in collecting glass plate photographs and stories of the west coast bush mill settlements, was in unfamiliar territory. Other writers were unable to access tribal records or talk with the people themselves, many of who had moved away from tribal areas like Te Henga and Piha.

It took me 40 years to learn something of the truth of the history of this so-called lost tribe of Te Kawerau ā Maki and their bond with Karekare. It is a journey that for me was both humbling and deeply emotional. When I became the Mayor of Waitakere City in 1992, I was able to open the door for their return. In a small way, I wanted to use the powers of my office to facilitate a process that would enable a reconciliation to take place, so that the healing might begin. This was simpler than I had expected. First, it required an acknowledgement of their rightful place as mana whenua; second, they were welcomed back to Karekare with a formal ceremony. This was done when the local community wished to place a rahui on the

(ABOVE) **THIS PRICELESS FLAX KETE CONTAINING ANCIENT MAORI FISH-HOOKS WAS DISCOVERED IN A CAVE AT KAREKARE IN 1933.** (BELOW) **HARIATA ARAPO EWE AT KAREKARE, 2000.**

shellfish, which had been decimated by new migrants to Auckland gathering them.

The dawn ceremony on 13 June 1993 was the significant beginning of the tribe's return to their ancestral papakainga and marae. From this pivotal moment their true story has unfolded, their own telling of their whakapapa or genealogy, their oral history and their spiritual guardianship of the land is revealed.

To understand the history of Te Kawerau ā Maki, it is necessary to go back to the 17th century and to the Kawhia Harbour. It was from this place on the west coast that their eponymous ancestor Maki decided to lead his people north. He travelled with his whanau, his two wives, Rotu and Paretutanganui, and their children Manuhiri, Ngawhetu and Maraeariki. He was accompanied by his younger brother Mataahu and 300 followers. It must have been quite a group. Maki takes his rightful place today as one of the carved figures of the Pouwhenua on the Arataki Visitor Centre.

Before Te Kawerau ā Maki came to the Waitakere Ranges, the hills and valleys and streams were inhabited by a spirit people, the Turehu, who possessed super-human attributes. The Turehu are regarded by Te Kawerau and other Maori as their earliest human ancestors in Aotearoa. Their legendary founding chief was Tiriwa. His name still echoes in chants and on marae today. The original name for the Waitakere Ranges was Te Wao o Nui a Tiriwa – the great forest of Tiriwa.

They were not alone for long. Voyagers from distant islands of Polynesia migrated to this land in small groups and some made the Waitakeres their home. From the 13th century, the people known as Ngaoho occupied the Karekare area for three centuries. They would have been either killed or assimilated into the new wave of migrants and it is this new group who will carry our story further.

On arrival in the Auckland region, Te Kawerau ā Maki first settled at Rarotonga, the volcanic cone that Aucklanders now know as Mt Smart. By the late 17th century, we find them moving towards the coast, first settling at Te Henga (Bethells Beach) and, as their tribe grows, moving north towards the Kaipara and spreading small pa sites along the coast. The food is abundant, with seafood obtained from the headlands jutting into the sea. Fishing from the rock ledges would always be hazardous. Large rolling combers swept many to their deaths, as still happens today. Māori legends abound in tragic loss from drowning.

They would not have used waka regularly on this coast, although occasionally even right up to the 1920s waka were seen here in good weather. Seaweed, such as bull kelp, would have been used as a food source, dried and stored for winter or for times of seige. The kelp was also used to store things like eel, which was plentiful in the wetlands, streams and rivers of the Waitakeres. Birds and their eggs were gathered, as was the meat of seals or the occasional whale after a stranding. The bones of these animals were turned into ornaments and weapons. The tangata whenua named headlands, rocks, streams, beaches and other geographic features. They consolidated through inter-tribal warfare and marriage as far south as the Huia Bay. The tribal confederation acknowledged their place and their mana and

(ABOVE) **TE WARENA TAUA (RIGHT) LEADS HIS PEOPLE IN A KARAKIA (PRAYER) ON THE OCCASION OF THE PLACING OF A RAHUI ON THE GATHERING OF SHELL-FISH AT KAREKARE, JULY 1993. ALSO SHOWN, FROM LEFT, ARE TUMAMAO EWE, MIHI TE RINA WETERE AND TANGIARO TAUA.**

(ABOVE) **KAWERAU A MAKI HEI TIKI, KNOWN AS TE MANU WHAKATAU, CARVED FROM WHALEBONE AND SECURED WITH FLAX FIBRE CORD.** (MIDDLE) **KAWERAU A MAKI PATU PARAOA (WHALEBONE CLUB) NAMED TE HAU PATU RAU, THE STRIKING OF A HUNDRED WINDS.** (LOWER) **ADZES FASHIONED FROM POUNAMU WERE HIGHLY PRIZED POSSESSIONS IN MAORI SOCIETY.** (OPPOSITE) **THE WARRIOR WEARS A KAHU TOI (WAR CAPE), AND A KAWERAU A MAKI HEI TIKI NAMED TE KANOHI ORA.**

for the most part, they lived peacefully, trading mainly with their Tainui relatives on the south side of the great Manukau Harbour.

At Karekare they established their main pa site on the Watchman, which was called Te Kaka Whakaara. They were led by Kowhatukiteuru, one of Te Kawerau ā Maki's great chiefs, who was a designer and builder of formidable fortified pa. Defence of the pa was of critical importance and a means of escape was often incorporated into the design. Below this pa, in what would later become the garden of the Murdoch homestead, was established Te Marae o Mana – the courtyard of Mana. This was the area for living, debate and all things domestic. Around this courtyard revolved the life of the whole community, for Māori discussed everything communally. As the tribe flourished, the Karekare Valley was planted in extensive gardens. The fertile soil of the valley floor produced renowned kumara harvests.

In those days, peace was hard to come by and at Karekare horrific and bloody battles were fought, probably by relatively small numbers of warriors, with slaughter or slavery inevitable. Fleeing, hiding and exile in the interior of the ranges was almost an annual occurrence. In the Maori calendar, all things were given a rightful place. Tattooing, cultivation and war all had their season. They knew the season for war: it fitted in between planting and harvesting.

After each battle, the pa would have been repaired or rebuilt with more reinforcing. A better warning system would be adopted, on both south and north headlands at the Pararaha and above Mercer Bay. The survival of the tribe depended on the effectiveness of its early warning system. No one was spared in the path of the taua or moving war party.

The protocols of the time required that during major conflicts, warriors would be drawn from the regional tribal pool. These warriors, seeking utu, would be recruited for the resolving of insult and retribution. Many would not return. Vengeance and its aftermath is part of Māori history and it was during a period of relative peace that a group of Ngati Whatua, accompanied by the warrior chief Kawharu and some of his visitors, made a visit to the South Kaipara. Just south of Woodhill, they found an elderly Te Kawerau ā Maki rangatira, Tawhiakiterangi. While his relatives were harvesting toheroa, this welcoming old man was set upon and mortally wounded. His death would herald several decades of fighting.

During these times Te Kawerau ā Maki travelled widely, venturing as far as the Kaipara and over the southwestern ranges to their gardens and gathering fields, but they always returned to their home marae for the season of war. A greater war was soon to come, this time from the Far North. The arrival of whalers and traders would introduce to Māori a weapon that would completely change the balance of inter-tribal power. The musket would enable smaller tribes to compete with larger, but Te Kawerau ā Maki, like most of the tribes of Aotearoa, were initially isolated from such trade and contact.

(ABOVE) **TE KAWERAU A MAKI SENTINEL WARRIORS ABOVE TAHORO (UNION BAY).**

Nga Pakanga a Te Pu – the Musket Wars – would eventually be recognised as the bloodiest in the country's history. It has been estimated that up to 200,000 lives were lost between 1820 and 1845. This period of our history has been largely ignored while other agendas have been addressed. Māori war parties armed with muskets retaliated against major transgressions and minor insults, bringing a European scale of warfare to almost every part of New Zealand. The art of war as practised by Māori had been based on a ritualised culture of hand-to-hand combat. Bravery in battle was paramount. The musket changed all that. Unable to resist this invisible assailant, those without weapons were slaughtered and the survivors deprived of ancestral rights and mana.

Although the Karekare dwellers had committed no direct hara or wrongdoing against the tribes of the North, that did not spare them from destruction. The Ngapuhi empire sought vengeance on all who they considered had transgressed or insulted them; often century-old grievances would now be avenged. Death might come from a relative's indiscretion, an unguarded comment or a broken tapu. It seemed any excuse would now warrant forceful retaliation: the death machine of the musket, the feasting and the capture of slaves changed the face of pre-settler Maori society into a warlord culture. Aotearoa was drenched in blood.

In early 1825 a large northern taua fought a major battle against the combined iwi of the Kaipara and the Mahurangi areas. Following a major victory by Ngapuhi at Mangawhai and then near Kaiwaka, the main force, led by Hongi Hika, travelled down the eastern coastline while another group headed inland to attack the main settlements on the southern Kaipara and south towards the Waitakere Ranges. This taua, headed by Te Kahakaha, a renowned warrior of a subtribe of Ngapuhi, easily defeated the traditionally armed defenders at various places in southern Kaipara, Muriwai and Te Henga. Slaughtering everyone in their path, they headed south to Karekare where the defenders of Te Kaka Whakaara awaited the onslaught.

The taua would have come over from Piha, past the sacred hill of Hikurangi above Mercer Bay to besiege the pa. It is recorded that many Ngapuhi were killed by rocks thrown from the pa. But the Kawerau warriors had no defence against the musket. Without 'throwing weapons', they were systematically slaughtered.

High above the beach, in the large palisaded cave known as Wharengarahi, the women, children and elders awaited the attack. The palisade platform was lowered as a defence. Armed with rocks but little else, they watched the brutality in the pa below, and then their turn came. The attack was launched from above. Manuka brush is said to have been stacked below the palisade and lit, as well as being lowered from the rock face above the cave. They were simply smoked and burnt out. They had no option but to leap from the platform or face death in the cave. Parents, knowing the fate of their children, would have killed them. Any remaining survivors would have soon been put to death, although strong men and beautiful women were taken as slaves. That was the way the war party operated.

This was the most tragic episode in Karekare history. Known simply as Te Tarukenga, or the slaughter, it resulted in the decimation of the Karekare people and only today are they recovering numerically. Several hundred dead lay scattered throughout the pa; the last defenders, driven over the palisade and up to the summit of the Watchman, would either have leapt or been thrown to their deaths 50m below on the sand. Many of the younger women and children were captured as slaves, and taken back north by the Ngapuhi. Karekare would be known by a new name, Mauaharanui, or the place of the great wrongdoing, and to Te Kawerau ā Maki it would take on a special tragic significance down through the generations.

What seems to be true is that the warning signals, coming down the coast, would have allowed a small number of the tribe chosen by rank and birth to be hidden in the huge caves at Mercer Bay. They survived the carnage in the great vaulted cavern known as Te Anaareare, and after waiting for the taua to move out of the district, they crossed the isthmus to Waikumete – the old name for Little Muddy Creek on the Manukau – and into the Waikato, where they would live in exile for a decade.

At Karekare the sole survivor legend emerged – the lone warrior who, escaping the muskets, seeking refuge in a crevasse high on the seaward cliff and under cover

(ABOVE) ON THE LOOKOUT FOR ENEMY, SIGNALLING THE TROOPS WITH A TEWHA TEWHA. (BELOW) THIS TRADITIONAL COMB IS MADE FROM DRIFTWOOD. COMBS LIKE THESE WERE MAINLY USED BY CHIEFS TO KEEP THEIR HAIR DRAWN UP IN A KNOT ON THE TOP OF THE HEAD. SUCH A HAIRSTYLE WAS KNOWN AS A TIKI TIKI.

of darkness, descended to the beach and joined the survivors in the Mercer Bay cave. His remarkable escape became known by the Kawerau as Te Heketarere, or the descent by rope. The large cave at Mercer Bay was also honoured with the name Te Ana Wai Ora Iti, the sea cave of the survivors.

The ancient home, the pa sites, the headland fortification, had become 'Karekare Kainga Whakarere', the abandoned settlement.

The aftermath of the Ngapuhi raid on Karekare has two interesting sequels. The first involves a woman of high rank, captured by Ngapuhi. She was Waiopare, and was indeed the sister of the sole survivor of the pa battle, Heketarere. Waiopare had a distinguished lineage of both Tainui and Kawerau. She would later marry a rangatira who had taken part in the raid on the Karekare pa. He was Tuhirangi, the elder brother of Hone Heke, famous in New Zealand history for his flagstaff assaults. Their union would create one of the North's largest and most esteemed family lines. Their grandson Hone Heke II would become a Member of Parliament and their granddaughter would return to the Waitakere Ranges and the Kawerau sites of bloodshed. Hongi Hika and Te Kahakaha would continue fighting with their muskets throughout the North Island. Te Kahakaha would die an old man, fighting alongside Hone Heke now, during Heke's rebellion against the British rule in 1845. The blood and the aftermath of feasting on the victims had seeped into the earth itself.

Te Kawerau were introduced to Christianity between 1836 and 1839 by the visiting missionaries of the Church Missionary Society from the Anglican Mission, based across the harbour in Orua Bay, Awhitu, on the southern shores of the Manukau. One of my wife's ancestors, the Wesleyan missionary Reverend Buller, probably was the man who did the final conversion, on 7 December 1845. It is recorded that the Reverend Buller visited the pa site Hikurangi at Piha, so it would be more than likely that Karekare Maori were also present when he baptised the rangatira Te Tuiau and gave him the Christian name John. They were to remain Wesleyans until they converted to the Pai Marire faith after the Land Wars of the 1860s, and they hold to that faith today.

By the late 1840s Te Kawerau would meet the first of the entrepreneurs, who were travelling through the ranges seeking cutting rights from Māori. Disconsolate, Kawerau were easy targets for unscrupulous negotiators, and it would be fair to say that the Crown was also a major player in the purchase of the ranges, which were then divided into five large blocks. The land was mostly sold by non-resident rangatira, often with no direct tie to the land.

Hikurangi, the name given to the Karekare block, was sold between 1853 and 1854. A small group of Te Kawerau retained kainga or small settlements at Piha and at Te Waiti on the Waitakere River at Te Henga. Karekare would not see the return of Te Kawerau ā Maki until the late 20th century. Heketarere, who had survived the

Karekare massacre, died at Piha. Following his death, the remainder of the tribe, now few in number, settled with their relatives at Te Henga.

Karekare, however, was never lost to the Te Kawerau mind or psyche. The people continued to visit Karekare to honour the dead, acknowledge their past and mourn for their lost ancestors and heritage. This small group inherited the role of kaitiake, or guardians of tribal mana from their tupuna who had passed on. This sacred knowledge, precious to Māori, involves the obligation to visit, nurture and to watch, often secretly or unobtrusively, over their ancient lands.

At the beginning of the 21st century, Te Kawerau ā Maki, regarding themselves as the rightful owners of so much of the ranges, retained formal ownership of only Taitomo Island at Piha and a small piece of land between Muriwai and Te Henga. After 160 years of European settlement, they still felt disadvantaged. Their tribal structure was broken and they were physically separated from their ancestral land, with no marae to call their own, nowhere to bury their dead; they were scattered and disempowered.

*    *    *    *

I am walking on Karekare Beach with Te Warena Taua, whose leadership has brought Te Kawerau ā Maki to prominence and partnerships that have spearheaded the renaissance of this iwi. We have been friends and have developed a strong bond since the rahui ceremony on this beach in 1993. He tells me that they are bringing their young people to this beach, in the company of their old people, naming the

(ABOVE) **TE KAWERAU A MAKI IWI, LOCAL RESIDENTS AND SUPPORTERS AT THE RAHUI, KAREKARE, 1993.**
(OPPOSITE) **THE CARVED CENTREPIECE OF ARATAKI VISITOR CENTRE FEATURES, FROM TOP, TIRIWA (TO WAO NUI A TIRIWA); HAPE (PRIEST OF THE TAINUI CANOE); HOTUROA; MAKI (TE KAWERAU A MAKI); TE AU O TE WHENUA, ALSO KNOWN AS TE HAWITI (GREAT-GRANDSON OF MAKI).**

(ABOVE) **TE UTIKA TE AROHA EWE CARRIES THE NAME OF HIS KAWERAU ANCESTOR WHO DIED IN 1910 AT TE HENGA.** (BELOW) **THIS CARVED TRITON SHELL IS KNOWN AS PU MOANA. SHELLS LIKE THESE WERE USED FOR WARNING AND SIGNALLING THE APPROACH OF ENEMY. MANY OF THESE TAONGA (TREASURES) WOULD HAVE BEEN CARRIED FROM POLYNESIAN HOMELANDS.** (OPPOSITE) **ESTEEMED RANGATIRA, NEGOTIATOR AND CUSTODIAN OF TE KAWERAU A MAKI'S WHAKAPAPA AND MANA, TE WARENA TAUA, AT UNION BAY.**

headlands, retelling the legends and unveiling the reality of what they need to do to work together, to claim their place in the sun. "We have to do this, to give them a sense of who they are and what is their ancestral heritage and legacy. So much has happened here; it has a terrible tragic past for us. Although time heals, this land will always remain tapu to us, and sacred."

When I point out to him that the battles here were Māori against Māori, he agrees, but adds with a grin: "Without the guns and the arrival of you lot, we would still be here, living in paradise."

He says that he first came out here when he was very young. "Auntie Hariata was here last week. She remembers Karekare as a big farm, with few trees.

"We are often out here," he adds, "and we always will come back. Sometimes if there is a drowning we are called. We don't make a big fuss, but we feel involved again. Sometimes if there are bones found, we are asked to come and retrieve the remains."

I ask Te Warena what it is that tells him this place is special.

"You remember the morning of the rahui, with that lone hawk flying around the Watchman? We believe it is a spirit ancestor."

"Have you ever seen a hawk up there before?" I ask.

"No, I have not. That tells me a lot about this place. And about you too."

Ka tangi te titi
Ka tangi te kaha
ka tangi hoki ahau
Tihei mauri ora!

Ki nga tini mate kua huri atu ki tua o te arai, ka mihia.
Ka nui te aroha ki a koutou kua wehe atu nei i a matou
No reira e nga mate, haere, haere, haere atu ra.
Apiti hono, tatai hono.
Te hunga wairua ki te hunga wairua
Apiti hono, tatai hono.
Tatou te hunga ora ki a tatou.

*The muttonbird calls, the kaka calls, I also call and lament.*
*Tihei mauri ora! (I breathe and I am alive.)*

*The many dead who have passed beyond the vale are remembered*
*and greeted. Great is our love for you who have been taken from us.*
*Therefore I bid farewell to the dead, farewell, farewell. Join together*
*the lines of humanity. Those of the spirit world to themselves, us*
*the Living to the Living.*

# THE COMING OF
# THE SETTLERS

(ABOVE RIGHT) **A HUNTING PARTY SHOWS OFF A BOUNTEOUS CATCH, WHATIPU WETLAND.** (TOP) **TABLET CARVED FROM KAURI GUM, KAREKARE MILL.** (OPPOSITE TOP LEFT) **COACHMAN GILL WOOD DROVE HORSE AND WAGON TEAM TO THE COAST.** (OPP. TOP RIGHT) **CRINOLINE LIFTER RAISED LADIES' HEMS TO AVOID MUD WHEN WALKING.** (OPP. MIDDLE) **'WILD' CATTLE BEAST WERE CONSIDERED FAIR GAME FOR EARLY VISITORS.** (OPP. LOWER) **NEAR WEST COAST (NOW PIHA) ROAD STRAIGHT, NIHOTUPU, 1889.** (OPP. BACKGROUND) **MAP OF KARANGAHAPE PARISH 1850, WHICH INCLUDED KAREKARE AND EXTENDED SOUTH TO WHATIPU AND EAST TO LAINGHOLM.**

FOR 60 YEARS after the destruction of the Karekare pa, the Karekare Valley lay fallow. The clay road to Piha was rarely travelled, and the Kawerau people now lived in small groups moving between Huia, Piha, Te Henga and Muriwai. These were desolate years following the Musket Wars: Karekare was a tapu place. For a decade from 1826 to 1836, the valley was virtually deserted. It was as if the land itself needed to heal. The westerly wind howled, shifting the sand from one side of the beach to the other, covering the bones.

The first record of European settlement at Karekare is from 1852. A Crown purchase document records the sale of land in 1853, "encompassing West by the Ocean at Hikurangi by the tree at the edge of the cliff of the Ahu". Seventeen Maori chiefs affixed their names or mark to this document. It was a large purchase and it

(ABOVE) **THE WEST COAST ROAD, ON THE WAY TO MANDER'S MILL.** (BELOW) **SILAS SHAW LONGED FOR THE WILDERNESS LIFE WITH HIS BROTHER JOHN, FINDING WHAT THEY WERE LOOKING FOR AT A SMALL BAY KNOWN TO PAKEHA AS 'KARKARE'.** (OPPOSITE TOP) **THE SHAW BROTHERS' COTTAGE AT KAREKARE, 1878.** (OPP. MIDDLE) **SHAW FAMILY DRESSED IN THEIR FINEST FOR JOURNEY TO ORATIA.** (OPP. LOWER) **ANOTHER SHAW FAMILY OCCASION.** (OPP. BACKGROUND) **FARLEY'S FURNITURE SALE NOTICE, 1882, PRIOR TO THEIR EMIGRATING TO NEW ZEALAND.**

was later challenged as invalid. It comprised 12,000 acres, stretching across West Auckland from the Tasman Sea to the Waitemata Harbour.

At this time, the Auckland Provincial Government maintained a free grant system of lands for settlement. Under this scheme, any settler or immigrant who could afford to get to New Zealand was entitled to a grant of 40 acres, with a further 40 acres for his wife and 20 for each member of the family between the ages of two and 18 years old. The grants of around £16 were extraordinarily generous. The only stipulation was that the recipient had to live as a resident somewhere in the Province of Auckland for a period of four years out of five after arrival. Many landowners in the Waitakere Ranges never moved out to their land, often sold it unseen, and in many instances they abandoned it. Surveys of the Karekare Valley were not completed until 1857, and blocks of land shown on the old linen maps record the names of some early grantees who never showed up.

The *Coromandel*, a sailing ship of 662 tons, was chartered by Thomas Spencer Forsaith. It sailed down the Thames on 14 January 1838 laden with trading goods and sawmilling machinery, heading for the South Pacific and New Zealand. On board were a young married couple, Elihu and Mary Shaw, who were destined to become the first Europeans to settle in the Karekare Valley. Elihu, a gardener, was considered no match for the daughter of a squire, and so he at 25 and she at 22 eloped. Now ostracised from the community and estranged from their families, they were sailing for a new life with their three small children, John, Silas and Emily.

As they headed out into the Atlantic the winds intensified, and near the Equator the *Coromandel* became engulfed in a raging storm. If this wasn't bad enough, smallpox broke out on board and 36 perished from the disease. When the survivors at last arrived at Port Jackson, Australia, the ship needed urgent repairs. Half the crew then deserted. Captain Thomas Neal and his first officer, a Mr French, combed the convict settlement for fresh crew. While they waited, Elihu found some work as a sawyer. He could have done better, for he was one of the few on board who could read and write.

They finally set sail again in the late spring and arrived on the Hokianga Harbour in the first week of December. Within a month, Captain Neal would die on the Hokianga. As a trader, Shaw became fluent in Māori, the language giving him an insight into the customs and culture of the country. It was to stand him in good stead when a fleet of canoes came down the river, its warriors performing a haka on the banks before wrecking Elihu's trading store. The object of their fury was a moko mokai or tattooed head taken by Shaw's business partner from a tapu burial cave for trading purposes. Only the intervention of the chief Te Tirarau saved Shaw's own skull from being split with a tomahawk.

In 1845 'Heke's War' came to the Bay of Islands. The Shaws decided to move south from the Hokianga to safety in the environs of the growing town of Auckland. They sailed in a brig down the river into the Kaipara with their few possessions and their only cow, disembarking at Helensville. They walked the remaining 20 miles to Auckland, and with their hard-earned savings they bought a 16-acre block known as Cabbage Tree Swamp. Today it is called Eden Park.

The inseparable Shaw sons, John and Silas, still longed for the wilderness life. These were pioneer times in a country where you could live the kind of life you wanted. The Shaw brothers were larger than life, 6 ft 4 inches or more. Powerful men, they were good at swimming and wrestling. Silas showed his strength by lifting an anvil weighing 5 hundredweight (254 kg).

Now both married, they found the remoteness they wanted on Auckland's west coast at a bay known to the Pakeha as Karkare. This tiny fertile valley, yet to be marked on a map, was given to them by the New Zealand Government as a free land grant, aimed at fostering rural settlements. It was located in the Parish of Karangahape.

The Shaws would have approached their new home along the coast from Whatipu. The valley was not bush-clad in those days – it had been cleared for cultivation by Te Kawerau for generations. The area had been heavily modified by fire, cultivation and settlement. The task of farming in this steep-sided valley would

have been daunting for most settlers, but not for this family. They got to work immediately, cutting timber to build two houses. What they did not cut, they burnt. Zion Hill, which the Shaws named, became the grazing farmland. The southern lower slopes were also grazed, as was the valley floor, and the Shaws commenced working on a bridle track which they cut into the steep side of the Karekare Valley. This would enable the Shaws' stock to be driven up and along the ridge trail and down to Henderson. Impassable in winter, the track would later become a road popularly known as the Cutting.

John Shaw and his wife Sarah would have 14 children and Silas and his wife, 10. Their Karekare life was tough, but for the times, relatively comfortable. Whether they would have been aware of what had gone before, we can only wonder. Would their contact with Māori travelling along the coastline have been such that they would have known of legends of battles and death, and if so, would they have been interested? Their Hokianga experience convinces me that they would have understood what had happened here. But the rigours of life and the harsh west coast winters would have simply meant a sun-up to sundown existence, with little time to contemplate anything other than their farm, their family and their faith.

By 1881, the Shaws in mid-life sought the comforts of a less rigorous existence. Charles Murdoch, the mill manager from the Pararaha, looking for a new site for

his mill and his family, would have made them an offer that they did not wish to pass by. The brothers accepted Murdoch's price. Still inseparable, together with their families, John and Silas first farmed at Whitford, but for only a short time. In a little over a year their brotherly bond changed. Did they fall out? We don't know. Perhaps the call of the Waitakere Ranges was too strong. For whatever reason, John took his family back west to Oratia, buying 80 acres in 1882 for £200 and farming in Carter Road. He is buried in the Oratia Cemetery and his memory is recorded on our maps in the name of Shaw Road.

This robust family is part of the rich tapestry of Karekare's past. I would like to know more of their complex relationships, when New Zealand was developing from a remote part of the British Empire to a nation in its own right. The story of the Shaw brothers is another fascinating footnote to our country's history.

In the 1950s, Tom McGuire, the new owner of Winchelsea House, searched one summer for the foundations of the Shaw homesteads, using the 1881 Charles Blomfield painting as a guide. But the wind and the elements had removed all surface evidence of the first European settlers in this valley.

(ABOVE) **MILL COTTAGE IN POHUTUKAWA GROVE AT FOOT OF ZION HILL IS BELIEVED TO HAVE BELONGED TO JOHN 'PA' BETHELL.** (BELOW) **MURDOCH FAMILY BLACKBERRYING BEHIND WINCHELSEA HOUSE.** (OPPOSITE TOP LEFT) **SHAW BROTHERS' BULLOCK TEAM.** (OPP. TOP RIGHT) **WINCHELSEA HOUSE, 1912.** (OPP. BELOW) **TWO MURDOCH DAUGHTERS UNSUITABLY DRESSED FOR FISHING.**

# THE MILLERS' TALES

AT THE HUIA Settlers Museum and hall in mid-winter 2000, the exuberant reunion of the Foote family was in full cry as people who had never met each other recognised their family likeness. Amid tables groaning with food and memorabilia, they had returned to their roots on the Manukau. Finlay Foote told me that his great-grandfather had been summoned to New Zealand by a persuasive letter from his father-in-law John Gibbons. Until they arrived, they did not realise just how difficult milling was in the young colony. The land was steep and hard to work. More than in their Newfoundland homeland, profitability here depended on winter rainfall in the ranges to fill the dams.

The history of the Waitakere coast was indelibly stamped by William Foote and two others, Charles Murdoch, the mill manager of Karekare and the Pararaha, and the other raw-boned Newfoundlander, John Gibbons. All were strangers in this land, but they readily adapted to it. Their financial success may have been debatable, but not so their determination to make a living from the timber of the ranges.

These days, it's easy to despise their deeds in destroying the vast tracts of virgin kauri *(Agathis australis)*, but their actions must be seen in the context of their own times. They were sawmillers, and their business was the supply of materials for the building of a new colony that was almost as far removed from the Old World as you could go. If only they could, by sweat and sheer ingenuity, get their saws and axes on some of the largest trees on earth, and then find a way to bring these behemoths to their mills by bullock team, by water, and later by bush rail, then their financial success would be assured.

The year was 1864 when the Gibbons sailed first from Newfoundland for the United Kingdom and from there to New Zealand. They arrived a year later on the shores of the Manukau Harbour. As the brigantine *Clara* tacked close to the coast, sailing south to the Manukau bar, they glimpsed their new home for the first time. They were expecting the sheds and houses of the settlement known as Auckland, which was their advertised destination. But the township had two ports and both

the Waitemata and the Manukau were navigable by sailing vessels. The crew were aware of the tragedy of *HMS Orpheus*, lost on the bar two years earlier, but the vessel flew through the turbulence and on 30 June they had cast anchor and landed on shore at Te Huia, or the Huia as it was then called.

The Gibbons were a large family. Their eldest son John, 26, had stayed in Newfoundland. Their daughter Elizabeth also remained in Newfoundland, married to a William Foote. With them came their other children: Ebenezer was 24, Mary Ann 21, James 18, Thomas 16, Nicholas 15, Robert 11, Sarah 8, and Emma Jane 4.

Within six months, the industrious John senior had summed up the potential for a milling operation in Huia Bay and had a timber licence for a 525-acre block in the Huia, which was gazetted in May 1853. Water was abundant, flowing from the steep hills and ravines behind the bay. It was a simple operation to construct a water-powered sawmill with the machinery that they had shipped with them on the

*Clara*. Not satisfied with one, Gibbons soon had two water-powered sawmills chugging away with timber from the hills on both sides of the Huia Valley.

John Gibbons knew how to build bush tramlines, which were vital for extracting the giant logs from deep in the forest. Shipping the iron rails from Auckland via Onehunga, he was able to construct a bush rail over three kilometres into the hinterland of the Huia Valley. It was a paying proposition and soon the Gibbons' Huia mill spawned a small settlement with cottages and a cookhouse whose morning smoke drifted across the valley. Mill workers were journeying up and down the harbour and soon the road which now takes you to the Lower Huia Dam was abuzz with activity.

Gibbons' second mill was built on the foreshore on the northern side of the Karamatura Stream. The mill had the interesting nickname Niagara, honouring the great 8m-diameter waterwheel which powered the 400m long flume from a reservoir behind an earth dam across the stream. Gibbons had seen these in Canada and introduced the concept to the Waitakeres. Not only was it a success, but it saved the logs from being damaged while they were being dragged and torn from the bush.

One of the visitors to the Gibbons mill was renowned naturalist Dr Ferdinand von Hochstetter. He was touring the Manukau coastline with the Reverend Purchas and Captain Ninnus of Onehunga. Hochstetter records in his diary his impressions of the Huia mill site, the peaks and the romantic mystery of the area:

I was extremely surprised at the romantic character of the landscape now

(TOP) **BRONZE MEDAL AWARDED TO WILLIAM FOOTE FOR HIS TIMBER ENTREPRENEURSHIP.** (MIDDLE) **FOOTE FAMILY CREST; LATIN TRANSLATION: 'ONE FOOT FORWARD'.** (LOWER) **WILLIAM FOOTE'S RESOLUTE CHARACTER IS SHOWN IN THIS PAINTING.** (ABOVE) **LONE BUSH WORKER AT THE COMPANY STREAM.** (OPPOSITE, CLOCKWISE FROM TOP LEFT) **ELIZABETH MURDOCH; CHARLES AND BROTHERS; LOGS WERE HAULED FROM PIHA ON RAIL INCLINE.**

surrounding us. A wild mountainous region covered in dusky woods, lofty sharp pointed peaks, steep and rugged precipices and gloomy ravines from which brooks and rivers of the clearest water are continually issuing forth.

Enterprising colonists have chosen this romantic wood region for the establishment of sawmills. The primaeval forests furnish in the powerful trunks of the kauri pine, excellent timber. Brooks and rivers provide abundant water power for the mills and are at the same time used for floating the timber.

Thus the busy life of the woodcutters' colony is developing itself here as in the wild coasts of California and Canada. The sawmills in Huia Bay and Henderson's mill on the Waitemata are the principal establishments of this kind for the preparation of boards and all kinds of timber in the vicinity of Auckland. We paid a visit to one of the sawmills here, which is constructed and managed in the best manner possible. Thence we followed a tramroad leading about three miles into the woods to a point whence the woodcutters were engaged in rolling the powerful kauri logs downhill to the road...

In June of 1865, on the shores of Huia Bay, the Gibbons were delighted to welcome their daughter Elizabeth and son-in-law William Foote. They had been writing to Elizabeth and no doubt she would have been enamoured with the idea of travelling to this idyll of plenty in New Zealand, considering that Newfoundland was in the grip of a depression and provisions were scarce.

Within a few days, William Foote and John Gibbons had started to look further inland at the vast kauri forest that stretched from the Huia through to Swanson. Although not as tall as the Californian redwood, the massive diameter of the New Zealand kauri provided the largest millable timber volume of any tree. The trees had an average diameter of 2m and a clear bore length of 12m. Many trees were measured with diameters close to 4m, which equates to 12.6m in girth. To the Gibbons and Foote partnership, this was gold waiting to be gathered.

Together they mapped out the accessible milling areas. It would have taken months of bush-bashing day after day – wading, climbing, possibly camping for days on end as they worked out the feasibility of damming and driving the logs downstream, and while they considered the practicalities of a bush rail system. When they had finished, they were convinced their project was feasible: it was to be one of New Zealand's foremost industrial undertakings of the 1870s, and included an export wharf on Paratutae Island at Whatipu, linked by a bush tramway line up the coast to the Pararaha Valley.

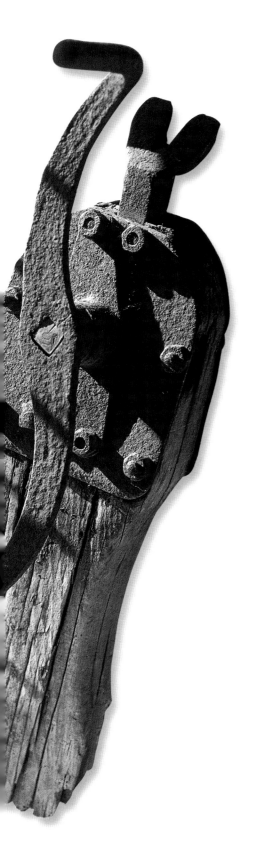

Charles Blomfield executed a superb oil painting of the mill, shown at the start of this chapter. All that remains today of that once industrious site is a large section of the earth dam, which is a 20-minute walk from the Whatipu Lodge.

The remains of the wharf can be still seen on the rock shelf used by people fishing on the eastern side of Paratutae. This massive timber wharf was tied to the imposing rock, and on it was laid a tramline that stretched back across the beach, at times covered by the high spring tides. It was continually being eroded by the black, shifting ironsand. Business was brisk and on any given day the cutters *Rose Ann*, *Dante*, *Rangatira* and *Tay* could be seen shipping the timber for the port of Onehunga, a distance of 12 miles (18 km) up the harbour. Once a month, the overseas and coastal cargoes were taken on the beautiful three-masted schooners with the evocative names *Fiery Cross* and *Atlanta*, the brigs *Derwent* and *Syphen* and every six weeks the ketch *Wild Duck* would be moored at the Gibbons wharf.

Two kilometres north of Whatipu, through wetlands alive with bittern, terns, ducks and other birdlife, past the great sea cave renowned for dances at the end of the 19th century, is the Pararaha Valley. The mouth of this beautiful gorge – for that's what lies beyond the two massive, guardian rock headlands – is hidden by a great ironsand dune, the largest on the west coast. From its sharp ridge is a breathtaking view inland: the swamp gives way to higher ground and here, close to the cliffs, near some giant yucca, was the site of the busy Pararaha timber mill. The high gorge was easy to dam, so the kauri, cut from the hills above, would have crashed through the undergrowth and plunged into huge man-made dams, ready for the spring release.

This mill was run by our second entrepreneur, William Foote, another weather-beaten Newfoundlander. It was not unusual for the dams to hold up to 300 kauri trunks. When the dam was released, the logs would be sent roaring down the gorge to the valley floor below. There they would be jacked up and sawn in the water-driven mill.

As the timber became more difficult to extract, the need to refinance became the

(ABOVE) **TIMBER JACK FOUND IN KAREKARE STREAM, 1965.** (TOP RIGHT) **MILL WORKERS AT BOTTOM OF THE CUTTING CONTEMPLATE AFTERMATH OF A FLOOD.** (OPPOSITE) **MURDOCH FAMILY INSPECT DEVASTATION CAUSED BY TRIPPING OF THE KAREKAU DAM.** (OPP., INSET) **CHARLES PRIMROSE MURDOCH: PIONEER MILLER, BUSINESSMAN AND COMMODORE.**

real priority, so Foote and Gibbons together brought in a third investor, Joseph Howard, who brought money and bad luck. The Pararaha Stream, which supplied the vital ingredient to drive the machinery, was that summer reduced to a mere trickle. The timber could not be processed and Howard now started to press Foote for repayments. What had begun so promisingly as a highly successful operation now became a squabbling mess between the financial partners. By 1875, Howard was demanding from Foote a sum of £857 for mill supplies. In his letter to Foote, he simply adds: "I cannot permit this state of affairs to go on any longer." It wouldn't. The mills were leased out and in 1877 Foote was given notice.

Finlay Foote recalls a family diary note explaining that when they left Whatipu, the family took a large four-wheeler bullock wagon, loaded with furniture, tools and the stock from the store, six head of cattle and four horses, along the sand to Kare-kare, then over the ranges to Opuawhanga north of Whangarei. The journey took six weeks.

Our final player in the Karekare mill saga is the resourceful Ayrshire-born Charles Primrose Murdoch who, while reading the *New Zealand Herald*, noted a vacancy for the position of mill manager on the west coast. The new owners were Guthrie and Larnach, builders from Dunedin. They needed someone they could trust to manage the two mill operations and it was Murdoch they selected.

Early photographs depict Murdoch as a clear-eyed and resolute man. He had an  extraordinary past. He had served his apprenticeship on the sailing clipper *Peter Denny* and at the age of 20 he was already a chief officer. The race was on to bring tea to Europe and these great ships were the pride of the fleet, plying the clipper route between China, Burma and Liverpool.

In 1870 Chief Officer Murdoch sailed on the *Robert Henderson* to distant New Zealand. The family of Major Wallace and his wife and seven daughters were aboard. Their destination was the southern port of Dunedin. Sometime during the voyage, Murdoch and Wallace's youngest daughter Elizabeth became friends and four years later in 1874, at Knox Church in Dunedin, he would return to marry her. It was to be a long and wonderful marriage. She lovingly supported him in both good times and bad, the mill years, the family and retirement: a true pioneer woman who probably had no idea at the time of her wedding of the trials and tribulations of the pioneer life she would share with her husband.

In 1877 Murdoch was sent to manage both the mills. The Footes were still living in the Pararaha Valley. They had moved to the other side of the stream and the enterprising William Foote, undaunted by his dismissal from his dream, was now running a small flax mill, supplying cut flax from the lower hills and valleys. It couldn't have been much of a business.

(ABOVE) MEN OF THE KAREKAU SAWMILL, CHRISTMAS 1886. CHARLES MURDOCH IS AT EXTREME LEFT; BOB GIBBONS AND JOHN 'PA' BETHELL ARE STANDING SIXTH AND SEVENTH FROM LEFT. (MIDDLE) MURDOCHS CUTTING FLAX FOR THEIR MILL. (LOWER) MURDOCH'S WOODTURNING FACTORY, 1890. THIS LATER BECAME HIS FLAX MILL, POWERED BY WATER-DRIVEN TURBINE WHICH ALSO SUPPLIED ELECTRICITY TO WINCHELSEA HOUSE, YEARS BEFORE AUCKLAND SAW THE LIGHT.

Murdoch was as ambitious as the Gibbons and Foote combination had been. He believed the valleys further to the north could be milled – but how? The high, crumbling and often treacherous cliffs proved inaccessible, so with the abundant funding of Guthrie and Larnach, it was decided to push the bush mill north around the two bluffs and then across Taranaki Bay to Karekare.

While this was still in the planning stage, disaster struck the Pararaha mill. On 25 March 1881 embers from the boiler chimney smothered in the shavings burst into flames, and before the mill hands, woken by the barking dogs, could form a bucket brigade from the dam, the mill was a total loss. Fate had taken a hand and Charles Primrose Murdoch had no option but to move his family and business to Karekare, as the best timber in the gorge had been felled by that stage. The mill's boiler was taken by the bush rail to be installed at the new mill, but at the tunnel entrance to the small pa headland known as Kawakawa it was rolled from the siding where it remains as a rusting hulk today.

At the Karekare Valley, Murdoch and his family found their nirvana. The Shaw brothers had left two small, neat cottages. There were two houses on the Shaw property, one of which was known as Doon Holme. It too is seen in the Blomfield painting. It looks to be a two-roomed, pitsawn, weatherboard cottage with attic accommodation. Murdoch decided that he would farm as well as running the mill. The hills around Karekare had been cleared and grassed. Horses that hauled trams in Auckland city streets were spelled out on Zion Hill. The Murdochs record that sometimes up to 60 horses were rested before returning to Auckland to be put back into harness.

Near the Karekare waterfall, below the great cave, Murdoch built the Karekau sawmill. It was a sizeable operation, sawing the timber brought down from the nearby valley. Out of the mill ran a rail towards the south rocks. On it ran the little engine built by George Fraser and Sons of Auckland, chugging down the coast, through the hewn tunnel at Kawakawa Pa Point, past the ruins of his old mill and on to Whatipu.

Seven children were born to Charles and Elizabeth at Karekare, but tragedy struck twice. The Shaw farmhouse burnt down, the family surviving with just a few possessions, one of which was a beautiful photograph album which records the family living in this exotic, green utopia. Soon after, their precious two-year-old toddler Florance drowned in the Karekare stream.

Murdoch had to put aside his grieving to build a new home for his family. He set his mind and limbs to building one of New Zealand's great coastal houses, which was later named Winchelsea. The house took almost a year to build and kauri pitsawn planks still bear Charles Murdoch's signature and the date, 29 November 1889. This house was built close to the flank of the Watchman, with a spacious lawn in front and a large macrocarpa casting its shadow on the grass. It was a beautiful house and behind it, on the site of the marae, Elizabeth and the family developed a glorious garden and two orchards. The remains of the Murdoch orchard are still to be seen as you walk up the small road beside the house towards Union Bay. The large Norfolk pine marks the grave of Florance.

When local historian Jack Diamond interviewed Charles Murdoch junior on his memories of Karekare, Charles described Doon Holme as clad in palings, split from logs of kauri and totara, with a shingle roof.

"When the house was burnt down, we saved few possessions," Charles recalled, "and we built the larger weatherboard house, for the foundation block and deckings for the verandah my father had some baulks of teak that had washed ashore from

(ABOVE) **KAURI LOG HAULED BY BULLOCK TEAM TO KAREKARE MILL, WHICH WAS SITUATED AT BOTTOM OF THE CUTTING; SAWN TIMBER DEPARTS PARARAHA FOR WHATIPU WHARF.** (BELOW LEFT AND BELOW) **THIS NEW ZEALAND-BUILT (1872) FRASER & TINNIE LOCOMOTIVE HAULED TIMBER AT KAREKARE AND IS NOW BURIED IN SAND BEHIND THE BEACH. PAINTING BY W.W. STEWART. COLOUR SLIDE** (BELOW) **TAKEN 1947.**

the wreck of the *Orpheus*. These were sawn into suitable sizes and used to block the verandah.

"Later, when necessary, we built in the valley behind the main house a barn with a hayloft, and stables for the horses. We gathered hay from the paddocks in the Karekare Valley for the winter feed for both the house cows and the horses. In spring, the valley behind the homestead was ablaze with fruit blossom. It was a marvellous garden, but needed to be well watered in summer as the sandy soil dried out quickly."

One of the guests at the Murdoch home was the poet Thomas Bracken, who composed the national anthem *God Defend New Zealand*. A memento of his visit is a signed copy of his poems, still in the Murdoch family. Another heirloom, of even more importance, is their precious family album, dated 1886, with photographs of the mill and timber workers.

The Karekare mill became unproductive as the logs were stripped from the hills. The Murdochs' love of Karekare was such that this resourceful man, reluctant to leave, set up a small factory across the road from the carpark, with a water turbine-driven machine to manufacture wooden spokes, axles and tool handles. The machinery would operate for many years, later driving the turbine for a flax mill, another concept of Murdoch's, and finally as a generator to supply electricity to the Karekare settlement, 10 years before Auckland would see electric light.

Elizabeth Murdoch appears fragile in the early photographs, but she must have

(ABOVE) **PARATUTAE ROCK AT WHATIPU WAS THE RAILHEAD FOR TIMBER FROM THE UNTAMED COAST. BARQUE NJORD DOCKS FOR A CARGO, 1909.** (BELOW) **MURDOCH FAMILY PROMENADE ON KAREKARE BEACH IN THEIR BUGGY.**

been amazingly strong. As each of her pregnancies neared full term, she would ride her mare down the coast to Whatipu, travelling by steamer up the Manukau to Onehunga and on to Auckland for her confinement. Within a week, she would return the same way with a newborn baby. In a Thomas Bracken photograph she is seen with her youngest child Celeste, in the glade by the bridge in the prime of her life.

The Murdochs would finally and reluctantly decide to leave Karekare in 1897: the family moved first to Ponsonby and then to 8 Garden Terrace, Devonport. With his sons Charles, Leslie and David and their knowledge of the woodworking industry, Murdoch set up in Customs Street West in the city. This time, the business flourished. Within two years, Murdoch was a wealthy and respected Aucklander. He was able to buy a Bailey-built rated racing yacht, *Zinita*, a classic of the Waitemata. *Zinita* and Murdoch would win the Auckland Yachting Club's Commodore Cup in December 1898 and the North Shore Sailing Club's Dunning Cup the following February. Murdoch the sailor was back in his element, with the hard years of Karekare behind him. In a howling nor'easter, Murdoch, with his new boat *Ida*, took a well-deserved victory in the Ponsonby Regatta and it was with pride that he became Commodore of the Auckland Yachting Club in 1901.

Through Murdoch's vision, the AYC became the New Zealand Yacht Squadron ('Royal' was added soon after when King Edward VII issued the Squadron a Royal Warrant) and he became one of the great yachting identities of Auckland. As wooden spokes gave way to steel and wire, Murdoch closed his business and returned to timber, becoming an official timber assessor for the Bank of New Zealand. In 1920 at the age of 70, he retired. With Elizabeth and his sons Leslie, David and Roy, he moved to Tangiteroria where he died of a heart attack in 1925. *Ida*, his prized yacht, continued racing into the 1950s, though she never reached the level of excellence that she had achieved with Murdoch at her helm. She still sails, having been restored in Sydney.

At Karekare, Murdoch's Winchelsea House has also been lovingly and beautifully refurbished, as we shall see.

(TOP) **IN ITS FINAL YEARS, TRESTLE RAILWAY SNAKES OUT OF VALLEY AND ACROSS THE BEACH.** (ABOVE) **FOOTE FAMILY PLOT, PUREWA CEMETARY, AUCKLAND.** (BELOW) **1999 FOOTE FAMILY REUNION OUTSIDE HUIA SETTLERS MUSEUM.**

# ROAD RUNNING WEST

(TOP) WAIKUMETE (GLEN EDEN) STATION, WHERE HOLIDAYMAKERS TRANSFERRED TO KAREKARE COACH. (LOWER) MR LLOYD AND HIS COACH AT 'WAIATA RUA' ACCOMMODATION HOUSE, NEAR SUMMIT OF THE WEST COAST ROAD. (OPPOSITE) IT WAS A LONG, TIRING AND MUDDY JOURNEY OUT TO THE COAST, BUT VICTORIAN TRAVELLERS INSISTED ON OBSERVING REFINED DRESS CODE.

FROM MY HOME in Glen Eden, a suburb that was called Waikumete until the 1920s when the name was changed because of its association with the cemetery, it's a good three-hour run to the coast. When I was training for the Rotorua marathon, it was my regular Sunday jaunt. Along this road ran some of the greatest runners New Zealand has ever produced, the Lydiard athletes Snell, Halberg, Magee and Baillie. The route to the west coast was part of the famous Waitakeres circuit where 'Arthur's boys' toughened up for their international triumphs. Never was I in their class, but like them I did some big miles, many sweated out on the road to Karekare.

The early colonial travellers also took the road west from Glen Eden, from the Waikumete railway station. Guests travelling to the west coast would alight here, then the train would go along a little further and a coffin would be off-loaded onto a handcart. The station clock would be approaching 10. Our tourists would be greeted by Gill Wood, a gruff but warm-hearted driver of the Karekare wagon. The vehicle seated eight people, some facing each other and others facing forward, and with a jerk and some creaking it would be drawn away by five horses and accompanied by as many barking dogs.

The West Coast Road was hell for these early travellers as well as for generations of runners to come. If it had rained, the wagon wheels would sink into the clay, and it hadn't even started climbing to Waiatarua yet. At Parrs Cross Road, the Parrs Orchards stretched north, almost to the township of Henderson. Part of this land is now Hoani Waititi Marae.

Down the hill towards Oratia stands the beautifully restored Harré homestead. It used to be the Town and Country Roadhouse, one of Auckland's first restaurants. Next to it is a small, almost forgotten cemetery where I've staked my claim, for the simple reason that it's on the way to Karekare, and I always seem to be on the way there. Across the road, the old school with its little white schoolhouse that was opened in 1886, stood at the corner of Shaw Road. It was destroyed by fire on 29

December 1974, but the historic gates are still there. Behind is a new school. All of my five kids went to Oratia School and on the centenary, I helped some local orchardists devise a time capsule for the school. We filled it with memorabilia and placed it under a huge rock by the dental clinic.

At the corner of Parker Road, before the road drops steeply to Kelly's Bridge, was the first stop, a small hotel near the church. Between the two oak trees stood the blacksmith's shop, which was still going until well into the 1930s.

Now came the dreaded hill, winding up to Waiatarua. On the right stood the home of John Taw, which would later be sold to Captain Peter Theet, a wily old sea-dog and great mate of the notorious Count Von Luckner, the sea devil, who stayed there with him. This house was later donated to the Girl Guide Association in 1927. They sold it to the Gash family, who took it up  Parker Road, where it still stands. Next door is the old property of Robert English, who joined Von Tempsky's Forest Rangers against Titokowaru. He should have stayed in Oratia, as he was killed and eaten. In 1914 old Theet built another house – a grand one across the road – and the Captain called it Lancedean. Today it serves as a rest home.

By midday, the mud-spattered coach and occupants would reach Waiatarua. The old homestead and large accommodation house, owned by the Judson family, was called 'Waiata Rua' – the song of two waters – and gave its name to the area. For an

hour, the guests would drink tea or ale here. Waiatarua homestead would finish its life as the Dutch Kiwi, where I once did a stint as a waiter. Soon after, it caught fire and was razed to the ground.

The worst was yet to come. In those days, the West Coast Road dropped steeply towards Nihotupu, down the long straight that was the first section to be tarsealed in the 1960s. Back in the 1880s, the mightiest kauri in the whole of the Waitakeres grew on each side of the road – and the road darkened through this glade, according to an early traveller. In this grove grew the fabled Glasgow tree, which was so immense that no saw was big enough to cut it. When it finally fell in 1897, a section was cut for display at the Great Auckland Exhibition in the Domain. You can see it today in the Christchurch Museum.

Our travellers were then in the great Forest of Tiriwa, the name that for a thousand years meant home to Waitakere Māori. Its dense forests held secrets and fear: inhabited by the legendary Turehu spirit people, it was not an easy place to move through.

(TOP) **'DARKIE' SANDERS, A JAMAICAN WHO LIVED AT THE FOOT OF DARKIE'S HILL. IT TOOK THIS CUP OF WHISKEY BEFORE HE WOULD POSE. (ABOVE LEFT) DARKIE AND AGNES AT THEIR BUSH WHARE. (ABOVE) ETCHING OF WAIATARUA, NIHOTUPU, BY E.W. PAYTON, 1887.**

At the bottom of the steepest hill lived Martin 'Darkie' Sanders (pronounced 'Saunders'), a Jamaican who boasted that he was the first 'white man' to cross the ranges. He lived in a paling shed with his Irish-born wife Agnes, who had been a housemaid to Governor Grey on Kawau Island. Pigs and goats were penned on the property and this unusual couple would regularly go to Henderson and the city for drinking sessions. This section of the road bears his name, Darkie's Hill. Agnes is buried there beside the road.

The road was developed and maintained by John 'Pa' Bethell and other Karekau mill workers and was referred to as the 'Breakneck Road' by the Waitemata County Council.

Just before the Karekare turnoff, the travellers would have sighted the famous lone kauri. There was a track to the Pararaha Valley which led to two sawmill

settlements, working the upper Para-raha. If the travellers looked closely, they would have noticed that the tree was dying. It was eventually felled by the council. The stump can still be seen today, 200m west of the turnoff from the Piha Road. The track became the Lone Kauri Road.

The journey must have seemed never-ending to the colonial travellers. Evening would be drawing in as the coach reached the top of the Karekare hill. They would continue on a little further, to drop off stores for the Piha mill.

The return coach departed at 5 am, the family rising at 3.30 to get the horses in and fed, and then breakfast for the drivers at 4.30. The horses needed a two-hour spell before the return trip, arriving at the coast at 5 pm. The coach drivers were Harry Wilkins, Gill Wood and Wally Farley.

As there was no telephone, carrier pigeons were kept lofted on the side of the stable. When the Karekare coach left, several of these birds were taken in a wicker box. If there were any unexpected arrivals at Waikumete, a message was attached to the leg of a bird and it was set free. Ten minutes later, the message would be at Kare-kare. Food fanciers were able to select from menus and organise their walks and recreation pursuits in advance by the courier pigeon post.

When I first moved to Glen Eden in the 1960s, Gill Wood lived on Oates Road. He'd lived in Glen Eden for 75 years, and apart from a stint of service in France during World War I, he'd never lived anywhere else. Sitting outside the Post Office,

(ABOVE) **FINAL MOMENTS OF THE LONE KAURI THAT HAD STOOD FOR 600 YEARS IN THE WAI-NUI-A-TIRIWA FOREST. IT WAS FELLED BY ORDER OF WAITEMATA COUNTY COUNCIL.** (ABOVE RIGHT) **A HAZARDOUS JOURNEY: SINKING IN A SEA OF MUD NEAR THE ANAWHATA TURNOFF.** (BELOW) **LOCALS TED BROWNE, TED BADHAM AND JIM LOCKETT CLEARING A TREE THAT FELL ACROSS THE CUTTING, WINTER OF 1925.**

he would reminisce about his daily chore at Karekare, hammering the soles of discarded hobnailed boots on the brake blocks of the Glen Eden to Karekare coach.

"In those days," Gill told me, "everyone in the ranges wore hobnail boots and when these were worn through, they would save them for me and leave them out tied to trees. I used to have a sackful which I kept by the Glen Eden railway station. My coach of four horses had such power I used to go through a lot of them."

When we talked in the 1970s, Gill was pushing 80 and in the last two years of his life. He remembered how the brakes were vital for getting the coach safely down the Cutting into Karekare. The incline was a breakneck four-in-one gradient, and the driver had to reassure the passengers at every clop of the horses' hooves that there was no likelihood of an accident.

"As they alighted from the train," Gill recalled, "it cheered them up to see me hammering a new set of hobnailed brake shoes before we set off. At 10 am, twice a week, Wednesday and Friday, I would set off for Karekare. About midday, we reached the Judsons' boarding house at Waiatarua. Here we had cake and tea and at 12.30 we hit the Piha road. We watered the horses in the stream which is at the end of the straight, and then we started to wind up and to negotiate the clay road all the way to the coast.

"In fine weather, we made good time. We carried a shovel and an axe – it got us through the rough bits. If a bullock team had been using the road, they would chew up the roots of trees buried under the clay and the wheels would be stuck. In winter, the mud caused the coach wheels to sink down to the axles, and that often happened. I used to unhitch the front horses, take them round the back and haul the coach out, and then we'd start off again. We'd get there to the boarding house around five. In winter, it would be dark and I only used to do the trip on Friday night."

His worst moment, he told me, was one night just after dusk. "The two horses had just been freed and I gave them a sharp slap, which frightened them, and they dived straight over the side of the valley and crashed down through the trees. It took

(TOP) MOTOR-CAR REALITY CHECK: WAITING FOR A HORSE-TOW. (BELOW) MOTORING ENTHUSIASTS DISCOVERED THE WEST COAST BEACHES WERE WITHIN EASY DRIVING DISTANCE OF AUCKLAND. (LOWER) THE *NEW ZEALAND MOTOR JOURNAL* OF 25 MARCH 1933 MISTAKENLY FEATURED THIS FLIPPED IMAGE OF KAREKARE CAMPERS.

me all weekend to find them in the gorge. I had to cut a path to them to free them – they were tangled in trees and ferns. In summer, in the 1920s, I used to have 60 people staying at Karekare. To get them out and home again, I needed the whole fleet – a 12-seater coach pulled by four horses, a nine-seater, a six-seater and a beautiful butterfly gig, all heading to the rail stop at Glen Eden."

Gill said he'd love to do it again, but cars had obliterated the leisurely, romantic but tiring coach ride to the coast.

It is relatively easy now to negotiate the Karekare incline. Though your brakes may still smell of rubber, and you have to approach the narrow bends with extreme caution, you will catch glimpses of the alluring valley below.

When I became the captain of the Karekare Surf Club, it was my duty to drive the club vehicle out to the coast every weekend. It would start under the clock of the Central Post Office in downtown Auckland and weave its way through the suburbs picking up club members and their girlfriends for the weekend patrol. It was a ex-US Army Ford V8 that had been used to track down AWOLs and drunks. It was the third vehicle that the club had owned. The first was a former Farmer's Trading Company bus that had been left on the grass carpark at Karekare when the club members went off to World War Two. Locals had taken its wheels off in case the Japanese landed and used it to attack Auckland. Rusty pieces of it were still stored in a shed at Karekare in the late 1950s. I was not the best driver; the machine was very heavy and reacted sharply to the pedal. The brakes were never brilliant, and heavily laden with clubbies, the vehicle swayed precariously on the gravel road to the coast. Accidents were frequent and the truck spent as much time in the panel-beaters as on the road.

Noticing a car cautiously rounding one of the S-bends, I slowed down, only to get into a skid, and side-swiped it into the ditch. The driver leapt out and took off into the bush. The stolen car was loaded with gelignite from the Waitemata County quarry, so the driver had more than one reason for his quick escape from the scene. The road was closed all day while army demolition experts removed the deadly booty, now dangerously melting in the hot February sun. We thought ourselves lucky to have survived what could have been an explosive end to our young lives.

As it was for coachman Gill, the Karekare incline was always a problem for me. The brakes would overheat and cease to function. If I missed a gear, I would have to slam the truck into the drain to slow it down to a chorus of thumps on the cab roof from the alarmed clubbies. This truck finished its working life on the beach outside the Surf Club, where I had carelessly left it, ignoring threatening storm-clouds behind the hills. As night fell, so did the rains. The stream came up and

(ABOVE) **PITSTOP WAS A BLOKEY RITUAL WHEN HEADING FOR THE COAST.** (ABOVE RIGHT) **FARMERS DEPARTMENT STORE FREE BUS BECAME THE FIRST KAREKARE SURF LIFESAVING CLUB TRUCK. WHEELS WERE REMOVED DURING WORLD WAR TWO TO FORESTALL AN EXPECTED JAPANESE INVASION.** (OPPOSITE) **JAUNTY CHAPS OF THE SURF LIFESAVING CLUB IN A FROZEN MOMENT OF TIME.**

drowned our precious transport. I was fired as club captain and honorary driver. We never had another club truck. It was back to hitchhiking or the Piha bus.

My friend the poet Sam Sampson, whose great-uncles were early club members, has dedicated this poem to his grandfather, who serviced the truck:

### The Cutting

for George (Sam) Sampson

Changing down. Gravel separating;
middle ridge sprayed from tyre.
Pumping brakes until high on fluid.
Smoking drums exhausted. Light
shafts breaking kauri and tea-tree.
Blind corners...a leap of faith...
swinging wheels caught in corrugations.

Springs resisting pitted folds....Velocity
brushing arched toe-toe....
                                    Foot pulsing.
Wheel arch nudging clay bank.

Boys on back, white knuckled grip
(holding on for dear life). Bumper
buffeting flax outcrops, slowing... stationary.

Boys leaping from tray.          *Alive!*

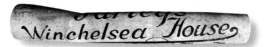

# GLORIOUS WINCHELSEA

IN 1906, *Harding and Billing's Guide to Auckland*, in a three-page advertorial for Winchelsea House, advertised "a salubrious climate, superb scenery, shooting and surf-bathing." Class-conscious, it added "select patronage and moderate terms." The *Guide* salso mentioned passage by Northern Steam Ship Company steamer from Onehunga to North Manukau Heads as an option.

On April 20 1907, the *New Zealand Graphic* ran a double page spread on the 'Rugged West Coast'. The Waitakere coastline attracts fulsome praise:

> The colouring is magnificent. The dark blue ocean, paling as it shoals into a broad fringe of white, stretches away to the horizon, and you know that there isn't a rock or an islet for 1200 miles – nothing but the "changeless, but ever-changing sea" between you and Australia. The black rocks, eroded into a phantasmagoria of sphinxes with the likeness of animals and other weird shapes, or perforated with reverberating caves, rise sheer for several hundred feet from the strand and are crowned with the sombre green of the native bush. Pohutukawa and a few windy-looking shrubs here and there find a niche of shelter in the face of the relentless cliffs of conglomerate rock, all nobby and boulder-studded. Toi-toi with its feathery tops, and tufty native grass, struggle vainly for a precarious existence on the great stretches of sand hills blown up by the winds into long hummocks, all ribbed on the seaward side and smooth and sleek on the shore side. The receding tide leaves the sand wet and shining, a mirror on which the craggy headlands cast great shadows of inky hue, and on which you can watch the reflections of the soft white clouds as they sail slowly across the ethereal blue.

The beautiful name Winchelsea was given to the Murdoch homestead by the matriarch of the Farleys, Maria Mary Farley, who named it after her home in England. Maria and Charlie Farley would bring the 20th century to Karekare. It was the start of a new and fascinating career for this beautiful residence which graces the southern end of the Karekare Valley.

On a spring morning in 1900, Charlie and his friend John 'Pa' Bethell, who had lived at Karekare in the pohutukawa glades, working as a mill worker and butcher, came down the Cutting from Te Henga to look at the property that Murdoch had for sale. By the afternoon, the deal was done: the new owners of the Karekare estate were Charlie and Maria, and their children Charlie, Wally, Laurie, Noel, Marjorie and Zoe.

The family moved to Karekare and realised that here was a resource, if they were prepared to work: a tourist accommodation house on the west coast. It was a grand idea – after all, Maria was famous for her cooking and Charlie had spent time teaching the Italians how to make cheese the New Zealand way. They would seize the opportunity and become renowned hosts.

Winchelsea House became a popular and very stylish weekend, Christmas and Easter destination, although it was hard going just simply getting there.

The Farley household would change considerably with the arrival of Edward Dudley Cust Badham. Born and raised in India and educated at St Paul's School in Jalapahar, Darjeeling, he arrived in New Zealand in 1909. He came with a return ticket, the other part of which he never used. He visited Karekare for the weekend in 1911 to ride down the coast to Whatipu, which was part of the weekend package of Winchelsea House. An excellent rider, Zoe Farley went with him, always riding side-saddle. Badham was a handsome man and Zoe fell in love with his dashing, debonair manner. They courted for three years and Badham became a part of the family at Karekare. It was inevitable that they would marry. The ceremony took place on the lawn at Winchelsea.

It was a splendid occasion. At 10 am, the wedding party and guests assembled in

(ABOVE) **PASSAGE BY STEAMER FROM ONEHUNGA TO THE MANUKAU HEADS WAS THE PREFERRED MEANS OF TRAVEL FOR THESE AUCKLANDERS ON A DAY TRIP TO KAREKARE.** (OPPOSITE TOP) **COAST SERVICE CAR DESTINATION ROLL.** (OPP. LOWER) **CHARLES FARLEY'S TOPHAT BOX.** (BELOW) **FLIMSY FOOTBRIDGE CONNECTED WINCHELSEA WITH BROWNES.**

Kare Kare, West Coast, Auckland. F.G.R. 5224.

# Albert St. Land Rooms
## Friday, December 17th
### at 2.30 p.m.

Favoured with instructions from **Mr. Charles T. D. Farley,** Karekare, West Coast, we will offer for Sale, by Public Auction,

## HIS PARTICULARLY WELL-KNOWN PROPERTY OF 478 ACRES
### Freehold, Seaside Resort, and Farm,

Capable of carrying 800 sheep when properly cleared. The Farm is ring-fenced and subdivided. About 200 acres in grass and rough feed, and in its present state will carry a small dairy herd, besides sheep and cattle. House, 8 rooms and offices; Bungalow, 11 rooms; 3 Cottages, 4 rooms each; and 21 small shelters: electric light and power; magnificent beach, good fishing and shooting; about 16 miles from Waikumete Station. Any quantity large pohutukawa trees, and thousands of tons of big tea-tree. Farm splendidly watered; post office on the property. A really good proposition to anyone running the boarding-house and farm in conjunction.

(FROM TOP) CHARLES THOMAS DALE FARLEY; ZOE KATHLEEN FARLEY, AGED ABOUT 20, 1909; EDWARD DUDLEY CUST BADHAM, AGED 25, 1912. (RIGHT) THESE VASES ARE THOUGHT TO HAVE BELONGED TO MARIA FARLEY IN ENGLAND. (OPPOSITE TOP) THE WEDDING OF EDWARD DUDLEY CUST BADHAM AND ZOE FARLEY, 1914. (OPP. LOWER) MARY MITCHELL, WHO MADE THIS CROSS-STITCH SAMPLER, WAS WIDOWED IN ENGLAND BEFORE EMIGRATING TO NEW ZEALAND WITH CHARLES AND MARIA FARLEY IN 1882.

the drawing room and joined in singing the bridal anthem. The Reverend Gatman united the happy couple as the sun streamed in through the French doors. Zoe was dressed in a white embroidered silk, wearing her mother's wedding veil. The best man, Culley Richardson, was the schoolteacher for the mill children at Piha and had ridden over earlier that morning. Fred Wiseman, one of the few people in Auckland with a large plate camera, had come out to record the event and we are indebted to him for the beautiful images he left for posterity.

The wedding breakfast was provided in the school hall. Afterwards the guests gathered under the pohutukawa trees for the official photographs. The bridal couple's destiny would be to live at Karekare with Zoe's father and mother, finally inheriting Winchelsea House in its golden years.

Their first child was Wallace Badham, who was born on 11 December 1914. His father was working for the tramway company, a long way from Darjeeling and the classy life of the English Raj. When I met Wally to talk about his life at Karekare, he was living in a small resthome in Pakuranga. His world had shrunk, but not his memory, nor his longing and love for Karekare. For he was brought up in the golden age of the 20th century; with the prosperity at the end of World War One, cars, planes, radios and jazz added a new excitement to life in New Zealand, and this all came to the stylish and sophisticated grand boarding house at Karekare.

As we sit in the sun, going through his treasured album, Wally's memories are lucid and keen. Over his bed is a photograph of him landing his fragile aircraft on Karekare Beach. At the home of his niece Lisa are the remaining treasures of the boarding house's grand dining room – the Chinese artifacts, vases, mirrors and screens that graced the sideboards and the walls, the cutlery, sterling silver cake knives, soup ladles and of course, the dinner gong, which sounded its call across the lawn into the stillness of the valley. It summoned the diners for lunch and for dinner from the rooms and from a group of eight cabins joined together up on the flank of the Watchman overlooking the tennis court. And in the cool evening, a gramophone on the verandah of Winchelsea House would play for guests who danced in the moonlight on the beautifully manicured lawn. And if there was no moon, they would dance just the same.

Wally first came to Karekare when he was just two months old. His parents wanted him christened at the coast, and they got their wish, on 7 February 1915, 52 years to

the day after the sinking of the *HMS Orpheus* on the Manukau bar. In 1918, we find Wally being given a ride on the Sandfly, a little mill steam engine, by the driver Jack Sergeant, and going up the Scotsman (the hill behind the house) with Elfreda Eyre, the mill manager's daughter, to catch her black mare Judy.

One of the joys of being a tourist in the 1920s was the popular game of tennis. Mr Charlie Hyde was employed to build a tennis court and pavilion on the lower flank of the Watchman. It took three men three months to cut the court out of the hillside, to make stone terraces and to surface it. The tennis court was finished in time for Christmas 1928 and lasted into the 1950s. The cabins above the court provided additional accommodation for the boarding house and later became the first Surf Club premises, appropriately renamed the Grand Hotel.

By 1920, Zoe and Dudley Badham have moved their household to the coast; they are staying in the grand house, and Wally is attending the schoolhouse across the road. It is every boy's dream: he rounds up the cows in the gorges before going to school; he accompanies his uncles on fishing trips to the rocks above the Cauldron, and he hunts pigs for the boarding house table.

In 1924 the valley is buzzing – the first motor car is coming to Karekare. The Ford Motor Company has sold a Model T Ford to Wally's grandfather, and after seven hours on the road, honking and tooting down the Cutting, it comes into view. Wally remembers it as a great moment at Karekare. The greatest fear was that it would never get back up the hill, and he says it was a hard task. With the long

(TOP) **A BIG BUZZ: THIS 1932 BEACH LANDING WAS GUARANTEED TO PULL A CROWD. CAPTAIN HEWITT CHARGED £1 FOR A RIDE IN HIS GYPSY MOTH.** (ABOVE) **SICK LEOPARD SEAL DEPARTS KAREKARE FOR AUCKLAND ZOO. IT DIED ON ARRIVAL.** (OPPOSITE, TOP) **CAPTAIN J.D. HEWITT FLANKED BY PASSENGERS MARIA MARY FARLEY, AGED 76 AND MR R. SHAW, AGED 84, 1932.**

climb out of the valley, all the pedals had to be held down to keep the vehicle in gear. The car would grind up the incline, the gears working in conjunction with the handbrake and the hand throttle. This was serious business, but it seemed a hell of a lot easier than the tricky coach trip. It was a monster of a car with a bus body at the back where eight people sat, four each side facing inward and one beside the driver. The early Model T did not have a vacuum pump for the petrol tank to enable the fuel to flow into the carburettor, so it would need to be driven up Slippery Rock, the steepest part of the Cutting, in reverse. On many occasions the passengers had to get out and push.

But if the new age of the automobile had arrived, so had aeroplanes. Nothing brought people out of their houses quicker, waving anything that came to hand, than the sight and sound of a small plane approaching. The Karekare Valley was first shaken awake in August 1922 when a noise they'd never heard before filled the air. A De Havilland Gypsy Moth was circling the beach, a lone amphibian from the flying school at Kohimarama. The pilot was George Bolt, whose name is remembered in the road to Auckland International Airport. Wally was transfixed: he felt he had to have a go. It would take him another nine years to make his dream come true, but he succeeded. His father was also enthusiastic, and on Wally's 16th birthday, he and his dad went out to the Auckland Aero Club at Mangere. "More than anything, I wanted to fly," Wally recalls.

SUCCESS OF AUCKLAND AERO CLUB PUPILS DURING YESTERDAY'S TESTS.
From left: Messrs. L. L. White, Auckland, W. Badham, Karekare, R. G. Tappenden, Auckland, and R. Kemp, Hamilton, all of whom gained their pilots A licences yesterday. The tests were conducted by Major L. M. Isitt.

His first instruction was going to cost £3 10s an hour, plus two quid (£2) a week to stay in the clubhouse. A mechanic was summoned to start up the plane, ZK-AAU, No. 1131. "With the plane warmed up, I put on my helmet, which turned out to be not the best, as it was only a motorbike helmet with the headphones put in. These were plugged into a socket and you spoke into a tube with the [instructor's] reply coming back in your earphones. At that time it was hard to get a good helmet and I had to manage with that one through my training. I had a job to hear what the instructor was saying above the roar of the engine and wind. I still have this helmet and had about 20 hours solo before better ones, designed for flying, came on the market."

His flying lessons continued for a month. His instructor, Flight Lieutenant D.M. Allan, was as good as they came. He was New Zealand's leading stunt pilot in the 1930s and 40s and under his guidance the novice Badham became a qualified pilot. At the end of the month, Allan handed his pupil the keys to ZK-AAU and he celebrated with a flight over the Manukau towards the ranges and Karekare. He always knew that was where he wanted to fly.

Wally and his brother Dudley became superb pilots. The machines were small but very reliable. They could take on anything from stunts to soaring, and over Karekare Beach they were regular visitors. They would land into the wind, pick up passengers from the guesthouse and give them a whirl over the island. The

## A BOY AIRMAN.

### SOLO FLIGHT AT SIXTEEN.

### PUPIL OF AUCKLAND CLUB.

### SAVED MONEY FOR LESSONS.

### AMBITION TO OBTAIN LICENCE.

The youngest pupil of the Auckland Aero Club, Wallace Badham, aged 16 years, made his first solo flight at the Mangere aerodrome yesterday. His first trip in an aeroplane was at Rotorua with Captain M. C. McGregor about 18 months ago, and the youth enjoyed the experience so much that he resolved to learn to fly. After saving the necessary money Badham left his home at Kare Kare, West Coast, last August and stayed at the clubhouse at Mangere for some time, receiving lessons each day from the instructor, Flight-Lieutenant D. M. Allan. After he had completed a period of instruction his training was interrupted, and he returned to his home. He returned to the aerodrome on Wednesday, and after taking one or two lessons, principally in landing, he flew solo yesterday morning, flying by himself for 15 minutes and making good landings. The new pilot hopes to extend his stay at the aerodrome until he has completed the five hours' solo flying necessary before he can sit for his A licence test.

Prior to Badham's performance yesterday the youngest club pilot to fly solo was G. M. Owen, who made his first solo flight on January 26, 1930, at the age of 17 years and qualified for his A licence four days later.

Two other aero club pupils, Messrs. R. G. Tappenden and L. L. White, also flew solo for the first time yesterday. Mr. White took his first lesson a month ago.

photographs of the guesthouse were full of souvenir snaps of the planes and the passengers.

The fleet of large touring cars became the new mode of transport to the coast – who cared about the condition of the road? From Fords to Essexes, the big tourers chewed up the miles. The Badhams' cars were a 1927 Essex and a 1931 Essex, and they were simply known as the "service cars". Business boomed; the guesthouse was on the tourist map.

The 1930s at Karekare were full of music and interesting guests. In the summer of 1935, the Badhams put a fountain on the lawn and New Year's Eve was their big event. Amplification of the gramophone sent the sound up to the Piha road as guests danced on the verandah and the lawn. The powerhouse ran smoothly that night, the stream generating electricity for coloured lights and the boarding house complex, while around them little baches flickered with candlelight and kerosene lamps. In the afternoon the male guests were invited to go shooting: there were pigs and goats in the hills and from time to time a cattle hunt was organised. The cattle were survivors of the brig *Orwell* which had gone aground on the Manukau bar. The animals had got ashore and wandered off into the bush. "Stringy beasts," Wally says.

It was a romantic time of dancing till dawn. Between the wars they drank a huge amount – beer was too common for this lot. Whisky, gin and the harder spirits were their energiser. They played hard – these were days and nights of extravagance, gaiety, bold escapades and energetic self-indulgence. It was also a time for getting your clothes off. By contrast, when the first tourists came out to Karekare and stayed in Winchelsea House, in the first decade of the 20th century, it was the Edwardian age of elegance: the women dressed up in big hats and squeezed into corsets, the remaining shackles of Victorian refinement.

The boarding house dog Sammy had been washed overboard from a scow entering the Manukau bar, bringing cattle to Onehunga in 1925. After swimming ashore, Sammy settled in as part of the Badham household.

Around the boarding house, the world was changing. The jazz era had arrived, and with it, the big band sound. Almost everyone owned a wind-up gramophone and a collection of scratchy 78 records. Fancy dress and dress-ups were popular and every Saturday night at Karekare, people brought out their best attire for dining and strolling. Because of the generator, the boarding house glowed in the dark. The Great Gatsby could have dined there. The team of cooks, Jessie, John and Wally Badham and Laurie Farley, produced good table fare and plenty of it; with it went silver service, gleaming white table napkins and linen tablecloths. In winter, the fire at the end of the main room lit the library and the oils in their large, gilt frames. It was elegant and beguiling and many of the guests returned again and again. The Badhams became friends with their guests. Badham was a genial host, charming, slightly pukka; he retained the civilised manners of a colonial gentleman. Straight-backed, aware of who he was; indeed, he was the perfect host.

Behind the scenes, Zoe and Maria – always known as Old Mrs Farley – supervised and bossed the maids and cooks relentlessly. The *Weekly News* and tourist magazines carried advertisements for Winchelsea House. The great resorts were in their prime: Chateau Tongariro, The Hermitage at Mt Cook and the Bay of Islands were important New Zealand destinations. Karekare got a small share of the trade.

The giant macrocarpa that stood in the centre of the lawn was felled in 1938. It was milled in Glen Eden and became the bridge to the Winchelsea guesthouse. Solid timbers were needed to carry the heavy touring cars of the age. The bridge over the Watchman road has lasted well and is still in use. Cutting the tree and getting it to the mill in Glen Eden was a massive task, done with timber jacks. It took two days to haul it over the ranges. It's ironic that here at Karekare where timber mills had existed for over 80 years, no milling equipment now remained.

Supplies to the boarding house were brought out from Glen Eden, but larger materials such as those for building were brought up the coast from Whatipu. Freight was transported by the launch *Outlaw*, winched onto the wharf and carted by dray to Karekare.

A much larger launch, *Te Toa*, sailed from Onehunga once a month with building supplies, sand, sacks of flour, sugar, wheat, oats and chaff for the horses. The southern point of Karekare Beach was dangerous. Five people had lost their lives attempting to bring logs and materials round the headland and had been caught by the surf. It also proived hazardous for the Badham vehicles. When their tourer got stuck, it was under the surf for six hours. It was stripped down, washed in kerosene, had £150 spent on it and was still running on the beach in 1932.

The boarding house was fully booked at Easter and on other public

(ABOVE) **HAMMING IT UP IN THE KITCHEN, 1938: FROM LEFT, LAURIE FARLEY, JESSIE, JOHN AND WALLACE BADHAM, PAT McPHILLIPS.** (BELOW) **SUNDAY EVENING SONGBOOK.** (OPPOSITE, FROM TOP) **WINCHELSEA NESTLES IN LEE OF THE WATCHMAN; BADHAM FAMILY GROUP, 1941. BACK ROW: WALLACE, EDWARD, ZOE, DUDLEY (HOLDING BABY LOIS); FRONT: JOHN, EILEEN, JESSIE; DANCING ON THE LAWN, NEW YEAR'S EVE 1935; DON, THE COOKHOUSE DOG.**

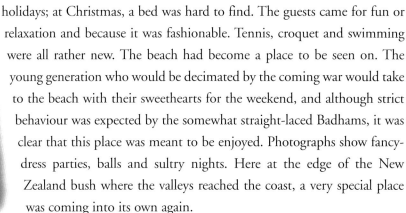

holidays; at Christmas, a bed was hard to find. The guests came for fun or relaxation and because it was fashionable. Tennis, croquet and swimming were all rather new. The beach had become a place to be seen on. The young generation who would be decimated by the coming war would take to the beach with their sweethearts for the weekend, and although strict behaviour was expected by the somewhat straight-laced Badhams, it was clear that this place was meant to be enjoyed. Photographs show fancy-dress parties, balls and sultry nights. Here at the edge of the New Zealand bush where the valleys reached the coast, a very special place was coming into its own again.

The beach was still unpatrolled and people were advised not to go swimming; New Zealanders did not yet understand the surf. Those who ventured into the breakers took enormous risks, and some paid with their lives. At Karekare, two drowned in 1927, one in 1931 and between 1932 and 1934, four people lost their lives. The Badhams advised their guests to swim at the waterfall.

They increased the size of the property. They burnt and then farmed Mt Zion

after buying it from Abel Lovett, who for many years had farmed a small part of what was called the Point. The Sugget family from the Pararaha travelled the beach to Karekare in what was known as a konaki, a strange contraption but good on the sand, with two wheels at the rear and a sledge runner or wheel at the front. It took four horses in harness. When the horses bolted, which they often did, the passengers would be thrown out on the sand, or if the vehicle hit a log it would likely overturn. It wasn't the most comfortable method of travelling, but on soft sand it worked for getting supplies along the coast. There are some beautiful photographs of the boarding house buggies on the beach. These sturdy vehicles with a single horse clopping on the deserted beach are glorious reminders of a bygone age.

When I became the secretary of the Karekare Ratepayers Association in 1957, we used to meet on a Sunday evening in the Winchelsea drawing room. The Croatian-born chairman could neither read nor write English, so at the age of 17, I became the local scribe, recording spats with the Waitemata County Council. It seems that not much has changed in my life.

Winchelsea, this grand old lady of the coast, was showing her age. The interior of this once stylish home was in desperate need of repair. The roof and the exterior walls were covered with peeling paint and rotting boards. The hallways were dark and lifeless. The paintings in the grand room were in need of restoration, while the books in the library were dusty and neglected.

(ABOVE) ANYONE FOR TENNIS? SHERRY EDEN, EILEEN BADHAM, BETTY BANKS AND WALLY BADHAM, 1940 OR 1941. (RIGHT) ONE OF THE FEW BIRDS TO SURVIVE GREAT TURKEY RAID OF 1964. (BELOW) MINIATURE CHEST MADE OF MOTTLED KAURI. (OPPOSITE) THESE STEREOSCOPE IMAGES OF KAREKARE ENABLED VIEWERS TO SEE THE BEACH IN 3D. LOWER IMAGE IS OF WOODCUTTER'S COTTAGE; MIDDLE, THE FAMOUS BENT-BACK POHUTUKAWA STILL SURVIVES ON THE WATCHMAN RIDGE.

Around the perimeter of the property were small, self-contained cottages. There was no silver service, no meals served any more. Dust and cobwebs seemed to clothe everything in a musty sadness. I remember thinking that these rooms had once echoed with laughter and dancing and the sound of jazz. By the 1950s, the music had stopped. The fun-loving Wally and Dudley Badham had long gone, as had their family. On 19 June 1950, on Zoe Badham's 61st birthday, the Badhams sold their beloved Winchelsea House to crusty Scotsman Tom McGuire. Tom was a no-nonsense master builder who saw the potential to cut up the property into quarter-acre sections. The valley road houses and baches are the end result of his plans. The Surf Club drove Tom to distraction with their irresponsible hijinks and in hindsight, I feel very sorry for the way we treated him.

He renamed Winchelsea The Karekare Guest House. During the 1960s the property hosted a flock of wild turkeys. Old, cranky birds, they waddled round the grounds during the day, and at night would roost in the pohutukawa. They were accompanied by half a dozen peacocks, birds not known for their friendliness. At Christmas 1964, the North Piha Surf Club decided that turkey should be on the menu. They came over in their club truck at night and proceeded to stuff the turkeys into sugar sacks, no easy task. The result was not too pleasant: some of the birds had half-wrung necks and others lost their heads to the club axe. It was turkeycide, beyond what was necessary for the Christmas treat. The truck ran out of gas going back up the Cutting, and the game was up. The furious owner of the turkeys, Tom McGuire, made the club pay a large bounty for the raid, and some 40 years later, the leader of the conspirators is still known affectionately by the nickname Turkey. I have to confess that I was a witness to this event, as our club was to be on the receiving end of the Christmas treat. Although wild turkeys had roosted at Karekare for 50 years, the raid led to their extinction here.

It would be 30 years, and two more owners, before Winchelsea House would be restored to its former elegance. Tom McGuire tore down much of the old wing to make room for another house (which for several years contained his makeshift shop), while an ungainly and squalid washhouse extension robbed the older house of any pretensions to grace or charm.

In the early 1960s the shop was run by Mr and Mrs Paul. You could rent the 'Barracks' rooms for five shillings a night at weekends and holidays. 'Talkie' Paul would collect guests in his truck from the Piha bus at the top of the Cutting. He was known to order in a batch of meat pies for Friday night dinner. When the Pauls left, the shop closed permanently.

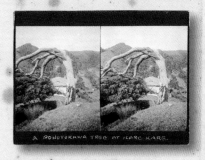

Shortly before the Butlers bought the property in 1972, 'Old Lady Winchelsea' had been declared a health hazard by the Waitemata County Council, and demolition seemed to be her likely fate. Fortunately, nothing was done about this edict, although the Butlers were at first inclined to agree with the decision. This was before they began to realise that under the layers of filthy, flaking paint and varnish, the original kauri ceilings, doors and floors were as good as ever.

'The barracks' as was
on purchase 1972

Winch

(ABOVE) **BY 1989 WINCHELSEA HOUSE WAS FULLY RESTORED, EXACTLY 100 YEARS AFTER CONSTRUCTION BY CHARLES PRIMROSE MURDOCH.** (OPPOSITE TOP RIGHT) **DOROTHY BUTLER GREETS WALLY BADHAM, WHO HAD RETURNED TO KAREKARE AFTER 60 YEARS, 2000.** (OPP. LOWER) **GRAMOPHONE MUSIC WAS POPULAR WITH PRE-WAR BOARDING HOUSE DANCE PARTIES. SHOWN IS 78 RPM RECORD *IF I HAD A TALKING PICTURE OF YOU:* FOX-TROT WITH VOCAL CHORUS, WILLARD YOUNG AND HIS ORCHESTRA.**

Winchelsea House had for years been used as a rubbish dump of sorts by the occupants of the shop-house next door.

The Butlers finally decided to restore and extend the other house on the property, which they fondly christened 'The Barracks' because of its long, thin shape and the number of doors which opened onto the front verandah. First they had to remove 28 truckloads of rubbish, replace the inadequate plumbing and drainage, and repair the roof.

Dorothy and Roy Butler were still undecided, although ready to begin restoration, when they met architect John Lewis, who at that time was president of the Waitakere Preservation Society. He suggested that they extend The Barracks, retaining the original character, and produced a sketch to show how this might be accomplished. The Butlers agreed to proceed with a gradual restoration, first transforming The Barracks into a comfortable family home.

By 1989, exactly 100 years after Charles Murdoch began its construction, the fine old house had regained its dignity. Dorothy admits to having become almost obsessed with the project, scouring demolition yards where she found an identical

Restoration of
Winchelsea House
1988

match for a lost window on the east wall, as well as several missing doors whose design fitted the period. She became a regular at antique and junk shops, always on the lookout for solid furniture. "Nothing flimsy; this had always been a *lived-in* house," Dorothy emphasises.

At first, the guest list was limited to family and friends, but the word soon got around, and the Butlers found themselves letting out the fine old house for weekends and holidays. The visitors' book reveals an impressive list of well-known names, from Anna Paquin and her father, during the filming of *The Piano*, to Neil Finn of Crowded House, a *Vogue* group from London and a *Marie Claire* group from Paris and New York, as well as a procession of writers, artists, academics, musicians, and theatrical people from near and far.

Thanks to the lovable and generous Dorothy and husband Roy, the music has at last returned to Winchelsea House.

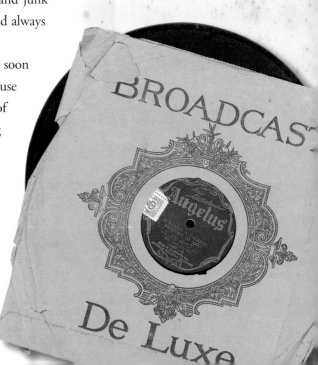

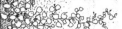  

# Trevor Lloyd: A Kiwi Icon

Whenever Trevor Lloyd came out to Karekare, he couldn't resist fosicking in every nook and cranny, searching for the lost Karekare treasure. Leading the expedition was one of his best and oldest friends, Charles Badham, the proprietor of Winchelsea House. Although they never found the motherlode, they did well on rock ledges and from digging in the caves above the waterfall, according to Charles' son Wally. After he had been digging all day in the Great Cave, Lloyd found a skull-sized piece of half-worked greenstone. This must have been hidden before a raid. A basket of ancient fish-hooks and sinkers found on the rock-face at Pararaha was his most important discovery, and encouraged him to continue searching. This beautiful collection is one the largest of its kind, and is in the Auckland War Memorial Museum.

Trevor Lloyd loved Karekare. He was one of New Zealand's greatest illustrators and cartoonists, and he gave the country its most enduring icon, the kiwi, as a cartoon character he drew when the All Blacks were defeated by Wales in 1905. Lloyd's kiwi captured the public imagination: the jaunty, flightless bird became symbolic of this country and its people.

Born on the Wade River near Orewa, Lloyd spent many of his weekends over a period of 50 years sketching the coastal bush. He worked from his small Piha bach, which he had built in the shape of a Maori meeting house, then carved and named Whare Tane.

Most of Lloyd's work was done for the Auckland *Weekly News*, but in the 1920s he began to be noticed with his superb pen and ink renderings in the *New Zealand Herald*. His sepia etchings now fetch thousands of dollars and illustrate the bush, the coast and the central North Island volcanic plateau. He had a close affinity with Maori, and although for the time respectful of their culture and rightful place in the New Zealand psyche, he was not bashful in creating his own mythology, of playful, cheerful elf-like Maori, dwelling in harmony with forest creatures and birds, which often graced the decorative borders of the bumper special issues of the *Weekly News*.

He introduced Maori cartoon imagery to politics. His obituary in the *Herald* made reference to the best-known cartoon that Lloyd ever drew, before the General Election of 1911, in which Sir Joseph Ward suffered defeat. It depicted the Prime Minister and his team steering a battered waka, heading for a rock under the escort of a large shark labelled SOCIALISM.

A second cartoon after the election showed the shark devouring the Honorable George Fowlds, who in the earlier cartoon was jumping overboard. I doubt if his cartoons would be appreciated as much in these more politically

*The Watchman. KareKare*                                        *Trevor Lloyd*

correct times, but his sense of humour, his good nature and his obvious affection for Maori, were always apparent. His cartoon dog Spot, which appeared in many of his works, gave New Zealand the term 'top dog' and countless fox terriers. Evidently he coined the name Spot, which has gone on to greater fame in recent times as the star of Telecom television commercials.

Exhibiting at the Auckland Society of Arts, he is said to have had lessons from the great epic painter of Maori mythology, Lewis John Steele.

Lloyd was disadvantaged by blindness in one eye, and lacked a thumb on his painting hand, yet nothing much daunted the fun-loving cartoonist, who saw much to laugh at in the society of his day. Dubbing the New Zealand Railways 'Snailways', he always had a quip or a new joke, and would turn up on a Saturday morning at Winchelsea House and stay until

long after dark. Charles Badham and Trevor Lloyd were life-long friends, and in 1936, New Zealand's grandest humorist and illustrator retired from both the *New Zealand Herald* and the Auckland *Weekly News*.

Lauded as a pioneer of etching, and a political cartoonist for 32 years, Lloyd's last trip to Karekare was on a weekend in September 1937 preceding his death at his stone fortress-like home that he designed and had built in Clive Road at the base of Mt Eden. It housed his collection of greenstone, Maori artifacts and found treasure, reputedly the largest private collection of its kind in the country. His legacy is seen in many of our current kiwiana icons.

Wally Badham recalls that at Karekare, following Trevor Lloyd's death, the place was in mourning all summer.

(ABOVE RIGHT) **LLOYD SKETCHES JUNE FARLEY ON WINCHELSEA HOUSE VERANDAH.**

# THE LITTLE SCHOOL
# IN THE VALLEY

(ABOVE) **KAREKARE SCHOOL PUPILS DRESSED IN PIONEER COSTUME FOR TWENTIETH ANNIVERSARY CELEBRATIONS, 1998.**

ON THE 20TH anniversary of the Lone Kauri Community School in 1998, we sat under a golden tent and looked out over the Pararaha Valley. It was one of those days when a community comes together to cheer itself on and to celebrate 20 years of hard work.

The Lone Kauri School is special. Not only is it a place of learning for the local children, but much of the community life revolves here around the young. The beginnings of the school grew out of the frustration of local parents, tired of braving the long, unsealed Lone Kauri and Piha roads to Oratia. Yet this was not the first school at Karekare.

The first school at Karekare opened in 1910, as an alternative to the journey over the ranges to the little wooden schoolhouse on the West Coast Road in Oratia, where a single teacher meted out strict discipline for the children of the orchardists and the other residents of the Oratia Valley.

At Karekare, the little schoolhouse of 1910 had a roll of six children of mill workers. It can be glimpsed in early photographs as a small, white building – more of a shed than a schoolhouse – but it served the purpose. It was located where the toilet block now stands. In those days the track to Karekare would have been long and slippery, but parents would have opted for a Karekare education. What lucky kids. You can walk the same track today, the Horoeka, down to Karekare.

The first teacher, Miss La Trobe, came out and lived with the Murdochs. She was also an accomplished artist. The school was open two days a week. On the other two days of the four-day school week, the children were given a lift on the train down to Whatipu, where there was another small school.

Although the roll was small, the Karekare School was excellent. The Murdochs, with their brood, believed in education and later, when the Farleys ran the boarding house, the children's governess Miss Elizabeth Lawrence became the second teacher. In 1921, the second schoolhouse opened across the dirt road leading to the bridge and the waterfall. This new building had been moved from further up the valley in

a flood, and was more of a workers' bunkhouse. After being gutted and painted, it looked quite elegant, and quickly became a place of great pride in the little valley community. Lit by a small fire in winter, it was also used for functions such as birthdays and weddings. The Farleys were married here.

The school in 1927 had a roll of Farleys, Badhams and Rules. All local, all growing up in a paradise relatively untouched by the changes that were happening in the wider world.

At 86, June Farley recalls the early schooldays at Karekare, when her father Wally worked at the boarding house. The long summer days dragged inside the one-room schoolhouse. Miss Lawrence had a habit of nodding off after a big boarding house lunch and a mug or two of the Farleys' home brew. As the usually strict teacher slumped in her seat, one of the young Farley boys would creep up and swing the clock hands forward by an hour or two. The banging of desks would wake up the woozy teacher, who would promptly exclaim about how time flies, before

(TOP) **THE TWENTIETH ANNIVERSARY CELEBRATIONS WERE ENLIVENED BY TWISTY WILLOW, A CELTIC BAND FROM ORATIA.**

proclaiming that school had finished for the day.

The pupils of Karekare School continued to be a mix of boarding house and itinerant workers' children and when it closed in 1932 it had served the local community for 21 years.

In the early 1970s, new residents were buying into the Lone Kauri Road properties after Gus Dean subdivided his farm into ten-acre blocks. The idea of a Karekare school really took off when local resident Kubi Witten-Hannah was accepted for teacher training. Jonathan Hunt, the Member of Parliament for New Lynn, suggested to Kubi and the local people that a part of his land could be used for a school. Jonathan's only conditions were that any child from Karekare must be able to attend, and that he didn't want any of the buildings to be in sight of his hilltop house. His final stipulation was that a bottle of Henderson wine once a year was the only payment necessary. The community swung into fundraising mode, organising barn dances, hangis, selling Christmas trees, and possum skin Davy Crockett hats which fathers made from on long winter nights. Fundraising seldom comes easy and by 1976, they had raised only $2000. Jonathan provided useful contacts, and one of the best was inviting the then Director-General of Education, Mr Bill Renwick, to come out to Karekare and meet the parents in May 1976.

The Education Department subsequently dangled the bait of re-opening the little Piha School. It didn't work; the Piha community wanted their own school, as did Karekare. It was agreed to start the school in Kubi Witten-Hannah's barn, with instruction provided initially by the Correspondence School. The first pupils were the local five-year-olds Sasha Gandy, Matthew Grove, Susan Humphries, Daniel Witten-Hannah and Cushla Yeoman. The barn provided plenty of space but few other amenities. There was one cold tap and a long-drop toilet and no electricity.

The barn served the purpose. Meanwhile local volunteers, mainly parents, laid the foundations of the new school building. Beautifully designed by local resident Bill Witten-Hannah (by good fortune architect to the Education Board), it fitted perfectly into the contour of the hill.

What was needed was the money to complete it. It was a balancing act, and it was a *New Zealand Herald* front page article that delivered the dream. The story on the Karekare pupils in a barn caught the imagination of businessman and philanthropist Mr Lewisham. He had $20,000 and a simple request: he wanted his gift to remain anonymous

for 20 years. For the children of Karekare, it was out of the barn and into the school.

In 1978, the Lone Kauri School opened officially in its own building. Under increasing pressure, the Education Board agreed on the legality of salary payments for a Correspondence Supervisor. Under this system, which was evaluated on classrooms outside a school district, the Lone Kauri School could operate in its own right. If this sounds simple, it wasn't. Kubi was appointed as the first teacher, assisted by a rostered group of local women. It was the beginning of a long list of committed school supervisors. Angela Patten was next, appointed in 1979, and when she left in 1980, there were 11 pupils. The July parents' meeting typically combined philosophic discussions with a working bee, and the meeting notice contained the somewhat alarming request to bring ideas for a statement of the school's special character, and an axe. The Department of Education's representative Mr John Joliff thought the school's ideas of community awareness and involvement would make it ineligible for integration into the

things I like best.
I like the peace. It's not too
crowded I like the work
and it's in the country
I do not have to go and wait
for cars when I go home. *Thomas*

(TOP) **KUBI WITTEN-HANNAH TAUGHT LESSONS IN THIS BARN.** (BELOW LEFT) **HAKA PERFORMED BY CLASS, DECEMBER 1978.** (OPP., BACKGROUND) **FIRST SCHOOL NEAR BEACH HAD THIS GRAND OLD CLOCK.**

system, so the school trustees were forced to consider establishing their own religion in order to qualify. Tongue in cheek, they called it the Pararaha Faith.

By 1982, the rising school roll at last reached a point where it outgrew the maximum size for a correspondence school, and although the Auckland Education Board was wary of developing the situation, it was decided to give the school a status: it would become part of the Oratia Primary School, 14 km down the West Coast and Piha roads.

In February 1984 the Lone Kauri Community School was opened as a classroom of the Oratia District School. Its new teacher was the historian and writer Peter Buffett, who would become their much-loved teacher. Jonathan Hunt donated a dinghy, which he allowed to be floated on his pond. Planting and landscaping was never a problem here. The little school in the valley flourished and has continued to do so.

(TOP) **PARENTS CELEBRATE SCHOOL'S ANNIVERSARY WITH A GLASS OF WINE BEHIND CLASSROOM.** (ABOVE) **TRADITIONAL EASTER TREAT FOR PARENTS AND FRIENDS AT WITTEN-HANNAHS.** (BELOW LEFT) **BEACH RACES AT SUMMER'S END BRINGS THE COMMUNITY TOGETHER AND INSPIRES THE SCHOOL'S ARTISTS.** (OPPOSITE) **PUPILS OF KAREKARE SCHOOL, 2000.**

# HAND OF THE MASTER

(ABOVE) **CHARLES BLOMFIELD USED KAREKARE AS A BASE FROM WHICH HE MADE FORAYS INTO THE WAITAKERES TO SKETCH KAURI AND BUSH SCENES, LATER RENDERING THESE INTO HIS PAINTINGS SUCH AS** (OPPOSITE) *TWO KAURIS;* **1901. OIL ON CANVAS; AUCKLAND ART GALLERY TOI O TAMAKI, PURCHASED 1967.** (TOP) **DETAIL OF BLOMFIELD'S BAPTIST TABERNACLE ROOF BEAM DESIGN.**

THE BLOMFIELD FAMILY emigrated to New Zealand as part of the Albertland Settlement Association, sailing from England on the *Gertrude* in 1862. Travelling with his widowed mother and eight siblings, the 14-year-old Charles Blomfield was already sketching ship life on the long passage to New Zealand. They arrived in Auckland in February 1863 after 97 days at sea. They never made it to Port Albert on the Kaipara, settling instead in a small house in Mt Eden. Auckland would be the artist's base until his death in 1926.

Blomfield gave us one of the great icons of 19th century New Zealand art, his paintings of the extraordinary formations of the Pink and White Terraces, which were destroyed in the Tarawera eruption of 10 June 1886, and known at the time as the eighth wonder of the world. He painted 12 versions of this scene.

Charles Blomfield, self-taught painter, signwriter and one of New Zealand's early environmentalists, created a legacy of beautiful landscape art. Blomfield's technique was without peer: his impact was such that he defined the grandeur of the New Zealand bush for generations. He struggled to make a living out of painting the outdoors. A fervent walker and traveller, he roamed widely in his new-found land. He held exhibitions during his travels, to sustain his family in often difficult times.

Based at the family home of 40 Wood Street in the inner city suburb of Ponsonby, Blomfield eventually outlived his popularity. Strange as it may seem, at the beginning of the 20th century, his great canvases were fetching as little as £1. By the century's end, his works were amongst the most valued and prized in New Zealand art. Blomfield and his large family would travel out to the west coast by train and coach, staying with the Murdochs for a week or two. Using Karekare as a base, he would sketch and photograph the dams, mill and beach.

I've always been fascinated by the variety of styles in his work. His Whatipu mill is a dazzling display of technique and almost photorealism, whereas his Karekare paintings are executed more in the French *primitif* style. His use of soft blue tones in sky and bush overlays a depth of feeling that has never been duplicated. He was

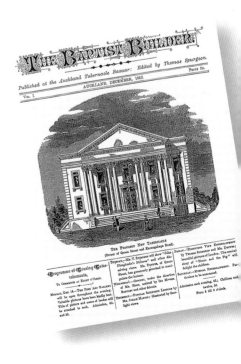

(LEFT) THE BLOMFIELD FAMILY OUTSIDE THE BAPTIST TABERNACLE IN 1909. CHARLES IS SECOND FROM LEFT IN SECOND BACK ROW. HE WAS ON BUILDING COMMITTEE, RAISING FUNDS AND LATER PAINTING THE HIGH CEILING WITH HIS INTRICATE DESIGNS. THE NEO-CLASSICAL BUILDING WITH GRECIAN TEMPLE-STYLE FRONT (BELOW) OPENED IN 1885. DECEMBER 1882 EDITION OF *THE BAPTIST BUILDER* (LOWER) SHOWS ARCHITECTURAL DRAWING OF PROPOSED STRUCTURE. (OPPOSITE) CHARLES BLOMFIELD, *WAITAKERE BUSH VIEW;* 1883, OIL ON CANVAS; PRIVATE COLLECTION. THIS STAND OF KAURI CAN STILL BE FOUND IN THE RANGES.

the Turner of the New Zealand landscape. His sense of light contrasted greatly with that of his friend, the moody and foreboding Petrus van der Velden, whom he in fact envied. If van der Velden's contribution to New Zealand's art was his menacing dark gorge, Blomfield's was the glory of the great kauri forests.

"The world is partly losing its meaning," he said. "I have never ceased to be thankful for two things. One is that I was born with a love for the beautiful in nature, and the other, that I came to New Zealand before the hand of man had spoiled most of its natural beauty. I love the bush. I delight to wander through it, hour after hour. I never tire of its wonderful charm. I love the glinting sunlight and the mysterious gloom, the sweet smell of moist air and the resinous perfume of the pines. I never feel lonely or a desire for company in the bush. I love to push my way up the spur of some steep bush range, or leap from stone to stone, travelling up some babbling creek."

At Karekare, Charles did exactly this. I followed his path up the Company Stream, crossing over the site of the bush millers' camp, down into the headwaters of the Pararaha, to the place where he sketched his Waitakere kauri. The painting was completed in his studio and the trees still stand today, high on a ridge above the gorge at Pararaha.

His grandest painting, now known as *Nature's Cathedral*, painted in 1921, was the work that broke his spirit. This large canvas (1.2 bys 1.5m) was entered by Blomfield as *The Vaulted Isles of Nature's Cathedral*, for the Jubilee Year Exhibition of the Auckland Society of Arts. It was a combination of elements from many of his previous paintings: kauri in light and shade overwhelm the viewer, almost dwarfing the spectator by their sheer size, as it would if you were standing in such a grove. It contains powerful religious symbolism: Charles was a deeply committed Christian and had painted the interior of the Baptist Tabernacle at the top of Auckland's Queen Street.

He considered *Nature's Cathedral* his masterpiece and he believed no New Zealand painter could have rivalled the work. The prize was that the painting would be purchased by the Auckland City Council and hung in the public gallery. He put on it one of the highest price tags for any New Zealand painting to that time. It gained only third place. Now in the Auckland War Memorial Museum, the painting hung on the stairway in his Ponsonby home for 40 years.

The rejection of his masterpiece as "old-fashioned" had a devastating effect on this proud man. His mental health deteriorated and the family was finally forced to commit him to the Avondale Asylum. By the time of his release, Blomfield's talent and confidence had sadly deserted him, and he was reduced to dabbing over his old canvases and his sketching became erratic. Attempting to sign his name to a painting, he dropped the brush and would never paint again.

(ABOVE RIGHT) **CHARLES BLOMFIELD,** *MURDOCH'S KAREKAU MILL*; DATE UNKNOWN; OIL ON CANVAS; COURTESY ESTATE OF MAURICE LEONARD.

While looking through a drawer at an Auckland art dealer's, I recognised Charles Blomfield in many of the photographs, and realised I was onto a real treasure, when I noticed that the photographs in this album had been taken at Piha and Karekare. Here was the recording of the Blomfield family on the coast at the turn of the 20th century, at a time when this prolific painter was gathering material for his exhibitions. Showing the family frolicking on the beach, on the sand dunes and in a makeshift tent, these summer photographs are a superb evocation of the life and times of this significant painter at Karekare. His painting *The Karekare Valley* is a simple rendering that serves accurately to place the Shaw homesteads.

Blomfield did not take too many liberties with his art. Often working from photographs, he evoked the living presence of the landscape. These were images that could not have been painted anywhere but in New Zealand: the light, the colouring and the feeling were opening people's eyes to see a new unpainted land that was radically different from anything in the Old World.

At his funeral, he was honoured as one of New Zealand's greatest sons. His son-in-law William Kendon penned a heartfelt obituary for the *New Zealand Herald*:

...for he has painted his country from north to south, in all her beauty and with all her changing moods... the magnificence of her sea coast, and above all, the witchery and wonder of her forests – all these, and much more than these have been flung into canvas by a master hand.

Charles Blomfield is buried in Hillsborough Cemetery, looking out towards the Manukau Heads and his blue, misty Waitakere Ranges.

(ABOVE AND OPPOSITE LOWER) **SNAPSHOTS FROM BLOMFIELD ALBUM SHOW HAPPY SUMMER DAYS AT KAREKARE.** (BELOW) **BLOMFIELD'S PONSONBY HOME IS COMMEMORATED WITH THIS PLAQUE.**

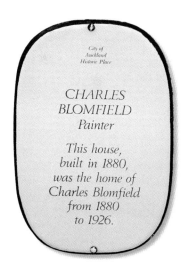

City of
Auckland
Historic Place

CHARLES
BLOMFIELD
Painter

This house,
built in 1880,
was the home of
Charles Blomfield
from 1880
to 1926.

# HONEYMOON
# AT KAREKARE

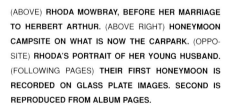

(ABOVE) **RHODA MOWBRAY, BEFORE HER MARRIAGE TO HERBERT ARTHUR.** (ABOVE RIGHT) **HONEYMOON CAMPSITE ON WHAT IS NOW THE CARPARK.** (OPPOSITE) **RHODA'S PORTRAIT OF HER YOUNG HUSBAND.** (FOLLOWING PAGES) **THEIR FIRST HONEYMOON IS RECORDED ON GLASS PLATE IMAGES. SECOND IS REPRODUCED FROM ALBUM PAGES.**

WHEN I FIRST saw the images, I was astonished at their beauty and elegance. Here in two albums in the Waitakere City Library were the images of the honeymoon of Herbert and Rhoda Arthur, dated 1897, Karekare, New Zealand.

The honeymoon of these two newly-weds in a canvas tent on what is now the parking area, provides a glimpse into the Karekare landscape as the 19th century ended. Herbert was 30 and Rhoda Mowbray 28 at the time of their wedding at the home of Rhoda's mother in Ring Terrace, Ponsonby. Rhoda was the beautiful daughter of a soldier who joined the 61st Regiment of Foot in the New Zealand Wars. At the time of her wedding, she was from Waiau Pa on the other side of the Manukau. Herbert, an enthusiastic photographer, took with him on their honeymoon a suitcase containing a Newman full plate camera, a British half-plate camera and a Ross and La Verne lens. They would have probably gone by train from Auckland to Glen Eden, before transferring by wagon to the Karekare Valley.

The photographs show that theirs was a true Victorian encampment. There are

*the breakers dash themselves to foam against the rocks nea...*

(ABOVE) **RHODA DRAWING WATER FROM THE KARE-KARE STREAM.**

bottles, clothes and trunks – the newly-weds were serious about their stay. The glass negatives capture the smoke of their cooking fire and the early morning light, with Herbert shaving and returning to the camp. This photograph, one of many, would have been taken by Rhoda. The photographs from the plate camera were placed in an album and captioned by Herbert.

Thirty-nine years on, the couple returned to Karekare to recreate the photographs of their honeymoon. These were also collected in an album and captioned in Herbert's unmistakable hand.

Years later, I was thrilled to hear that a number of glass plate photographs had been discovered in an antique shop in Dominion Road, and that they were of the Waitakere and Waiatarua area. The images are outstanding: bush mill camps, tracks that would one day become roads and a skyline now obliterated by scrub – but who was the photographer? There was no clue on the brown-enveloped plates, other than some basic description in elegant copperplate handwriting.

*We find the stream now takes a straight line for the distant sand hills,*

1936

Waitakere City purchased as many of the slides as they were able to. One of the photographs was published in a local newspaper in an effort to seek out the source of the plates. Fortunately, David Arthur – Herbert's grandson – recognised the style and image and contacted the Waitakere Library. The connection was made by the handwriting and the two albums from 1897 and 1936 became priceless mementos of the Karekare honeymoon. After his death, Herbert's collection of 10,000 glass plates was divided, some of the plates being donated to the Auckland War Memorial Museum and some to the Alexander Turnbull Library. The rest were sold to Auckland antique dealers.

When Herbert Arthur married, he was already fascinated by the photographic image. He was a founding member of

(ABOVE) **HERBERT, PHOTOGRAPHED BY RHODA AT THE HEAD OF THE VALLEY.**

*Come with me while I recall old, and form new impression*

*Crossing the bridge to the main road,*

the Auckland Photographic Society and Secretary of the Auckland Gas Company. He had a remarkable eye for composition and light and he was also passionate about the west coast. Here, in a pure landscape, he was able to explore structure and form as the soft dawn gives way to strong coastal light and later turns into a dramatic sundown with the giant orb sliding into the sea, directly out from the Watchman rock in January and February.

Glimpsed in the background behind their encampment is the bare, sandy hillock of the Watchman flank, nowadays covered in grass, flax and weekend houses. Towards the beach is the prominent rock-face that was known in those times as Queen Victoria, but now is simply a protruding buttress of rock. In those days, the Karekare Stream meandered between the pohutakawa and the Arthurs would have crossed to their campsite by a small bridge to the apron of grass where we now park.

By the time of their return in 1936 (Herbert aged 69 and Rhoda, 67), the valley and stream had been realigned by Depression work gangs. The Number Five

Scheme, as it was called, consisted of men from Auckland City working in the countryside. They transformed the valley. The green, two metre-wide track was cleared by men who lived in tents for the summer. Work was also progressed on the approaching roads, including the road into the Lone Kauri farmhouse from the Piha Road.

The stream was dug out and realigned, and near its end it then swung in a gentle arc towards the beach. A small bridge took over where the road finished, leaving campers to walk around the corner to Brownes' Boarding House. The tree that had held the tent guy ropes had died and the Watchman flank was covered in grass. The tennis court changing sheds of the Farley Boarding House now served as the first Surf Club and guests filled the accommodation to capacity.

Herbert again records the beach, this time under winter skies, then takes his camera high up into the Karekare Stream. His eye is as good as ever as he poetically describes the peace and serenity of the bush. These two albums are the bookends of their lives together.

Rhoda and Herbert are buried together in Waikumete Cemetery. Their great-grandson Max is a fine surfer and most summers when the surf is roaring, he can be seen off the North Point, riding the left-handers.

(ABOVE) **HERBERT ARTHUR HAD A KEEN EYE FOR COMPOSITION AND UNDERSTOOD THAT THE PHOTOGRAPHIC IMAGE WAS ESSENTIALLY A PAINTING WITH LIGHT.** (TOP RIGHT AND LOWER RIGHT) **RHODA AND HERBERT RETURN TO KAREKARE TO COMPLETE THE BOOKENDS.**

PROTECT
NEW ZEALAND

capture of the German submarine U 570 by a Lockheed "Hudson" of the British Coastal C

WITH

BACK THEM UP

3% NATIONAL SAVINGS

or a healthy, happy job

Join the

WOMEN'S
LAND
ARMY

# ROAD TO THE RADAR

IN WINTER, one of my favourite runs is from the end of Te Ahu Ahu Road. From this promontory there's a view that seems to go on forever, up the coast north to the Kaipara, and south to Raglan. It takes in the Karekare Valley below, the Lone Kauri and the ridgeline behind it .

Before you is a a small tower with a seaward light and a panorama of the Tasman. The foundations of buildings can be seen. This was Wartime Radar Station No. 4. Others were scattered along the coastline, part of the defence network established to detect a Japanese airborne invasion of New Zealand. The West Coast Road (now called the Piha Road) had trenches, and below in the Karekare Valley a home guard of four was ready to fight them on the beaches. Fortunately, they waited in vain. The radar station was the longest-serving coastal defence unit in the country. Situated at 841 feet above sea level, the facility opened in 1942 and did not close until 1959. Its other interesting feature was that it had one of the longest ranges of any coastal alert, at 200 miles. It was linked by telephone direct to the underground bunkers cut from the lava tunnels beneath the Epsom Training College in Auckland, which served as the headquarters of the New Zealand command.

When I first started to go out to the coast in 1956, Ken Craig was the resident caretaker of the radar station. Barbed wire and large, forbidding gates gave the impression of Stalag 17, our only reference in those days. He told me that their greatest fear was of submarine invasion, and the searchlight that swept the sea was manned constantly during the war years. There was a crew of six to eight men on each shift during the early part of the war, on constant vigil. Later, the Women's Auxiliary Airforce, the WAAFs, which included my mother, joined the unit.

The most prominent feature was the gantry supporting a 30-foot by 10-foot reflector screen for the aerial array. This system rotated several times a minute and both the speed and direction were controlled by the operator in the adjacent room. Housed in another room near the gates were four Lister diesel-driven alternators which provided power to the system.

My late mate Rex Head, for many years the art teacher of Kelston Boys High School, and an accomplished painter of this coastline, was a wireless operator here. Rex, a great lover of life, bemoaned the lack of entertainment. He told me that the only enjoyment he got during his years at the station were his visits to the Piha Hotel and the dances at the hall on the beach.

My mother told me that it was like a small community out on the headland. Although they were isolated, they were very much in touch with the ongoing war. Military aircraft based at Whenuapai would use the signal to home in as they returned from their missions.

The skies over Karekare were busy with aircraft picking their flight paths from the radar. Many were from the No. 40 Transport Squadron, which maintained a magnificent record over the later war years, following its formation in 1943. This unit, with its full quota of Dakotas and Lodestars, would fly from Whenuapai each Monday to the war zones of Guadalcanal in the Solomon Islands and Espiritu Santo in the New Hebrides, as Vanuatu was known then. Retracing the route, they would arrive back over the beacon on Thursdays. Two Lodestars departed from Whenuapai each Wednesday and Sunday, making calls at Tontouta, New Caledonia. A fourth left the airfield carrying RNZAF personnel of all ranks and trades.

(ABOVE) **WARTIME RADAR STATION NO. 4: VITAL LINK IN THE COMMAND CHAIN.** (BELOW) **PILOT'S VIEW OF RADAR NO. 4, LOOKING SOUTH TOWARDS KAREKARE.**

The aircraft often flew so low over Te Ahu Ahu Road that my mother recalled identifying the Dakota NZ 3501 with its Popeye cartoon character painted large and bold on the fuselage. As the Pacific War escalated, the Whenuapai base became a strategic hub and Radar No. 4 was a vital link in the air command chain.

My mother recalls that many of these planes were badly damaged, limping survivors of aerial battles in the Coral Sea and the Solomons and elsewhere in the Pacific theatre.

On one historic occasion, a low-flying aircraft was spotted and plotted on the radar screens. It was a Japanese reconnaissance plane launched from a submarine. While personnel throughout the radar and military network reacted with disbelief, the plane eluded capture, returning to its mother-ship. Enemy submarines were reported on two occasions by No. 4 Radar Station. In response to one reporting, an aircraft sent from Whenuapai failed to confirm the sighting.

By 1952, technology was rapidly advancing, and the base's last major surveillance was on the first and possibly only non-stop return flight to Australia by a Hastings bomber. This unauthorised flight was a nervous 12 hours and five minutes for the crew as they flew direct to Newcastle, down the coast to Sydney, and returned on a sniff of aviation fuel to land safely back at base.

These days, the new high-tech beacon, unlike its revolving predecessor, sweeps seaward only every 20 seconds, a warning that the coast is near, a sign almost as old as navigation and sea travel itself. It illuminates the clouds and on stormy nights it is great to behold from the Karekare Valley. While I'm standing on the deck of my bach in the valley below, it cuts the black night like the swathe of searchlights from the opening credits of a 20th Century Fox movie.

The track to Mercer Bay goes gently down from the carpark, swinging around the headland. There's a seat for a quick breather and a view down the coast. In July and August migrating whales can be seen heading south. In summer, dolphins play in the surf.

Below, out of sight, is the Gap at Piha. Keep moving, and you'll come to a great lookout, high above the cliffs at Te Ahu Ahu Point. Directly ahead is a massive rock face with a chiselled likeness of Hinerangi, the lone watchful mourning Turehu chieftainess. I'm not one to see shapes in rocks or even the man in the moon, but the face of Hinerangi, from which Ahu Ahu – the Likeness – takes its name, is unmistakable. She gazes sphinx-like, waiting for her lost lover, a warrior from Karekare, who was washed from the rocks below. At sunrise as the first shafts of morning light give dramatic form to the rock, it is quite eerie. The face seems so Polynesian. For me it's a far better example of a landform resembling a lifeform than the crouching warrior who gave his name to Whakaari, later known as Lion Rock. And as for that, I've never really worked out the lion either.

(TOP AND MIDDLE) ANZAC DAY IS USUALLY CELE-BRATED ON THIS COAST AT PIHA, BUT IN 1995, 60 YEARS AFTER SURF LIFESAVING CLUB'S FOUNDING, CLUB MEMBERS WHO SERVED WERE HONOURED WITH A SPECIAL ANZAC CEREMONY AT KAREKARE, WHERE (BELOW) THERE WAS A PLAQUE SET INTO THE WATCHMAN ROCK IN 1947. (OPPOSITE) RADAR NO. 4 KEPT A LONELY VIGIL ON THIS HEADLAND THROUGH THE WAR YEARS.

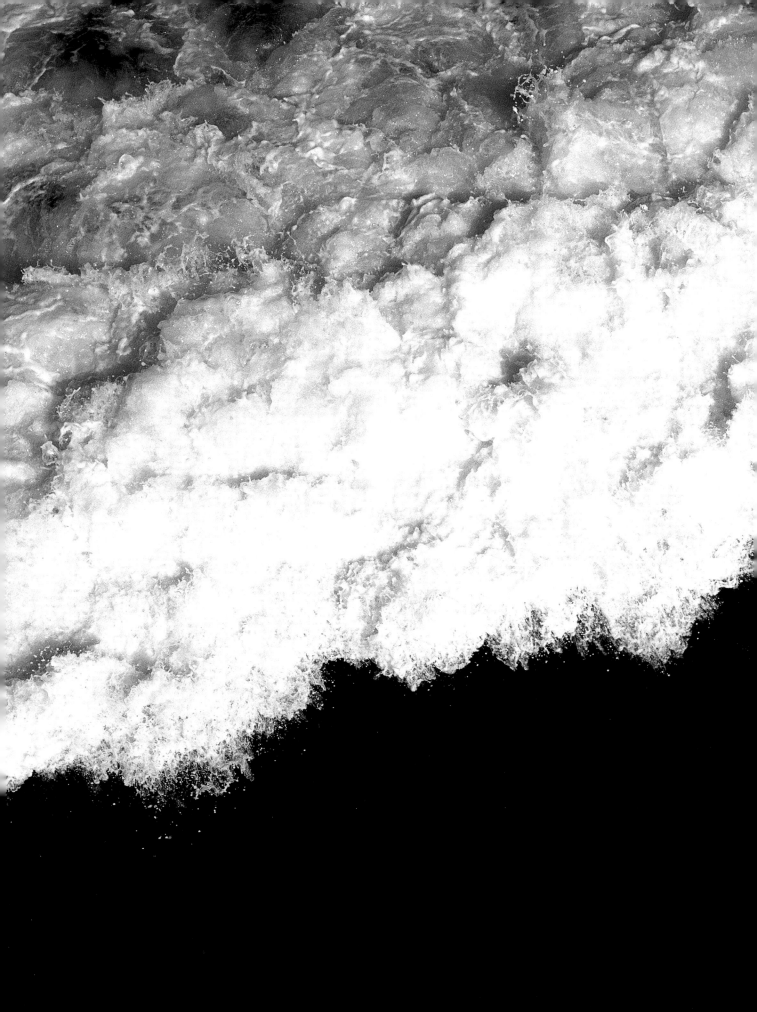

THE
ENERGY
OF WAVES

# THE GOLDEN MOMENT

(ABOVE) **ALL LIFEGUARDS NEEDED TO QUALIFY FOR THESE MEDALS OF THE ROYAL LIFESAVING SOCIETY AND THE NEW ZEALAND SURF LIFESAVING ASSOCI- ATION. THE CODES HAD DIFFERENT DISCIPLINES: ROYAL LIFE EMPHASISED PATIENT RECOVERY AND POOL SWIMMING SKILLS; NEW ZEALAND SURF LIFESAVING FAVOURED MILITARY-STYLE BEACH AND DRILL EXAMINATIONS. (TOP) CLUB'S COMPETITION SWIMMING COSTUME INSIGNIA. (OPPOSITE) TODAY'S LIFEGUARD NEEDS SKILLS IN FAST INFLATABLE CRAFT WHERE RAPID RETRIEVAL OF THE PATIENT TAKES A FRACTION OF THE TIME OF OLD METHODS.**

THE KAREKARE SURF CLUB is like a family. This is a life-and-death business, and although we don't make a big deal of this aspect, we have an emotional bond from working together in often extremely difficult and dangerous situations, where seconds count in the saving of a life. There is a great comradeship involved. It involves lifelong friendships that extend beyond the weekend beach commitments.

As we don't get paid, you might say that we're not professionals, but lifeguards are damn good at what they do, because they have to be, and although it's about youth and fitness, it's also about understanding the beach, its tidal currents, its rips and moods. It's also about wanting to do something positive for the community. Being in a surf club is also about belonging to a beach tribe which has its own rituals. There is no room for those who cannot face fear or who can't be trusted in an emergency.

The true lifeguard never goes to the beach or any area of water to simply enjoy a day's relaxation. No matter how tranquil the scene may appear, the lifeguard remains vigilant, knowing that hidden dangers may suddenly be exposed. A young lifeguard is forever changed by the experience of being involved in a rescue where a life is saved – or lost. That ultimate fulfilment of the lifeguard mission binds the individual to his or her calling.

Karekare still retains its strong family-based tradition that has given us able club captains and administrators for almost 70 years. Now our children, as adults, are taking over the role of lifeguards on this beach. In many ways, they are better, fitter and more able to cope with technology, which has revolutionised surf lifesaving in New Zealand. Whereas we manfully swam antiquated lines to the drowning, new technology enables people to be rescued within seconds.

Following the widely-publicised rescue of Hazel Bentham by seaplane at Karekare in February 1935, the club was founded in the old YMCA building in Wellesley Street in downtown Auckland, in a small back room on 14 March of that year. The minutes record that nearly all of those present were members of the

The Minutes of the First
meeting of the
re Kare Surf Life-Saving Club
held at the Y.M.C.A. Auckland
on
Thursday 14th Mar. 1935

Messrs. S. Wales, R. Wales, W. Aldred, I. Thom
H. Robinson, I. Robinson, V. Sanders, I. Sand
L. Reed, I. Reale, S. Jones, H. Liddle, L. Gun

Mr. S. Wales was elected chairman of the meetin

moved Mr. Gunson, seconded Mr Reed, that the
of the club be "The Kare Kare Surf Life-Saving

Manukau Amateur Cycling Club, who had been present at the remarkable rescue a month before. Subsequently they had talked with the newly-formed Piha Surf Club, who advised them to get a portable box reel.

Ted Browne, the erstwhile proprietor of the small guesthouse by the waterfall, had brought the group together and booked the room. Harry Liddle, a natural choice as the first club captain, was passionate about its formation. An excellent swimmer, and someone with a job – that's all they really needed; Ted came away from the meeting as the first president. They decided on a logo of eagle wings encasing a cycle wheel. It had echoes of Italian and German neo-classical culture, which was fashionable in the 1930s and would eventually represent a world at war. They would later put this symbol on their new reel, on their uniforms, their letterhead and their club march-past pendant.

In the first correspondence to the newly formed club was an account from the Air Force for £40, a considerable amount in those days, for the rescue of Hazel Bentham. They returned the account to the Air Force, but promised to pay when they could raise the funds. After 65 years, the Air Force is still waiting for the money.

Over that first winter they raised enough funds to buy the first surf reel. It arrived from Australia in kitset form, a beautiful laminated, wooden, bowed-frame construction with drum and 440 yards of Indian cotton, which had become hopelessly entangled in transit. The line first needed to be stretched and run through a vat of candle wax to allow it to float on the surface. With it came a cork belt which the designated beltman jumped into and took off with into the surf. The cork belt was a death trap: once in it, the swimmer could not take it off, and if the line became snagged, which it sometimes did, the beltman would be pulled underwater and drowned, or in desperate need of resuscitation. It would be 10 years before the belt would be redesigned as a canvas chest harness that was made up of three pieces held together with one steel pin. If the line became snagged, the beltman would simply pull the pin and the belt would disengage. Designed in 1948 by a New Zealander, the Ross Safety Belt would be the main lifesaving device, with the reel and line, for nearly 50 years.

Ted Browne provided a free lunch and from his property, kauri rickers were used to build the first patrol tower. In 1936 the club, now acting like a "real surf patrol",

started to cast around for good swimmers to teach and train the members in the very precise drill, which was part of the lifesaving competition ritual in those days. These competitions, known as surf carnivals, were important events, the national championships attended by the Governor-General or the Prime Minister.

The grand march-past was impressive and very much in keeping with the militaristic ideal of strapping young men with massive silk banners and gleaming stainless steel poles, topped by their grand Teutonic club insignia. Often they were accompanied by a military band and the effect on the thousands of spectators was electrifying.

Even during an actual rescue, everything was designed to be carried out with military precision. The reel was lifted, run down the beach and set down. The three linesmen lifted the racing line gently between the fingers, placing it on their heads and paying out rapidly to keep pace with the dashing beltman who was heading for the drowning swimmer. Even while the rescue was being enacted, legwork in the surf was done in unison. The reelman, who allowed the reel to fly free, would shout instructions to the team. When the beltman had reached the victim, the three linesmen, moving as one man, would then bring both the beltman and victim to shore with a swing-arm motion, moving in synch. No other individuals were allowed to touch the line, and once close to the shore all four would race down and lift the patient up and bring him or her to the beach, face down. Mock resuscitation was then performed, with a technique known as the Shaeffer method, borrowed from the United States Police. This rigid discipline dominated surf life-saving competition in New Zealand and Australia.

In a real rescue, it was very different. Shaeffer was replaced by the

Holga Neilson method, where pressure was used on the victim's back, while their arms were placed in a wing-like position. This was supposed to force water from the lungs, but if the victim had been too long in the surf, they simply did not revive. The medical world kept its distance from surf lifesaving, although this was changing by the time mouth-to-mouth was introduced as a first response in 1981. In 2000, the 'ultimate' surf lifesaving device was brought to the beach – the defibrillator, a small machine that can 'jump-start' a stopped heart.

Les Reed, a butcher from New Lynn, was an experienced member of the Waitemata Swimming Club and had patrolled the Oneroa Beach on Waiheke Island. He was a superb swimmer, and as the second club captain he brought a sense of discipline and competition to the team. He knew some of Auckland's top swimmers, like the dazzling Shanahan brothers, top competitors from Auckland University, and signed them up. By 1939 the club owned two reels, two surf skis and a 30-seater bus purchased from the Farmers Trading Company. The generous Farley family allowed the Surf Club to use the tennis court changing sheds and rooms at the base of the Watchman as their clubhouse. They called it the Grand Hotel. It served the club well until 1951 when a cigarette left in one of the bunks saw it destroyed by fire.

They found a sponsor in Dominion Breweries and the club became known for its keen competition and enthusiastic drinking teams. The ever-popular Karekare patrol of Shanahans and other top Auckland swimmers like Gim Tane and Jim Ferguson toured the summer carnivals, winning events and taking the honours for the new club.

In 1939, following the outbreak of war, every club member who was of age, enlisted together, and were sent overseas to the various conflicts. At Easter 1940 the remaining members agreed to put the club into recession. Petrol restrictions meant that transport to the coast would be difficult. The club bus was parked under the large pohutakawa tree on the green and in 1943 the wheels were removed to render

the vehicle useless if the Japanese invaded from the sea. There was no patrol on the Karekare beach during the war years. At the cessation of hostilities, the vice-captain from those pre-war days, Pat Shanahan, revived the club.

Winchelsea House proprietor Ted Badham agreed to be their post-war president. In 1937 the club had built a gear shed on the large rock in the centre of the beach. With Harry Liddle's building skills in stone, the handsome structure, with its large cedar door, served both as a patrol tower and as storage for the wooden surf skis. These days, the rising sand, 10 metres deep, has all but covered the building. With the loss of the Grand Hotel, the members guaranteed the funding, all of £150, for a new surf club, and the aged Maria Farley donated the last section on the Farley estate of the Watchman. In the summer of 1953, members spent four months

The Boys at Kare Kare
may be tough—

but for TENDERNESS try

QUALITY MEAT

from

LES. REED

the BUTCHER

TOTARA AVENUE, NEW LYNN
(opposite the Railway Station)

building a creosoted, rough-sawn timber, one-room clubhouse on the sand dune with a glorious view over the beach. This was their first real headquarters. Lit by paraffin lamps, and with eight bunks, it was the perfect weekend haven and the centre of fun in my life when I first joined.

In 1963, the owner of Winchelsea House, Tom McGuire, offered to build the Surf Club a new clubhouse in return for removing the existing structure, situated on the sand dune, to the carpark for use as a general store. Some of us felt strongly against this, and the day before the removal on rollers of the clubhouse, the struts supporting the roof and walls were partly sawn through and concealed with putty and paint. As the bulldozer winching the building forward onto the rollers took the strain, the whole bloody thing collapsed inwards on itself in a shower of glass, splintering beams and Fibrolite. McGuire was livid, but to his dying day, blamed himself and the dozer driver for putting too much strain on the hawsers. Bugger!

Built on a concrete base foundation, the new clubhouse, with all mod cons, was opened in the summer of 1974. The membership grew, nippers added to the growing base of lifeguards and a new sense of professionalism was adopted. Teams became patrols, patrols grew into rescue units and lifeguarding came into its own in New Zealand.

In the 1970s, with surfing on the crest of a new wave of popularity, surf clubs expanded. For the first time, women were accepted in New Zealand as members of mixed patrols. Except for competition, the reel and line were abandoned for the more speedy fins and neoprene rescue tubes. Rescue helicopters became a back-up in the main centres, and surf clubs on the west coast experimented with jet boats and other motorised rescue craft.

The Karekare patrol has maintained a magnificent record of lifesaving. It's an unpredictable and hazardous beach to patrol. The flags often need to be moved during the day with the rise and fall of the tides.

Few rescues could match that made by Ray Baillie in 1979 at Karekare. Alone in the clubhouse, he was awoken in the morning by cries alerting him to the fact that three people had got into difficulties in big surf off the Cauldron. Baillie attempted a solo rescue, diving 10 metres off rocks into boiling surf. Although two of the three were drowned, his outstanding effort was recognised when he was awarded New Zealand Surf Rescue of the Year.

In 1982 the club again won this award, this time for a mass rescue by lifeguards Andrew Pedersen and Stephen Pye, after a group of surfers were swept into the Cauldron.

When women joined the Karekare Surf Club in the 1980s, the first on the west coast to admit them, the club took a lot of flak, though it was the beginning of a fresh, family approach to lifeguarding. The macho era of bronzed males who spent a great deal of time showing off was superseded by serious commitment to new lifeguarding techniques. Clumsy jetboats were tried but proved unsatisfactory and were replaced by fast inflatables that were capable of cutting the rescue time down to seconds.

(ABOVE) **REGIONAL GUARDS FRASER HARVEY AND ROBERT HAMMOND PATROLLING BEACH DURING SUMMER HOLIDAYS.** (BELOW) **CORK BELT WAS AN ESSENTIAL BUT DANGEROUS ITEM OF EQUIPMENT UNTIL 1948 WHEN THE ROSS SAFETY BELT WAS INTRODUCED.** (LOWER) **JOHN SHANAHAN, 1946 AUCKLAND AND NEW ZEALAND BELTMAN CHAMPION.** (BELOW LEFT) **KAREKARE SURF BOAT *MISS UEB* IN ACTION.** (OPPOSITE, CLOCKWISE FROM TOP LEFT) **PATROLLING FROM GEAR SHED ROOF, 1947; KAREKARE TEAM CROSS-DRESS FUN SURF CHALLENGE; DRINKING RACE, KAREKARE VS PIHA, ON TENNIS COURTS, FOR THE DRINKING BONE; ROCK GEAR STORAGE SHED IS NOW TOTALLY COVERED BY SAND DUNES; OPENING OF SECOND KAREKARE SURF CLUBHOUSE, 1974.**

(TOP AND LOWER) KAREKARE BEACH WILL OFTEN PRODUCE A SHEER WALL OF WATER, WHICH CAN BE FATAL TO SWIMMERS; IN A DAY OF HUGE SURF AND MULTIPLE RESCUES, A LATE AFTERNOON RESCUE OF TWO KOREAN SWIMMERS WHO WERE HAULED UNCONSCIOUS FROM THE SEA, RESUSCITATED AND FLOWN TO HOSPITAL BY WESTPAC RESCUE HELI-COPTER, WINNING THE CLUB'S VETERAN PATROL THE 2000 NEW ZEALAND RESCUE OF THE YEAR.

The rescue helicopter service was one of my missions in life. I found a sponsor for the first one, with a farm helicopter that had been used for topdressing. Fitted with two floats and with the doors taken off, it allowed us to jump into the surf and attach the victim by swinging ropes and clips. It was terribly risky.

This ingenious Kiwi innovation worked too well and although it pioneered one of the great rescue services in New Zealand, it was simply too expensive to base a helicopter near the beach, waiting for a rescue to happen. The helicopter service, which has grown into a large organisation and is in the air constantly, is not involved primarily in surf rescues. Attending to road accidents, film shoots and medical emergencies are its priorities and although it is on call at the west coast beaches, with a helipad at Piha, it is now part of surf rescue history. I feel proud of my years involved in setting up the rescue helicopter service and recall the fun of leaping from the open door into a raging surf. In fact, there was more adrenaline in those precious moments than most people probably experience in a lifetime.

Although surf rescues are dramatic, there is the occasional lighter moment to relieve the tension. My happiest memory of such an occasion goes back to a mass rescue of French advertising film crew people in the 1970s. None of us knew the French word for *Help!* so their desperate cries were ignored for a time. The leader of the group was a pale, portly Gallic businessman whom we resuscitated and carried by stretcher to the clubhouse. As this rescue happened after hours on the night of the annual prizegiving, the place was in full swing. When he revived he must have thought he'd gone to French heaven, as the clubhouse was full of wine, song, and scantily-clad femmes. *Zut alors!* A near-drowning was never this good.

The toughest ocean swim in New Zealand must be the annual race around Paratahi. Held since 1980, it is the main event of the Karekare Surf Club's annual club day. The race starts at midday, and rarely is it without drama or a great deal of trepidation among the competitors and the boat crews, who must keep a tally of all swimmers. The event starts at the centre of the beach with an 800m race to the southern rocks. The smart competitors will equip themselves with running shoes and race around the rocks to take advantage of the fierce rip that snakes out towards the island. Those who risk going round to the next bay, Pari Whakaruro, generally finish up heading for the Manukau bar.

Around the back of the island, the surf has a habit of swinging back off the long, flat seaward face, which cannot be seen from the beach. This shelf will send a wave back into the oncoming surf and can reach 10 or 15 metres; it's a problem just to cope with such a clash of water. Once the swimmer is around the tip, it's often best to put the effort into gaining the beach rather than take a short-cut home, as this can send you back into the rip and the exercise then needs to be repeated.

The victors have included Olympic rowing triallist Steve Westlake, who has won the race 10 times, and former club captain Stephen Pye, whose surf ability is phenomenal. The reward for completing this exhausting event is a simple certificate, which is greatly prized.

Some clubbies pray for a light surf, which is sometimes delivered, but most club days are held in heavy surf, which makes this gruelling event even more difficult and leaves many of the certificates unpresented.

The Karekare club continues to flourish, with some of the best known lifeguard heroes of the west coast. Stephen Pye, twice winner of major rescue awards, still patrols. Stuart Hammond and his sons John, Lance and Robert combine more than 130 years of lifeguard skill and surf know-how. They are one of several families who will spend six months on the beach in the patrol season, which stretches from Labour Weekend to Easter. Eight former club captains are still on patrol and the junior surf squad will give us senior members for the next 20 years. Surf conditions at Karekare are constantly changing; lifeguards can never afford to take their eyes off the beach for a moment.

I've been involved in around 200 rescues. Each one is different and none is easy. They happen so suddenly: one minute there is a group of people swimming, the next, someone's in trouble. In the old days these dramas seemed to last for hours, but now with inflatable boats and crews on standby, rescues are over in seconds.

(ABOVE AND MIDDLE) **THE HOLGA NEILSON METHOD IS USED TO SAVE A LIFE, 1959. (BELOW) THIS 1986 NEWSPAPER CLIPPING DESCRIBES A LIFEGUARD'S WORST NIGHTMARE.**

Surf Lifesaving Club arrived.

### Blackest Day

Shore searches for the bodies of both men will resume this morning.

The Karekare club patrol captain on duty yesterday, Mr Mark Engel, said it was one of the blackest days in the club's 50-year history.

The worst part had been seeing Mr Edgar's body on the beach.

"When CPR [cardio-pulmonary resuscitation] does not revive the guy, it is a terrible feeling.

"And when the second guy goes missing, you just cannot believe it."

Mr Edgar had been swimming apparently with ease outside the patrolled area when the club captain, Mr Peter Connor, spotted him, and told those on duty.

(TOP, ABOVE AND OPPOSITE TOP) **ANNUAL ROUND THE ISLAND RACE IS CONSIDERED ONE OF THE TOUGHEST OCEAN SWIMS IN NEW ZEALAND.** (BELOW RIGHT) **THE DIRECTION OF THE VICTIM IS SIGNALLED TO RESCUE BOAT.** (BELOW FAR RIGHT ) **MILLENNIUM LINE-UP FOR ROUND THE ISLAND SWIM.**

The surf plays the biggest role in any rescue, but the sun is also a significant factor at Karekare. On an outgoing tide in late afternoon, the harsh glare of a setting sun and haze can blind the patrol, concealing a swimmer in trouble. There is a terrible moment when you realise someone is out there and you simply can't pinpoint them. The struggle is too great, the waves too strong, time moves too fast. The golden moment of life is over for the victim, and the family, friends and lifeguards are left to mourn.

I believe that you have about three minutes to spot the swimmer and to mount a speedy rescue. On a big surf day, maybe one minute. Some swimmers just disappear and our rescue book over the years also bears testament to those, who for whatever reason, never surfaced at this beach again.

There have been days from hell, when we have lost two people. One time I was talking to a young swimmer, explaining to him where not to swim. About 20 minutes later, at the southern end of the beach, the lifeguard spotted his body in the shallows. No sooner had we been confronted with his family's grief and anger at our inability to mount a rescue, while we were debriefing our team, and trying to find an explanation for what had happened on the crowded beach, than a group

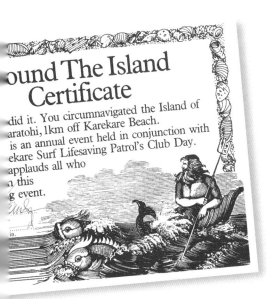

ound The Island
Certificate

did it. You circumnavigated the Island of
aratohi, 1km off Karekare Beach.
is an annual event held in conjunction with
ekare Surf Lifesaving Patrol's Club Day.
applauds all who
n this
g event.

of people running from the surf raised the alarm again. One of their friends had vanished in the waves.

This scene is often tragically repeated. We search into the night, often assisted by the helicopter hovering above, until we are exhausted. The current moves up the coast and days later it gives up the body. Yet our rescue records are impressive – we probably pull more people from the water here than actually swim on many other New Zealand beaches. We estimate that since 1935, around 5000 people have been rescued at Karekare Beach. Since the 1990s we have been moving people before they get swept away. Lifeguards call these actions 'preventatives', which means we put lifeguards into the surf and not on distant, fixed patrol platforms on the beach. This successful technique has been copied throughout New Zealand. Although it has removed some of the former heroics of the dash of the strapping lifeguard through the admiring swimmers, it has quickly averted many life-threatening situations.

Over the years, I have been left with many unanswered questions. Victims who have seemingly been pulled under, or merely been found on the bottom on calm days. When lifeguards talk in the bar of the Karekare Surf Club at the end of the

(ABOVE) **SOLID AS A ROCK: FORMER CLUB CAPTAINS POSE ON TOKAPIRI (SPLIT PIN), UNION BAY.** (BELOW, FROM FAR LEFT) **FORMER CLUB CAPTAIN DEAN BUNBURY; CLUB CAPTAIN STEFAN GABOR; STEVE WESTLAKE, FIVE-TIME WINNER OF ISLAND SWIM, NEW ZEALAND SINGLE SCULLS CHAMPION AND TRANS-ATLANTIC ROWER; IRB CAPTAIN SHAWN WANDEN.**

(TOP AND MIDDLE) **KAREKARE CLUB HAD A SECRET WEAPON IT EMPLOYED TO DEFEAT RIVALS IN ANNUAL DRINKING RACE.** (BELOW) **FAMOUS WEST COAST TROPHY, THE BONE OF CONTENTION.** (ABOVE RIGHT ) **KAREKARE SURF LIIFESAVING CLUB, 2001.** (OPPOSITE) **ORIGINAL SURF CLUB MEMBERS AND THEIR SWEETHEARTS POSED FOR A BOX BROWNIE PHOTOGRAPH, SUMMER OF 1935-36.**

day, their discussions are centred around the seamless teamwork that has made the day's rescues work. As all are volunteers, and that's the way we want it to be, it's not always straightforward.

With more sophisticated medical assistance available, including oxygen support and heart starting defibrillators, weekend lifeguards have become paramedics; we are very hard on ourselves if we lose someone or if we fail to pull someone on board the inflatable, when seconds count between the breakers. The adrenaline surges; mates shout commands at each other; we all work together when there is so much at stake. This has been my weekend life since I first rode out to Karekare Beach at 15. Those of us who have stayed the distance are now relegated to a veteran's patrol. Collectively, we have over 500 years of lifeguarding in our small group. There is a bond of comradeship that has grown with the years.

Few people see the inner life of a surf club. Here the family of lifeguards attempts to resolve their individual and collective grief over a failed rescue. It is intensely personal. The public image of superbly built young men and women, courageous and fearless in the surf, hides the reality of personal trauma as they come to grips at a young age, with death by drowning. Many who join surf clubs probably don't give a thought to the fact that their life will change in the first few seconds of their first rescue. I have always felt this is a huge burden to place on any young person, as the emotion of the moment will never leave you. It has certainly stayed with me.

This hidden side of the lifeguard's world probably helps to explain why there is so much partying when the sun goes down. After the darkness and tears, you need light and laughter and loud music.

The famous drinking race, which always concluded the Club Day, was inevitably won by Karekare over all contending clubs, particularly our arch-rival Piha. Our secret weapon was the Dunn brothers, identical twins, excellent lifeguards and legendary drinkers. Their place in the lineup was subject to change, if the other team could be distracted for a second.

The trophy has been competed for since 1935, and although the club bowed to local pressure to limit the number of races, we have now returned to the best of 10. These days I'm too slow, so I've been appointed an untrustworthy judge.

Karekare Surf Patrol 1935

I        not of that era but intimate
with locale     with photographs of dead
lifesavers who once saved swimmers
disabled by the fearsome Karekare rip.

Reconstruct     a stone surf club cut into
speckled dunes. Today buried under
onshore dumps. Iron roof barely visible
rusted-out – holed – by the Tasman Sea.

                        Omnipotent
a body of tumbling silver
weathered under cyclic sun and moon
pulse.          Etched west.     Tangled signs;
black and white images, lifesavers patrolling

heated planes. 1935 *you* feet skip-hopping
among patchwork towels and sleeping dogs.

                                    Sam Sampson

# THE GOVERNOR
# AT THE BEACH

Back in the 1930s, the British Empire still stretched all the way to New Zealand and the black sands of Karekare Beach. Imperialist ideology intimidated many New Zealanders, and Governors-General personified the natural world order according to the British class system. The King's gift to the Dominion of New Zealand in 1935 was the decorated World War One hero and cavalry commander Viscount George Vere Arundel Mockington-Arundel Galway.

The eighth Viscount, Eton College and Christ Church College, Oxford-educated,

Somme survivor, Knight of Grace of the Order of St John of Jerusalem, six foot six with a bad knee, the Right Honourable Viscount Lord Galway, PC, GCM, DSO, OBE, arrived in 1935 and departed in 1942. During his term, Karekare Beach cast its spell over him. It was soon apparent that Galway wanted to be regarded as the first people's Governor-General. Passionate about the outdoors, he fished at Taupo and the Huka Falls with his wife. A friend of the Maori renaissance, he quickly came to love New Zealand. On most summer Saturdays he would play a round of golf on the Titirangi

course. On Sundays, the Vice-Regal family would head for the beach.

The honorable Lucia Emily Margaret White, daughter of the third Baron Annaly, like her husband George, shared his love of hunting, fishing and golf. They were also enthusiastic tree lovers, the *New Zealand Herald* reported, and the Governor-General urged New Zealand to conserve its native bush. His first task was to give the 1935 All Blacks a rousing farewell before their tour of Britain. Even the tallest All Black looked up to the imposing figure of Galway, and with his military uniform topped by a plumed cockade, he reached seven feet.

Based for the summer in Old Government House in Symonds Street, he started to drive out to Karekare for the occasional picnic and became a regular visitor. His transport was the Vice-Regal Bentley, a wonderful, gleaming but heavy machine. The car would travel down the creek, turn right at the Watchman and park in the shade on the tidal sands near the Split Pin in Union Bay. The Governor-General and his three daughters and heir, the Honorable Simon Mockington-Arundel, would spread out a picnic fit for a king: wicker hampers, silver service and the very best of meats and bakery. English ale, warming in the sun, would be consumed. Departing was not such an easy exercise. Inevitably, the wet sand would bog the vehicle and the fledgling Surf Club patrol, watching the beach theatre with some envy, would be summoned to push the stranded car. This they accomplished successfully many times over the pre-war summers; they were rewarded with the remains of the day – beer and the contents of the hampers.

During the summer of 1935, the original Surf Club members and their sweethearts got to know the Governor-General well, and in an age of rigid formality, he willingly agreed to pose with the foundation members. Scantily attired in his beach costume, Viscount Galway was photographed by Marge Wales on a Kodak Box Brownie. This image has become one of the icons of surf lifesaving in New Zealand. Noticeable in the centre of the photograph is the first lifesaving reel, the popular wooden

surfboard used extensively at that time for riding the broken surf line, and the gammy knee of the Governor.

In the year 2000, after five years of negotiating with Government House, the club enticed Governor-General Sir Michael Hardie-Boys to come to Karekare and re-enact the visit of his famous predecessor. Like Viscount Galway, Sir Michael let himself be swept into the fun of the surf and for the first time in his life, joined a surf patrol on duty, taking part in a rescue demonstration and enjoying a personal

tour of the beach in the club's rescue craft. It was a great occasion when the whole club, whose members now numbered more than one hundred, recreated the famous photograph of that summer afternoon of 65 years earlier.

As for George Mockington-Arundel, he and Lucia departed New Zealand's shores in 1942, returning to his heritage, his ancestral home, the 5000-acre estate Serlby Hall in Bawtry, Yorkshire. I have often wondered if he remembered with affection his long hot summer days at Karekare.

(ABOVE) **SENIOR LIFEGUARD JOHN McLARIN EXPLAINS RESCUE TECHNIQUES TO SIR MICHAEL HARDIE-BOYS.** (RIGHT) **VISCOUNT GALWAY, AS SEEN BY COUNIHAN IN THE *NEW ZEALAND OBSERVER*, 1939.**

# THE GREEN ROOM

WHEN I FIRST MET Californians Rick Stoner and Bing Copland, they had been told to come out to our west coast by someone towing the Piha surf boat along Customs Street in downtown Auckland. They had two Dale Velzy balsa boards, an innovative design with tail fins. They were on their way to Australia after sailing from the Marquesas and their yacht was moored near the Ferry Terminal on the waterfront. They were looking for crew, and I desperately wanted to go with them.

The desire to surf, to glide up and down the waves, mastering the ocean, would change our lives. Stoner and Copland stayed all of that summer of 1958. Using basic materials, they ran a small custom-made surfboard shop from the back of the Piha Surf Club, with Piha local Peter Byers, who made a mould from the Californians' best gun board in his fruit shed on Garden Road. This was the beginning of the surfboard industry in New Zealand. From Piha Beach, surfing would spread throughout the country.

Surfing, the art of standing upright on a moving plank sliding down a giant wave, is harder than it looks. This was the ancient sport of the Hawaiian monarchy, which spread throughout the Pacific centuries before the coming of the Europeans. The knowledge of surfing was probably carried throughout Polynesia, wherever a good surf was running, by the great navigational fleets. We know that surfing flourished in Hawaii, Tahiti and the South Pacific, before the gambling culture associated with surfing in the Hawaiian Islands was frowned upon by the 19th century missionaries.

Surfing was practised in old New Zealand too. The ancient Maori, a maritime people who lived close to the coastline, became skilled in the waves. At Karekare,

(FROM TOP) **DANIEL DAVIE PADDLES OUT THROUGH THE NORTHERN RIP; SURFERS RESPECT KAREKARE WAVES FOR RAW POWER: DAN SCOTT MISCALCULATES; NEW ZEALAND'S BEST SURFER MAZ QUINN RATES KAREKARE AS A FAVOURITE BREAK; MAZ QUINN FLYING; MAZ'S BROTHER JAY GETS A DEEP BARREL OFF THE WATCHMAN.** (ABOVE TITLE) **UNCHANGED FOR FOUR DECADES, THE SURFER'S BEST FRIEND IS USED FOR BOARD WAXING SO FEET CAN GRIP.** (OPPOSITE TOP) **JAI EARNSHAW PERFORMS DIFFICULT BACKHAND 'PIGDOG' BARREL AT 'ISLAND', KAREKARE.** (OPP. LOWER) **DAMON GUINNESS AT 'ISLAND', WHICH PRODUCES WORLD-CLASS LEFT-HANDERS.**

GREEN ROOM

surfing may well have been a daily summer pastime. The sport was known to Maori as whakahekeheke. The historian Elsdon Best obtained oral reports from Maori of their prowess in the water, and two early surf planks found in sand dunes in the South Island give credence to this claim. He provides further fascinating detail:

> On our own shores three forms were practised, *viz.*, with and without a board, and also in small canoes called *kopapa*, a name which seems to belong to the surf board. This board appears to have been called a *moki* in the north, a name also applied to rude floats formerly used in crossing rivers.

Best quotes Tuta Nihoniho of the East Coast who stated that the board or plank was about three feet long and the sport was enjoyed "by both youth and adults, including females, and one might see thirty or forty riders coming in together on a big wave. Sometimes a performer dispensed with the board and rode in on the wave with his arms stretched out before him."

Captain James Cook, in his diligent manner, recorded "the elegant savages" surfing in the Sandwich Islands (the Hawaiian group), Tahiti and the Marquesas. Early missionaries record that the boards were large and cumbersome, but effective. Only the chiefly élite in the Hawaiian Islands were permitted to perform this ritual wave-riding on an 'olo' board about 5m long. Others rode a shorter, more common 'alaia' board. Men and women took part in the fun, using the waves and the beach for sport and the sheer love of the surf.

The great Californian writer and adventurer Jack London, visiting Honolulu in 1910, saw surfing as a metaphor for man's ability to harness the power of nature.

His Hawaiian surfer is "a member of the kingly species that has mastered matter and the brutes and lorded it over creation." In a superb essay entitled 'A Royal Sport: Surfing at Waikiki' penned when he was confined to bed with painful sunburn the day after he first attempted to ride a board, London described the interaction of man, board and wave:

And suddenly, out there where a big smoker lifts skyward, rising like a sea-god from out of the welter of spume and churning white, on the giddy, toppling, overhanging and downfalling, precarious crest appears the dark head of a man. Swiftly he rises through the rushing white. His black shoulders, his chest, his loins, his limbs – all is abruptly projected on one's vision. Where but the moment before was only the wide desolation and invincible roar, is now a man, erect, full-statured, not struggling frantically in that wild movement, not buried and crushed and buffeted by those mighty monsters, but standing above them all, calm and superb, poised on the giddy summit, his feet buried in the churning foam, the salt smoke rising to his knees, and all the rest of him in the free air and flashing sunlight, and he is flying through the air, flying forward, flying fast as the surge on which he stands. He is a Mercury – a brown Mercury. His heels are winged, and in them is the swiftness of the sea. In truth, from out of the sea he has leaped upon the back of the sea, and he is riding the sea that roars and bellows and cannot shake him from its back. But no frantic outreaching and balancing is his. He is impassive, motionless as a statue carved suddenly by some miracle out of the sea's depth from which he rose. And straight on towards shore he flies on his winged heels and the white crest of the breaker. There is a wild burst of foam, a long tumultuous rushing sound as the breaker falls futile and spent on the beach at your feet; and there, at your feet, steps calmly ashore a Kanaka, burnt golden and brown by the tropic sun. He has "bitted the bull-mouthed breaker" and ridden it in, and the pride in the feat shows in the carriage of his magnificent body as he glances for a moment carelessly at you who sit in the shade of the shore.

In 1910 tourists in Honolulu, like Jack London, would see stacks of 12-foot (4m) wooden boards under the palm trees. Surf gambling had gone (spectators used to bet on the length of a ride), the missionaries were losing their influence and the Hawaiians were enthusiastically rediscovering their traditional pastimes. Although they would not return to their ritual swimming and canoe races until much later, their surfboard skills would inspire a renaissance that saw surfing become the most glamorous 'new' water sport of the 20th century.

The most famous surfer of all time was Honolulu's own adored Olympic swimming champion, the dashing, debonair Duke Kahanamoku of Waikiki. In 1915 he was a culture bearer who visited California and Australia, demonstrating the sport on a hastily-hewn board. But it was always Hawaii and the romantic Waikiki Beach that held the culture of surfing and the cult of the Hawaiian beach

(ABOVE) ONE OF NEW ZEALAND'S FIRST AND MOST INFLUENTIAL BOARD SHAPERS IS PETER BYERS, WHO HAS DEVOTED A LIFETIME TO HIS CRAFT AND IS REGARDED AS THE MASTER. (BELOW) DUKE PAOA KAHANAMOKU (1890-1968) IS KNOWN AS THE FATHER OF INTERNATIONAL SURFING. THIS MULTI-TALENTED HAWAIIAN WON ONE BRONZE, TWO SILVER AND THREE GOLD MEDALS IN FOUR OLYMPICS; INTRO-DUCED SURFING TO THE EASTERN USA, EUROPE, AND AUSTRALIA AND RE-INTRODUCED IT TO NEW ZEALAND, AND WAS SHERIFF OF HONOLULU FOR 13 CONSECUTIVE TERMS. HE WAS PHOTOGRAPHED ON A VISIT TO AUCKLAND IN MARCH 1915, WHEN HE SET 50 YARDS RECORD OF 22.6 SECONDS IN A RACE AT THE DEVONPORT DRY DOCK.

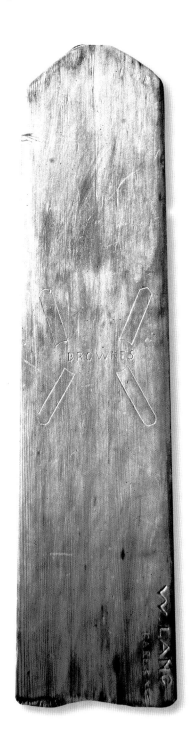

boys. Many were legendary for their ability to tandem ride, holding aloft American women tourists. Early movies of Waikiki, in the great days of the Matson Shipping Line and Pan Am Clippers, brought romance to surfing. It failed to ignite and become universally popular, probably because the boards were huge and heavy, so they were neither easily transportable nor very manoeuvrable in the surf.

Elvis Presley would help to change all this with his movie *Blue Hawaii* in 1961. Suddenly, all things Hawaiian became fashionable. The spin-off was surfing, made possible by a revolutionary new product called fibreglass. It combined all the qualities that were needed for the sport – it was lightweight, waterproof, flexible and virtually unbreakable. From the mid-1950s a youthful cultural revolution spread across the world, ignited by rock 'n roll. Surfing leapt from the Hawaiian Islands to California in the early 1960s, carried on a wave of popular music, led by the phenomenal success of The Beach Boys.

A natural-born surfer is rare. Surfing demands endless practice to harmonise the

symbiosis of board and rider. There's no finer art on water. Here in the 'green room' of life, the wave curls in a funnel around you. The zen of surfing is to give yourself totally to the experience, becoming one with the wave. Defying gravity, and exerting control, aware of your surroundings yet poised in space with all your proprioceptors firing, never are you more aware of your self.

If you believe that water has a pulse, as some Swedish scientific researchers claim, you can sense it at this moment. You are inside an iridescent, unfurling carpet of water, playing with an energy that engulfs you while at the same time setting you free. Adrenalin pumps as you hurtle like a comet across the cosmos. Endorphins flood your system, a natural high that gives the devotees of waves their satori.

As part of their rescue equipment, surf clubs had surf-skis, big, clumsy but stable Australian-designed plywood craft. Like surfboats, these barges were supposed to be used in rescues, but rarely were. They had no manoeuvrability and they were propelled by a large double-headed paddle.

At Karekare we began to shape our own surfboards in the winter of 1962. We first shaped them out of polyurethane foam; the keel and centrepiece were matched carefully to the form we required. The whole lot was then spread with polyester resin over fibreglass cloth, giving a light transparent coating. They were dream machines. Surfboards became prized for their shapes and shapers, who inspired a cult of surfers-turned-boardmakers. If you caught the right wave, you could stand quite quickly, but only months of constant practice would give you the confidence and skill. Three generations later, the longboard is prized anew and dearly loved by ageing surfers everywhere. Another cult has grown around these grand whoppers,

(TOP LEFT) THESE KAREKARE LIFEGUARDS WERE ALSO KEEN WAVE-HUNTERS. BARRY ROBERTS, DON WATERER AND BRUCE KEATLY ATOP MODEL A TRUCK WHICH WAS USED FOR BEACH RESCUE AND SURFING TRIPS. (ABOVE) PETER WAY, ROGER LAND AND DENIS QUANE WERE EARLY SURFBOARD SHAPERS AND ENTREPRENEURS. (BELOW) BING COPLAND AND RICK STONER HELPED INTRODUCE CALIFORNIAN SURFING CULTURE TO NEW ZEALAND. (OPPOSITE) AMERICANS R.H.T. SILVER AND S.M. DEICHELMANN ARRIVE ON YACHT *AWANEE*, INTRODUCING THE REVOLUTIONARY FIBREGLASS-ON-POLYSTYRENE SURFBOARD TO NEW ZEALAND, JANUARY 1962. (OPP. FAR LEFT) 'SURF-O-PLANE' MADE OF OREGON TIMBER AND USED BY GOVERNOR-GENERAL GALWAY AT KAREKARE WAS KNOWN AS THE 'BOARDING HOUSE BOARD' AND KEPT AT BROWNES'. (OPP. LOWER) KAREKARE'S FIRST SURF CLUB CAPTAIN HARRY LIDDLE (AT LEFT), LEADS PATROL INTO SURF USING SURF-O-PLANE BOARDS.

(ABOVE) **ONE OF THE FIRST ADVERTISEMENTS IN THE NEW MAGAZINE** NEW ZEALAND SURFER, **1965.** (BELOW, FROM LEFT) NEW ZEALAND SURFER **BECAME** NEW ZEALAND SURF MAGAZINE **AND SURVIVED FOR ONE YEAR.** SURFING NEW ZEALAND **ARRIVED 1968 AND DEPARTED SOON AFTER.** NEW ZEALAND SURFING **HAS BEEN GOING STRONG SINCE 1985.** SURFABOUT **WAS AN EARLY AUSTRALIAN PUBLICATION, WHILE JOHN SEVERSON'S** SURFER **CONTINUES TO INFLUENCE SURFING STYLES DECADES AFTER ITS DEBUT.** (OPPOSITE) **NAT BARON AND TWIN BROTHER CHRIS WERE INTRODUCED TO SURFING ON THE WEST COAST BY SURF-MAD DAD CLIVE, WHO FOUND TIME BETWEEN SETS TO BUILD HOUSES AT KAREKARE, WITH NAT'S HELP.**

while the young grommets still flick and turn on small, multi-finned fibreglass bullets.

We loved our big boards more than anything; more than our girlfriends or mates. We lived for waves, and although the sport waned in the 1970s, surfing is experiencing a global renaissance, bigger than ever. Board revolution continues: fins and shape are endlessly redefined and style is still everything.

Music and film played an enormous role in popularising the surfing life. In those days, rarely did we see free-form style on film. Surfing movies were played in halls at the beaches or in run-down suburban cinemas hired for the night, usually with the director-producer-writer-and-surfer narrating. A turntable played current hits, sometimes totally unrelated to the performer on the waves. These low-budget beach epics, beautifully shot, introduced New Zealanders to the thrill of surfing.

Filmmakers like Bud Browne, John Severson and Bruce Brown came to New Zealand to capture the green magic. We went with them in beat-up Holdens and woodies (wooden panel vans); we toured the coastline and their 16mm Bolexes with zoom lenses made us feel like movie stars. Bruce Brown was still five years away from making the greatest surfing movie ever, *The Endless Summer*, but we did get to see *Slippery When Wet*, the first clipped-together, squeaky-clean big surf movie, and we were truly awed. Later, we would buy a dated copy of the American *Surfer* magazine and see our New Zealand beaches rated as world-class surfing locations.

Surfing helped transform the way the world saw young people. Youth culture was being revolutionised by surfing style and language, by clothes, hair, dope and especially by the music of the 1960s. All these ingredients came together in a new beach culture, shocking and challenging the values of parents and the establishment.

Amongst surfers, it would also start a search for the ultimate wave, the holy grail of the new culture, which would reach all the way from California to Karekare. The quest for this nirvana would make Karekare one of the Pacific's most appealing surfing destinations.

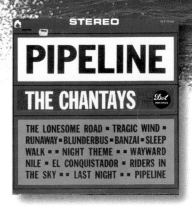

(ABOVE) **THE EXUBERANT SOUND OF SURF ROCK WAS CALIFORNIAN-DRIVEN BUT WENT GLOBAL IN EARLY 1960S. SOARING HARMONIES AND INFECTIOUS BEAT OF THE BEACH BOYS GAVE THE GROUP A STACK OF NO. 1 HITS AND PHENOMENAL SUCCESS IN NEW ZEALAND, WHERE THEIR POPULARITY CONTINUES TODAY. (LOWER) KAREKARE'S BLACK SAND LIFTS THE BURN RATE, MAKING SUNSCREEN ESSENTIAL.**

At Karekare the surfing lifestyle flourished as board riders hired baches, rode the waves and grew cannabis in private plots dotted around the hills. The warm, moist conditions in the valley produced its own distinctive product before helicopter spotter planes with infrared equipment and local rangers were instructed to seek and destroy. A fantastic surfer from Baja took up residency in the Surf Club gear shed right on the beach, transforming the humble stone structure into a Buddhist temple with Californian furnishings. A draft-dodger, he became our local hero until the police and immigration authorities moved him on.

On a good day, the surf at Karekare Beach is exceptional. Green, glorious, unbelievable gifts from the ocean gods rise out of the Tasman and give a ride either right or left, depending on the day or the wind, pulling stunts and tricks as good as any beach in the world. From the top of the Cutting, you can see which way it's peeling or pulling. The delivery is phenomenal and a long hot summer is yours.

Surfers gave their own codenames to the points and tracks at Karekare. The Watchman Road is Homestead Track leading to North Bay. The North Point was known in the early 1970s as Point X – never to be spoken of in public, and to keep its secret intact, published photographs were never captioned with a placename. The centre of the beach was simply called Ocean; it took its wave shape from the Karekare Stream which releases its energy into the water. The Island called the shots at the south end. It gave its name to the surf off its northern tip, the configuration of the green magic before Wastelands, the stretch of coastline which goes from the south point towards the Pararaha, a ghost strip of surf heaving out of nowhere, but driven in from the Manukau bar.

But nothing comes from nothing. The strong westerly wind lifts waves into a gentle but heavy lip which sends the surfer on a quick descent. It's not easy to ride the Karekare break, which changes from week to week and from season to season.

An outer break, behind the island, now dominates the beach and will do so for maybe a decade, maybe a lifetime. The Cauldron, as deadly as it always is, waits to snare the exhausted surfer who uses the rip that races from Union Bay down the side of Farley Point, past Mussel Rock and then dies 20m past the point. Here, you must pick up a wave to take you to the beach; if you don't, you're into the merciless Cauldron, the scene of the most dramatic rescues and most of the drownings at Karekare. The Cauldron is a surfer's kelp-filled nightmare: the cliffs are too steep to scale, and the large sea cave, although mostly filled with sand, creates a suction that still brings beads of sweat to me, just thinking of it. But on a good morning, the North Bay is awesome. Autumn brings the kind of surf that the Californians dream of, but without the crowds.

The southern surf line, inshore from the island, is a rare, superb right, lifting from way out at sea and catching a sharp, quick fall that will often deliver a 500m

(ABOVE) ANDY McALPINE GRADUATED FROM DIRECTING TV COMMERCIALS TO HIS HIGHLY SUCCESSFUL SURFING FILM *CHILDREN OF THE SUN*, WITH CREATIVE CAMERA WORK AND AN ENGAGING SOUNDTRACK. (LOWER) LURE OF THE SURF HAS A LUNAR EFFECT ON WAVE-RIDERS.

ride that's effortless and pure pleasure. On big days, the adrenaline pumps. The rides are steep, furious, punishing without mercy.

New Zealand's most famous surfing photographer is CPL, whose credits appear under some of the world's best surf photographs. His real name is Craig Levers and when he's not surfing and taking pictures, he edits *New Zealand Surfing*. He has spent a lifetime catching waves at Karekare. He rates it as good as it ever gets. He talks of sets that he remembers from 10 years ago, of days racing down from the carpark and leaping into the rip to catch a ride that will last in his memory forever. At the same time, he also goes along with the code of silence. When the photographs appear in the magazine, there's often no indication of location. Only a glimpse of a headland reveals to the cognoscente where it is. This is how it has to be – the beach is too small, the surf too good to be shared.

Eti Eaves, Superwaterman, has surfed since he was 12. At 28, he's one of the best in New Zealand. He lives in his grandfather's bach – a third generation has grown from surf prat to genius. He plays the waves, a minted master of every move – he's truly an original in the way he rides. Flicking and scudding, a maestro of green magic. Like his older brother Tui, Eti has graduated from a rusty bike to get to the surf after work, to a pick-up truck. Eti is so obsessed with his beach and his waves that he works locally so he can knock off early and race out to the surf. Guys like Eti may find it difficult to settle down – who could compete with this lifestyle and these waves?

(ABOVE) **SURFERS FROM AUCKLAND'S NORTH SHORE LOVE THE BLACK SAND AND BIG SURF OF KAREKARE. PAUL 'DURRIE' McMURRAY IS A REGULAR VISITOR.** (BELOW) **MANY EARLY SURFERS RODE BOARDS BUILT BY RODNEY DAVIDSON AT HIS NORTH SHORE FACTORY.** (LOWER) **NORTH REEF BOARD CLUB WAS FOUNDED 1962 AT TAKAPUNA.** (OPPOSITE) **CHAMPION SURFER CHRIS MALONE PULLS INTO AN ISLAND BARREL WITH EASE.**

# SURFING TERMS

**AERIAL** – TO LAUNCH OFF LIP OF WAVE, TURN MID-AIR AND LAND SUCCESSFULLY

**BACKHAND** – TO SURF WITH YOUR BACK TO THE WAVE FACE

**BARREL** – INSIDE THE WAVE

**BOTTOM TURN** – TO TURN FROM THE BOTTOM OF THE WAVE UP THE FACE

**CHUNDER** – TO VOMIT

**CUTBACK** – TO TURN BACK TO STEEPEST PART OF WAVE

**DECK** – THE TOP OF THE SURFBOARD

**DING** – CRACK OR BREAK IN THE SURFBOARD

**DOWN THE MINE** – WIPEOUT

**DUMPER** – A HUGE BREAKING WAVE

**FLOATER** – TO GLIDE OVER TOP OF BREAKING LIP OF WAVE THEN FREE-FALL WITH THE LIP TO THE BOTTOM

**FOREHAND** – TO SURF FACING THE WAVE

**GOAT BOAT** – WAVE SKI (RIDER IS A 'PARALITE')

**GOOFY** – LEFT FOOT FRONT STANCE

**GREEN ROOM** – THE BARREL OF A WAVE

**GROMET** – NOVICE SURFER

**INSIDE** – BETWEEN THE BEACH AND THE BREAK

**INTO THE PIT** – WIPEOUT

**JACK-UP** – WHEN WAVE HITS A SHALLOW SAND BANK, THE WAVE APPEARS TO SUDDENLY GROW IN HEIGHT

**KOOK** – NOVICE SURFER

**MRS PALMER'S** – SURF WAX BRAND

**NIPPER** – VERY JUNIOR LIFEGUARD (6 YEARS UP)

**OUTSIDE** – BEYOND THE SURF BREAK

**OVER THE FALLS** – FALLING OVER THE FACE OF THE BREAKING WAVE WITH THE WHITE WASH

**PIG DOG** – TO CROUCH GRABBING OUTSIDE RAIL OF BOARD WHILE IN THE BARREL: THIS STEADIES AND CENTRES THE RIDER'S BALANCE

**PRONE** – FOOT FORWARD

**RAIL** – SIDES OR EDGES OF A SURFBOARD

**REGULAR OR NATURAL FOOT** – LEFT FOOT FRONT STANCE

**REO** – TO TURN SHARPLY OFF TOP OF WAVE. ALSO KNOWN AS AN 'OFF THE LIP'

**SURFARI** – A SURF TRIP BY CAR

**SET** – A GROUP OF WAVES

**SWELL** – THE WAVE BEFORE IT BREAKS

**TAKE-OFF** – THE FIRST STAND POSITION

**TAKING THE DROP** – A SHEER DESCENT

**TUBES** – PERFECT FUNNEL FORM OF WAVES

**WAGGON** – A SURFER CAR

**WESTIE** – SURFER (OR HOON) FROM WEST SIDE OF CITY

**WIPEOUT** – FALL OFF

**WOODY** – OLD PANEL CAR

In surfing, you take what the water gives you and you get what the wave will deliver. Nothing less is acceptable.

My old fibreglass dunga lasted 10 years. The resin, spread over the polyurethane core, was indestructible and when I finally lost interest, I cut the board in half and used the top part in the garden as a tombstone for my dog Chester.

(TOP) **CANTERBURY'S DAN GARBES FLOATS OVER AND THROUGH THE LIP JUST NORTH OF THE ISLAND.** (MIDDLE AND LOWER) **WEST COAST RESIDENT HOLLY QUINN IN ACTION OFF THE WATCHMAN.**

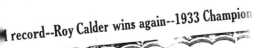

record--Roy Calder wins again--1933 Champion

# GETTING IT OFF

IF THE BEACH existed in watercolours and oils, it still lacked the most important ingredient – people. Our colonial forebears saw the beach as a sandy, messy place to be walked on while fully clothed. That all changed with the advent of swimming as a popular leisuretime activity.

Apparently the idea of going to the beach and actually splashing about in the water had not occurred to the general populace. Can you blame them? Clothing for bathing was more designed to drown in than to float. In Australia, beach inspectors measured clothes for acceptable dress standards and arrested offenders. In New Zealand, we also frowned on those who exposed their flesh. Only swimming clubs encouraged a looseness of costume, but their membership was small and so was their audience. That changed in the 1930s when a practical swimming suit became available on the market. Admittedly, it was a long way from the bikini, but it made swimwear fashionable, an important advance in developing a beach culture.

Before that time, women walked the beach under parasols in full-length dresses, while men promenaded in suits or jackets with boaters or bowlers. As ridiculous as this may seem, the guests at Karekare did just that. Over the little bridge and down onto the beach they walked or rode in the gig, resplendent in their formal attire.

In the late 1920s, suddenly it became acceptable to stretch out on a towel on the beach to cultivate a tan. The folding wooden deckchair with sagging striped canvas was an essential accoutrement. It became a sign of health and wellbeing. The sun gradually ceased being regarded with trepidation and was welcomed, literally with open arms, first by the rich and then progressively by everyone else. The discovery and subsequent worship of the sun changed a lot of things in New Zealand society. People were gradually liberated from their self-consciousness and cloying modesty. The repressed clothing of the Victorian era gave way to sexy, clinging, lighter fabrics and fashion statements about who we were. Our arms and legs were liberated at last. Bodies were to be enjoyed and even flaunted.

Resorts and beaches became a hot ticket to go to. This was reflected in art, in film

and in advertising, as the cigarette and liquor industries also adopted this imagery. The new magazines announced the arrival of the sexy beach belle. Women and teenage girls celebrated their femininity coquettishly, often with props like beach balls and umbrellas. The most photogenic would later become the pin-ups for the soldiers of World War Two. Generations of young men would adore the image of the beach bunny.

Tanned skin became the anti-depressant that was needed to address the woes of the Great Depression. The next best thing that happened was the introduction by the U.S. Rubber Company of the fabled product Lastex. This new latex rubber thread could be woven with other fabrics such as wool, cotton and rayon. It stretched and hugged the body and was a must for both men and women: it smoothed out bodies, including the naughty zones that you weren't supposed to look at. It would make us look slimmer, sexier, accentuating bosom in women and muscle in men. In the 1930s, latex was a household word and it would remain so through to the end of the century and beyond. The cult would give us names like

(ABOVE AND OPPPOSITE LOWER) **HOT BLACK SAND COATED NECK-TO-KNEE WOOLLEN COVERALLS.** (OPPOSITE TOP LEFT) **JUST FOR A LAUGH, MEN OF THE SCENIC PRESERVATION SOCIETY FAKE NUDITY IN KAREKARE STREAM IN THIS EARLY GLASS PLATE IMAGE.** (OPP. TOP RIGHT) **BEACH FASHIONS, 1912, WHATIPU: VICTORIAN MODESTY HUNG OVER NEW ZEALAND FOR DECADES AFTER HER MAJESTY DIED IN 1901.** (OPP. MIDDLE) **DIVING CHAMPION ROY CALDER ENDORSES PRE-WAR SPEEDO ADVERTISEMENT.**

Speedo, Jantzen, Cole, Catalina, and later, Nike and other aerobic gear brands would be the curse of those who were somewhat overweight.

At Karekare, the guests moved their base of courting, romancing and falling in love from the boarding house lawn and the great verandah to the beach. An all-day affair started at 10 am: after breakfast the guests would wander down the beach, not in crinolines but with towels. No longer were they daunted by the surf; they would actually brave it. Proper surfboards were foreign and unobtainable, but the small wooden bodyboard, about a metre long, curved at the tip, was a must. For those who didn't swim – and most did not – they simply went out to waist-deep and pushed themselves forward, lying on the board. They got a decent thrill and a ride to shore. If they got a little out of their depth and held onto the board, they could get a ride in.

By 1932, the Germans had developed the airbed. Swimmers could now lie on a inflatable rubber mattress. You simply inflated it at one end, sealed it and used it as a bodyboard. It was really designed for swimming pools, but at Karekare and other local beaches it was used in the surf. They punctured very easily and perished within weeks in the hot New Zealand sun.

In 1932, the cellophane industry launched its new paper sunblankets. They were the latest word in tanning protection, but in New Zealand the first rays of spring sun gave everyone sunburn. As painful as it may have been in the first few days, it gave the wearer a certain sense of pride and of health. No one cared or even considered that it would age the skin or lead to skin cancer. They worried only about the short-term effects of blistering, peeling and freckling. Little was known about the devastating toll ultra-violet light would take on our bodies. It was the age of innocence, and not until the 1980s would we begin to wise up.

The surf clubs would develop their own tribal coatings. Apart from the heavy cooking oil used to tan up quicker, the hot brand in New Zealand was Q-tol. Coppertone would not emerge as one of the most successful brands of all time until the 1960s. Surf club members would coat their noses and lips with zinc oxide. A

(ABOVE) **THE EVER-POPULAR SHAPED KAURI PLANK WAS USED AS A BODYBOARD.** (RIGHT) **THE SWIM-TEAM LOOK OF 1913, KAREKARE STREAM.**

dazzling white, it gave an all-day protection to the nose, but it was very much a lifeguard thing. Others wearing it were frowned upon. It gave the dark, rich, tanned skin of an all-summer lifeguard a special aura and it was not to be messed with.

In the 1930s, men and women would spend time getting ready for summer and the beach. The cult of the body affected virtually all New Zealanders under the age of 30. The beach became a hunting ground for partners – marriage and otherwise. Where the Edwardians were indifferent to a puny body, the new culture demanded that men be muscular and women lithe. A small bodybuilding movement grew into a huge new cult in New Zealand cities. Gymnasiums like the YMCAs, the police and fire stations added weights and ropes to their training. Charles Atlas advertised his personally endorsed body-enhancement system extensively, in the most popular medium for young people, comics. Generations of young men, including me and my mates coming of age in the 1950s, were obsessed with obtaining the ideal body shape. We were secretly afraid of meeting the same fate as that of the helpless victim of the beach bully in the Atlas ads, who had sand kicked in his face, to the delight of the onlooking beach bunnies. The idea was that if you started looking good for summer, you would eventually attract members of the opposite sex.

The only question that needed to be asked was where would you go to strut your stuff. It was simple: a beach was the only acceptable, non-threatening place to show off your body. Karekare and the other west coast beaches were challenging, rugged and quintessentially New Zealand. They had big surf, miles of sand and great back-drops for photographs of your friends and prospects. And like all surf beaches, the crashing of the waves charged the air with ozone, that intoxicating ingredient that is like dynamite to the senses.

Anything could happen, and I would think it probably did, when night fell over Karekare Beach in those golden days of summer.

(TOP LEFT AND ABOVE) JANTZEN WAS THE GREATEST NAME IN SWIMWEAR IN THE IMMEDIATE POST-WAR YEARS. THE COMPANY'S LOGO WAS A POWERFUL FASHION STATEMENT. (BELOW) FORM-FITTING LATEX WAS PROMOTED POST-WAR AS AN IRRESISTIBLE ACCOUTREMENT WHEN STEPPING OUT ON THE BEACH.

# The Bach Grows Up

(TOP AND BELOW) QUIRKY LETTERBOXES OF KARE-
KARE RESIDENTS ARE A CLUE TO THE INDIVIDUALITY
OF THEIR OWNERS. (OPPOSITE, FROM TOP LEFT)
BUILDING MATERIALS FOR THIS MORE RECENT RESI-
DENCE WERE HAND-CARRIED UP 100 STEPS; DEAN
BUCHANAN'S STUDIO COTTAGE; A 1930S FIBROLITE
DREAM HAS HAD A FACE-LIFT; KAREKARE BACHES
GREW OUT OF PRE-WAR SUMMER ENCAMPMENTS;
BACKROUND DETAIL OF 1927 AUCKLAND AUTOMOBILE
ASSOCIATION LINEN AND PAPER MAP.

I BOUGHT my bach at Karekare in 1972 for $5000. That seemed a lot of money then, but I'd bought two sections in 1961 for £25 ($50). They were unusable before the days of pole houses, and I was able to flick them in a quick sale. I couldn't have been happier. My bach had been built in 1946 by Frank Casey (who had made a fortune from American soldiers stationed near Onehunga, where he had a menswear store) of untanalised, untreated pine; the borer held hands, keeping the cladding on. I didn't care. It was gloriously unpretentious with its creosote exterior. The windows were large and in winter there was a small fire.

All my children learned to walk at the bach, as we spent so much time there. Every weekend, we would simply decamp from our home in Glen Eden, driving over the ranges, dragging cats and dogs and kids. Winter and summer, it didn't matter; this was our home away from home. Over the years we've done so little to our bach, I'm almost ashamed. With five kids, we got a serious dose of cabin fever and needed to expand the one-room-everything to stop us from falling over one another. Our major renovations involved extending the deck and changing the shower nozzle. Apart from that, it's much as it was when we first stayed here. All around us, a similar story unfolded.

In the 1930s, people started to come out to Karekare for weekends, really liked it, and came back. They camped under the trees at either end of the beach. They became regulars, some arriving before Christmas, creating small tent villages beside the streams. Before tents tried to mimic houses with separate rooms, there was the great Indian Army tent – spacious, high, forever dripping water on the occupants, with camp stretchers, billies and primuses, and it smelt wonderful. Anchored to trees or guy-roped to the ground, these canvas caverns created the atmosphere of the holiday, while the pohutakawa trees shed their Christmas blossoms over everybody and everything.

It was inevitable that the campers would start searching for a piece of land on which to build the mandatory bach. It became a status symbol. The early baches

Anawhata

Piha

Karekare

THE CASCADES

Te Atatau

ENDERSON

Oratia

Glen Eden

Man

arbour

9

MAP OF

AUCKLAND
and 40 mile Radius

Supplementary to

*Day and
Week-end*

MOTOR TOURS"

Compiled and Published by

The AUCKLAND AUTOMOBILE
ASSOCIATION (Inc.)

roughout
Automobile Associa-
ront motorists wherever
if not already members,
the Organization, which
of the motorists of the

THE BACH AT KARE KARE

(TOP) **THE SIMPSON-HOSKIN FAMILY BACH, BUILT BY THE LYONS FAMILY, HAS CHANGED LITTLE SINCE THE MANUKAU CYCLING CLUB STAYED THERE IN THE 1930S, WHEN THESE STEREOSCOPE IMAGES WERE PHOTOGRAPHED. (ABOVE) ARTIST DEAN BUCHANAN'S HOUSE HAS A COMMANDING VIEW OF THE TASMAN.**

were Fibrolite flimsies, rough as guts and often erected on scrubby land. There was one all-purpose room with a long-drop dunny and a water tank out the back. There were no lawns to cut – that would come later – but kikuyu and buffalo grass would rise like surf around the footings, and the worst damage would come when cuttings from the back yard in town were brought to the bach to make a small garden. The smart cuttings would flourish as weeds and flee into the bush to create an organic menace to the ranges.

As New Zealand became prosperous and entered its golden era of the 1950s, the bach came into its own with the New Zealand bent for do-it-yourself. Pockets of coastline were transformed with ugly little structures that in places replicated our suburban sprawl. For three decades, the bach remained a supreme status symbol.

What a bizarre word 'bach' is. It derives from the word bachelor. In Otago and Southland, they have a different word for holiday houses, which they call cribs. Karekare survived the onslaught of money that Piha, just over the hill, accepted as the norm. Here in our small valley, generally we missed out on the full concrete block basement, the garage rumpus room and the ugly outdoor furniture.

The little Fibrolite cottage with its tiny deck sat all winter waiting for the holiday invasion. Most baches were in desperate need of a paint job. Usually there was a garden of spinifex and ice plants, white painted rocks and tyres filled with mum's succulents which flourished on nothing. Generations of kids grew up at the beach this way. The New Zealand bach was never very romantic or private but it felt like a palace after you had been pent up for the winter. It never lasted that long: by the end of January, most family members had had a gutsful of one another and were happy to return to the suburbs.

The 1950s bach might have been a scourge on the pristine New Zealand land-

scape, but at the same time, I think it expressed something of our identity, or at least our national character as it was back then: unsophisticated, a little rough around the edges, but with a sturdy frame and a warm heart.

Harry Turbott is a quiet, unsung hero of New Zealand architecture and one of the first environmental architects to introduce landscape design and the planting of trees and shrubs along the Auckland motorway system. He has taught for years at the Auckland School of Architecture, and hundreds of bright young designers, planners and shapers of our environment hold Harry in high regard.

Many of his students have spent time with him at his beautiful open-plan barn-like home, which is folded into the ridge of the Watchman. I helped to carry the massive demolition beams up to the building site and on Sunday mornings the Surf Club members would form a human chain, passing bricks and other materials up the steep, winding path. Such was our admiration for the man and his vision. It looked like the first new dwelling that made sense to us back in the 1960s. It was purpose-built to fit into this particular landscape.

UNDER THE DIRECTION OF INSPIRATIONAL ARCHITECT IAN ATHFIELD, THE OLD COMMUNITY HALL (TOP AND INSET) WAS TRANSFORMED INTO THIS GRACIOUS COASTAL HOME (ABOVE) FOR THE McSHANES.

Harry first came to Karekare with his late wife, the painter Nan Manchester. Her paintings still hang on the walls, while the house has aged beautifully. Harry and Nan were a much-loved couple locally, for their commitment to keeping sub-division development away from Karekare. As I sit with him in the winter sun, we reminisce about the 40 years that we have been involved in battles to ensure that this place retains its unique quality. We agree that not having even a store here has been accepted by the community and by the thousands of visitors, who don't seem to miss even the traditional New Zealand beach ice cream.

Harry Turbott has made an indelible impact on the ranges with his signature work, the Arataki Visitor Centre on Scenic Drive. Working closely with Te Kawerau ā Maki carvers, he and the iwi produced one of the most popular and admired buildings in New Zealand.

As Harry describes it, the challenge in designing Arataki was "to make the beautiful landscape of the Waitakere Ranges more approachable and understandable both in Maori and Pakeha terms. It was a deliberate attempt to synthesise both Māori and European traditions into a unified bi-racial design. The building is very directly related to the spectacular landscape, but it is also centred on a thousand-year-old tradition of the tangata whenua. It also attempts to link the past with the present."

Harry has redesigned a number of Catholic parish churches to make them suitable for modern liturgy. He redesigned the Mary McKillop Chapel to make it suitable for women's worship. Another commission involved designing the interior of the Marae Church at Mangere where the problem was to unite traditional Anglican religious symbols with contemporary carving, kowhaiwhai and tukutuku panels.

On a visit to Rarotonga, Harry was confronted with a massive stone marae and large coral walled structures that the local people had built in the 19th century. The Are Ariki (chief's palace) of the Ngati Makea at Taputapuatea Marae was a massive ruin destroyed by a hurricane in the early 20th century. Harry put a proposition to restore the Are Ariki to the paramount chief Makea Nui Teremoana Ariki and the Ngati Makea.

After the proposal was accepted, Harry organised combined working parties of the local people, the Auckland School of Architecture, and Unitec carpentry students who set out to work together to restore the building using 19th century building methods. A massive pit was dug and filled with tightly packed coral and then burnt for a month to create lime to mortar the walls. Six years later, the restored and refurnished Are Ariki was opened at a massive feast. Makea Nui Teremoana Ariki subsequently bestowed the Cook Island Maori name of Tama Ta'Unga O Makea on Harry, possibly the only Pakeha so honoured.

Standing on the Watchman with Saul Roberts, Te Kawerau ā Maki architect and consultant to the Waitakere City Council, we discuss why, by and large, there is no distinctive Pacific feel to our coastal dwellings, why we have taken English architecture and dumped it onto very different landscapes here. Saul is working with resource consents, trying to raise the awareness of what could be a Polynesian feel to buildings: space, openness and an ease unrestricted by small, closed rooms, as he says "a flow of bodies and spirit." It sounds good to me. He is working with other members of Te Kawerau ā Maki and the council on a set of protocols on what to do when someone finds human remains, which many people are doing on this coast. With the Auckland Regional Council, the tribe have a secret burial site, where the recovered remains are reburied with ceremony and respect.

Harry Turbott and Saul Roberts are visionaries, leading us in fresh approaches to what and how we build on our coastal landscapes.

(OPPOSITE) ARCHITECT HARRY TURBOTT AT HIS HOME ON THE WATCHMAN RIDGE. (ABOVE) RENOWNED PHOTOGRAPHER MARTI FRIEDLANDER CRAFTED THESE IMAGES OF THE TURBOTT FAMILY AT KARE-KARE BEACH IN THE 1960S.

## SEASONS IN THE VALLEY

THE CLIMATE at Karekare enhances the environment: if it looks a lush viridian green from a distance, up close there are a million variations on the theme of lushness. Although massive fires have raged at times during the past two centuries, the regeneration is phenomenal. On the hills and in the gorges the big trees have survived the intense heat.

The vegetation ranges from small, exquisite plants, fungi and ferns to centuries-old kauri, rata and puriri. There's always a mystery with kauri as to how some trees survived the axe – what tender mercies were delivered by the brutal, unrelenting merchants of timber? Somehow, magnificent trees did make it. Such are the trees at the head of the Karekare Valley, where a small but important grove flourishes above the stream, and in the Liddles' family estate the kauri stood tall above the rainforest canopy. It is this way in the gorges too, where the kauri is returning majestically, shrugging off all challengers. Its remarkable shedding skin, like that of a giant snake, ensures nothing sticks, and it remains the king of all our forests.

This stretch of coast is part of the Waitakere Ranges ecological catchment area and what makes it astonishing and unique is that it contains no fewer than 111 species of the fern family; 60 percent of all New Zealand fern species are found here. The bad news is that 21 percent are categorised as either rare or endangered.

These coastal hills, valleys, headlands and wetlands also host an impressive variety of wildlife, with 27 bird species flourishing. In addition there are five lizard species, three types of frogs, and 100 species of land snails, or 20 percent of all known New Zealand snails.

Just as climate affects the land, so geography modifies the weather, causing moisture-laden clouds from the Tasman Sea to collide with the Waitakere Ranges before moving across the Auckland isthmus to the Hauraki Gulf and beyond, saving the city from higher precipitation while filling its western reservoirs. It's appropriate then to take a brief look at the geological structure of the area.

The Karekare beach sits within one of the colossal Waitakere volcanoes, formed

in the Miocene period, which ranged from about 22 to 15 million years ago. According to geologist and historian Bruce Hayward, the volcano was pushed up out of the sea, and from deep within the earth's crust, the vents discharged massive lava flows which now cap the Waitakere Ranges. The lava from the flanks of the volcano can be seen striping the cliffs around the northern end of the beach, near the Cauldron.

Nowhere are remnants of the ancient crater more visible than in Union Bay, where you are standing in it. The Watchman and all the other rocks are simply the eroded remains of cathedral-like projections that have been extruded into the crater. In the 15 million years since the eruptions abruptly ceased, the Tasman Sea has battered its way in, and when the sea rose to its present level a mere 7000 years ago, the Karekare beach was flooded and the dunes were formed.

The Whatipu sands, stretching from the Manukau bar to Karekare, are the largest sand accretion in the Auckland region. An area of 650 hectares of shifting unvegetated dunes is mixed with prolific vegetation zones of pingao, spinifex and herbfields around the ephemeral freshwater lakes near Pascoe and Ohaka Points.

Inland, the Karekare Valley is a true rainforest. It drips with moisture for nine months of the year and vegetation flourishes because of it. But if the kauri is still making its comeback, the giant pohutukawa groves are the great gift of the last millennium. For some are 600 to 800 years old, and when you put this in context, these trees were alive when the Vikings were still raiding England and the great fleet of Polynesian navigators was heading southward. It is to their credit that our early settlers built around these gnarled, twisted giants. At the entrance to Pohutukawa Glade there are numerous large pohutukawa and three huge specimens where the valley opens out towards the beach. They are coastal residents, so you don't find

them putting down roots too far inland. Two giants sit comfortably almost side by side to the right of the Ahu Ahu track. There are peaceful glades everywhere in the Karekare valleys; like spindly cathedrals, the pohutukawa invite you to climb into them, sit and meditate. The knees and ribs were prized for their strength in boat building and the groves at Karekare were often raided for this purpose. Some of these ancient pohutukawa have had a new lease of life, thanks to a major campaign to eradicate possums in the coastal settlements and ranges. Operation Forest Save is a ten-year, million-dollar extermination programme. The first stage has already shown results, with new shoots on

(OPPOSITE, TOP AND RIGHT) **BENEFITS OF OPPOSUM ERADICATION PROGRAMME 'OPERATION FOREST SAVE' CAN BE SEEN AROUND THE STREAMS AND WATERFALLS, WHERE REGENERATION OF NATIVE BUSH IS TAKING PLACE.**

the old trees and the spectacular displays of flowers in the first half of December are evidence of the plan working.

Puriri is a handsome tree, with dark, glossy foliage. This is the tree that the Murdochs and Farleys used for house blocks at Winchelsea, for fenceposts and timber for the outhouses and stables. Māori used puriri for the storage of human bones, so respect the giant puriri on the Buck Taylor Track as they may be tapu.

In spring the clematis bursts into white dazzling rivulets across the treetops on Mt Zion. Up close it's hard to find, but from a distance, it presents a magnificent display.

Close by, you'll find the northern rata, which starts life as an epiphyte, perching among the branches of all our great trees including the kauri. It germinates in the accumulated vegetable debris and then begins its deadly descent. Dropping its aerial roots, these soon become trunks that in turn send out their insistent, encircling arms. Folklore has it that they then simply crush the supporting tree. This is the houseguest from hell. The decaying heart of the host is eventually replaced by the rata's own massive, irregular trunk, itself often covered by climbing plants and epiphytic vegetation. This is seething, multi-occupancy, high-rise accommodation.

Orchids flourish in this climate. The common dendrobe or perching orchid is beautiful and delicate; a metre or more long, it's a spring gem.

Only two trees, the kauri and the puriri, are able to survive the rata's fatal embrace. There are some impressive rata and puriri on the Horoeka and the Taraire tracks. Named after the taraire, with its large characteristic impressed veins and the leaf edges curved back, it is of the same family as the kauri.

The stately, majestic nikau was a great resource for Māori. The fronds were used for the making of kete, for weaving and lashing. Nikau is common in the Karekare wetness. Its heart was a food source, but was rationed for special occasions and the feeding of guests, for its removal killed the tree.

The valley behind the sand dunes floods in winter, and when Cyclone Bola

deluged the upper half of the North Island in 1987, Karekare almost disappeared beneath floodwaters. The dunes trapped the water pouring down from Zion, and the three-metre-high cabbage trees were barely visible. We paddled and swam like kids in this lake all that winter.

Māori would have found Karekare an abundant source of food. The valleys provided the modestly populated pa on the Watchman with food for immediate consumption of the tribe as well as for storage. Kumara, the sweet potato, was propagated and grown on the valley floor in extensive gardens alongside the present road. Cakes and a type of bread were made from the pollen of the raupo or bullrush which can be found in the lagoons behind the sand dunes between Karekare and the Pararaha.

The sea provided a bounty with fish and other seafood caught from the north rocks and from small waka. From the size and type of fish-hooks found along the coast, it would seem that they were after large fish that came in to feed near the kelp beds. The hooks are designed and shaped beautifully, and must have taken considerable time to craft.

Eels are still common in the deep pools and are not difficult to catch. Every summer the local kids can be seen eagerly fishing for eel off the bridge at the bottom of Lone Kauri Road.

The introduction of millers, mynahs, magpies and mustelids took a heavy toll on birdlife in the area. The Murdochs and other boarding house proprietors kept caged birds, some of which escaped into the bush. Some of the rosellas and cockatiels are descendants of these freedom fliers, as are the pheasants that you may surprise while you are walking over the dunes at dusk.

Around the south point past Paratahi Island both the New Zealand and the banded dotterel, oystercatchers and flocks of gulls can be observed. At Mercer Bay there is a colony of spotted shags that have made their nest in the ledges on the sphinx rock just round the corner from the Cauldron. When I have been swimming past on my way to Mercer Bay they peer down at me inquisitively, as if wondering what I could possibly be doing. Apparently this colony has been here for almost a century.

Weka and the brown kiwi are both now gone from the Waitakere Ranges, as is the korimako or bellbird. Fortunately, the haunting call of the ruru or morepork can still be heard in the valley. In winter, blue penguins come ashore along much of

the coastline, and occasionally the threatened New Zealand falcon can be sighted.

In spring the tui returns from the interior to the warmer beach areas and the abundant kowhai tree covers both sides of the valley in golden hues.

Around my bach in the karaka trees are a pair of kereru or native pigeons. These same birds seem to have been there for 20 years, each summer getting intoxicated on the fermenting berries on which they gorge. They have survived the feral cats dumped in the ranges as well as the onslaught of stoats, ferrets and weasels. These species were misguidedly introduced to New Zealand in the 1880s to control rabbits and became a major predator of native birds. Mustelids, as they are collectively called, are known predators of kaka, yellowhead and saddleback and have led to the decline of kakapo, takahe and the little spotted kiwi in other parts of New Zealand. They are also carriers of bovine tuberculosis, parasites and toxoplasmosis. The Auckland Regional Council has declared mustelids 'animal pests' in the Auckland Regional Animal Pest Management Strategy. Further information on these threats to the environment in the ranges and elsewhere in the region can be found at: www.arc.govt.nz

Rabbits are common; many are the descendants of pets abandoned by city dwellers who grew tired of them. Another mammal found in the ranges is the long-tailed bat, which prefers to hide out under the cliffs in coastal caves.

Many plants brought out to the beach by bach owners derive from garden centres and school fairs, and have migrated into the bush. Introduced species including two varieties of wild ginger and climbing vines like old man's beard, jasmine and climbing asparagus are strangling the native flora and changing the character of the bush.

The natural world is delicately balanced in this part of the Waitakeres. Yet although fragile and vulnerable, the Karekare Valley appears to be thriving, thanks primarily to the caring concern of residents, as well as to policies developed and implemented at local, regional and government levels. Although the long-term outcome is unknown, there is reason for cautious optimism.

(TOP) PAUL JACKSON, *WHATIPU SOAK*, 2000, OIL ON LINEN, 770x3004MM. COURTESY MILFORD GALLERIES. (MIDDLE) SONG OF THE TUI RETURNS TO THE VALLEY IN SPRINGTIME. (LOWER) ENDANGERED KERERU OR NATIVE PIGEON IS NOW BEING SEEN IN GREATER NUMBERS IN THE WAITAKERE RANGES. (OPPOSITE) THE CLIFFS, REEFS AND ISLAND ARE COMPOSED OF ROCK KNOWN AS MANUKAU BRECCIA. (OPP. FAR LEFT) PLANTING OF MARRAM GRASSES IN THE 1960S HELPED RAISE KAREKARE FROM A FLAT BEACH TO ONE WITH DUNES 15 METRES HIGH. WIND PATTERNS CONTINUALLY CHANGE THE FORM OF THE DUNES.

# UNDER YOUR TOWEL

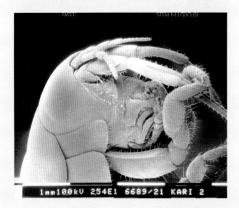

(ABOVE AND OPPOSITE) "TO SEE A WORLD IN A GRAIN OF SAND..." WILLIAM BLAKE KNEW NOTHING OF MEIO-FAUNA WHEN HE WROTE THIS AROUND 1803, BUT HIS VISION ANTICIPATED THE MICROSCOPIC WORLD OF THESE 'BIBLIOCRYPTOZOANS'.

As you stretch out on the beach at Karekare, basking in the heat of the sun radiating off the black sand, you are probably not aware that under your towel lives a teeming world of creatures that Hollywood's zaniest special effects people would be proud of having created.

Right underneath you, clinging to grains of sand with tentacles and claws tearing and chewing, these microscopic animals, which inhabit the deep sand on both shore and sea-floor, are some of the oldest on this planet. Yet they remained undiscovered until the 1920s. They are known collectively as meiofauna, meaning 'lesser animals', a classification system that zoologists use to describe them.

I went digging for these mysterious meiofauna over two summers. The first time I did not go deep enough. But the following summer I discovered a 'new' 40 million year old species whose science fiction-like appearance seemed appropriate when I observed its ferocious homicidal behaviour. Down in the dark under two metres of black sand is a busy world in miniature, whose denizens are visible only with the aid of an electron microscope.

One study calculates that a handful of wet sand can contain as many as 10,000 of these creatures. They play an important role in the conservation of our coastal marine ecosystem. These prodigious eaters consume pollutants and detritus, and in turn serve as a primary food source for small shrimp, molluscs, and bottom-feeding fish. Relatively unknown even to the scientific world, they are also described by the term bibliocryptozoans – animals that are extremely common on Earth but difficult to find.

With the help of a spade and a fine-meshed screen, I discovered four new species. Peering into the petri dish, I observed the meiofauna moving amongst the sand, magnified up to 25,000 times so each grain appeared like a diamond rock. They crawled and writhed, electrified by the light. What surprised me was not their numbers but the variety of their forms.

The most common is what is known as the peanut worm. It dates back a mere 530 million years, forming its own phylum or classification of animals. It has the unusual feature of being able to retract its head completely as it moves through the sand.

The more common variety found at Karekare, so far unnamed, is a large shrimp-like creature with a feather-plumed body covering and a big lance for sucking the living juices out of any like rival that comes near its patch. These are all serious predators, sticking their body to the sand with a glue-like substance, mating or killing before releasing their grip, then moving off to do the same to the next animal.

Under the electron microscope, each one seems so different to the next, a myriad variety of extraordinary forms. Their colours are also remin-iscent of sci-fi fantasy: metallic gold, blue and green, as if they were tiny extras from an aliens-from-outer-space movie. Their plumes, fins and

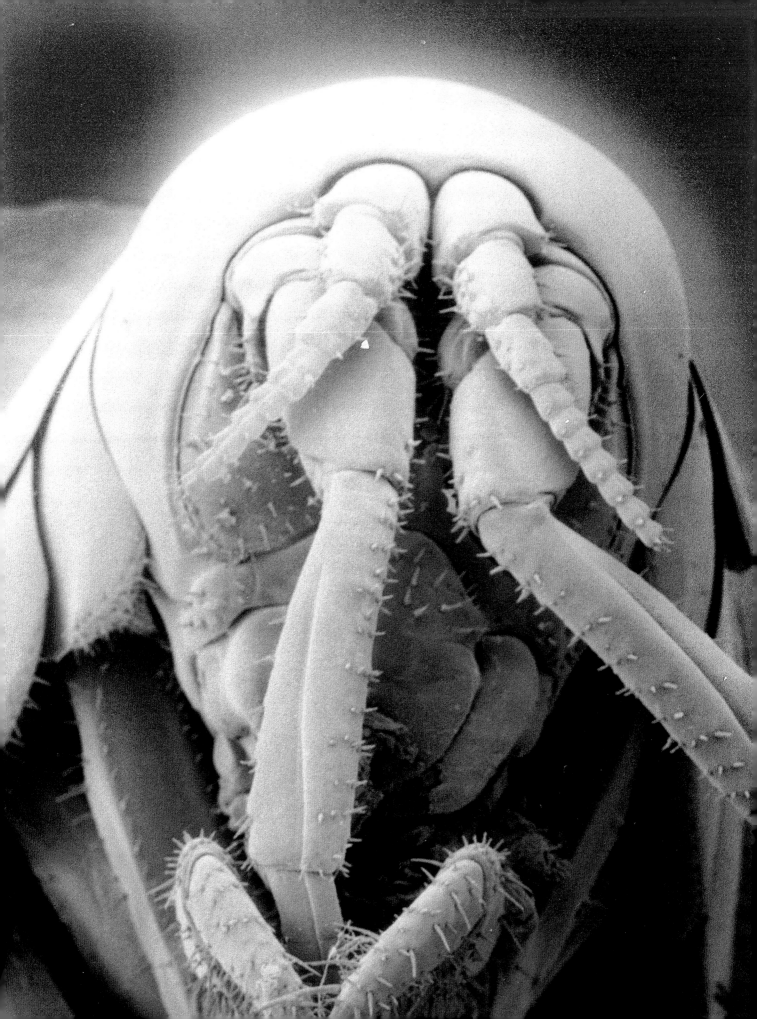

rugged-looking bodies are a scientific curiosity and a visionary nightmare.

They have the smallest known cells of any animal on the planet, with a total length of only 40 micrometres, and as many as seven specialised cells for the muscles and nerves. Each seems to have devised a method of propelling itself with jets or stabilisers, able to move rapidly or glide through difficult, hostile terrain. The males have enormous testes that take up to as much as 75 percent of their body size, and the females produce an egg occupying half of the abdomen, and understandably produce just the one egg at a time.

In the surf, a newer and hardier variety has evolved. They are found closer to the surface than their land-based cousins. Here they resemble large shell-like creatures, and appear under the microscope to be more translucent and skeletal. Their locomotion is like a gentle swan, while that of their neighbours, loosened from the sand, is more like that of a jet-ski.

A healthy beach is one that has a thriving meiofaunal population. Their vacuum cleaner-like ability enables them to suck up bacteria, algae and other organic material from the sand. When we think of the food chain and its function in the global ecosystem, few of us may have considered that to appreciate this vital link requires an electron microscope image magnification in the thousands.

I intend to continue digging for these fascinating little wonders. Zoologists believe that the variety could encompass some 600 species. Seventy have so far been identified, one having been discovered eight kilometres below the surface of the Pacific Ocean.

As for the Karekare varieties, they will be graced with the names of local historic identities. Were these people still around to enjoy the unusual honour conferred on them, they might quote a line from Shakespeare: "A small thing, but mine own."

(ABOVE AND OPPOSITE) MEIOFAUNA CAN BE FOUND ON EVERY BEACH, BUT UNTIL THE 1920S NO ONE KNEW OF THEIR EXISTENCE.

PEOPLE
OF THE
VALLEY

# THE FAMILIES

(ABOVE) **THE WITTEN-HANNAH LIFEGUARD PATROL IS A CLOSE-KNIT GROUP OF FAMILY AND FRIENDS.** (OPPOSITE) **WITTEN-HANNAH PYRAMID RECREATES SUMMER OF 1935-36 PHOTOGRAPH OF ORIGINAL KAREKARE LIFEGUARDS. FROM LEFT, KAREL, BECKY, SHALEMA AND TOMAS WITTEN-HANNAH AND SHAWN WANDEN.**

## THE WITTEN-HANNAHS

Karekare was a magnet for the three Witten-Hannah brothers Alexander, Karel and Kubi, sons of Anna Maria Witten-Hannah, who emigrated to New Zealand from Czechoslovakia in 1946.

Anna Maria was a marvellous woman whose home in Titirangi was a centre for all things art and politic. Her second husband Bill was the chief architect for the Education Department. She was first married to Bill's brother James, who fathered the three sons, and when the boys discovered Karekare and moved onto ten-acre blocks up on the Lone Kauri farm estate in the 1970s, Anna Maria and Bill also relocated to Karekare Beach.

Bill designed the Karekare schoolhouse and helped with the extensions to the Surf Club. His designs for small public buildings like these use space effectively and reflect his belief that houses should also be related to their environment. Kubi settled on the steep, unsealed La Trobe Track in a small three-bedroomed house designed by Bill and nestling in thick regrowth.

The lives of the Witten-Hannahs have revolved around the Surf Club and the local community. Karel and Kubi have been major contributors to the establishment of the Karekare Rural Fire Party and the First Response Unit, which is able to rapidly respond on a 24-hour basis to a medical emergency, a vital service in a remote community like this.

Kubi became the first teacher at the Lone Kauri School while Alex initially practised law from his home on the Lone Kauri Road. Kubi's son Tomas and daughter Emily are lifeguards. Alex's son Sasha has become one of the country's leading exponents of classical guitar after training with a master in Europe.

Karel's daughters Shalema and Rebecca are members of the Surf Club, First Response Unit and Fire Party. Shalema was one of the youngest of 100 New Zealanders to be chosen to attend the first constitutional conference in Wellington. This event, staged in the old chamber of Parliament, brought together a diverse

group to visualise a more productive and harmonious society. I can see Shalema taking a leadership role in a larger forum one day.

Anna Maria's three sons and their families have had a huge impact on the community. They have fronted up to any challenge, from surf rescues to environmental threats. They are a kind of local dynasty which is part custodian and part kaitiake (guardian) to the area. Familes such as this are like wheels that oil communities. When Bill died in 1998, the locals planted trees and placed a seat by the bridge, in his memory. His Management Plan, developed over a decade in consultation with the local community in the 1980s, remains the blueprint for this small coastal settlement.

### THE LIDDLES

Harry Liddle was a stonemason who built the Paihia Church that stands on the foreshore at Waitangi. During the Depression years he worked at Karekare, fencing high in the hills, and as the day closed he would look down on the Karekare Valley and dream of one day owning a part of it.

Harry, his wife Noma and their three daughters camped every summer in the late 1940s under the great rata which still stands on the edge of what is now McCready's Paddock. As his business grew, installing petrol pumps and tanks, Harry continued to dream of buying a big piece of valley. When 100 acres became available in what looked like an inaccessible area, he knew this was what he was looking for, and it would be his. Using his skill as a builder, he started to construct a ford across the stream. With slabs of aggregate which he had dug from service station forecourts, the indomitable Harry built an access road into the valley. Metre by metre, he was able to bring his truck and digging equipment to an ideal building site where he

(TOP) CLASSICAL GUITARIST SASHA WITTEN-HANNAH AND CELLIST NATARANI THEOBALD TUNE UP FOR A WEDDING PERFORMANCE AT THE BEACH. NATARANI TRAINED AT TRINITY COLLEGE, LONDON AND WITH RUSSIAN VIRTUOSOS ALEXANDER IVASHKIN AND NATALYA PAVLUTSKAYA. (ABOVE) ALEX WITTEN-HANNAH IN HIS BARONIAL MANSION. (OPPOSITE) THE FIRE PARTY IS AN INVALUABLE PART OF THE KAREKARE COMMUNITY. TOMAS WITTEN-HANNAH AND VANESSA FERGUSON ON A MONDAY TRAINING NIGHT.

Mum & Dad in Sissy

Photographs

and Noma built their dream house – a long, low, riverstone-based home with a huge fireplace also made of locally gathered rocks. It overlooked the stream, which they dammed regularly to create a swimming hole at the head of the Karekare Valley.

The Liddles hated change. They campaigned against electricity reticulation and opposed the introduction of telephone lines. I adored them for it and I used to spend long hours sitting by their fire, discussing how we could lobby against the road being sealed, to keep down the number of visitors. We visualised hordes of people using up 'our' space on the beach. Harry became my first environmental mentor: although he wasn't aware of the term and would probably have hated it, he was an advocate of sustainability. His honesty and integrity greatly impressed me. His ability to build things himself inspired me. Whether it was in rock work or a days' hard yakker on the end of a shovel, we would share in the building of the Surf Club and he taught me a lot about being resourceful. Following a swim in his pool after surf patrol, I would be rewarded with a beer and a lecture on the perils of working in advertising, which he didn't see as a real job. He once loaned me a spanner for a small job in the Surf Club. I left it on the beach and I think he never trusted me again. At his funeral, I couldn't resist reminding Harry that I was still looking for his spanner. The sand always returns what's lost, and I hope that one day that spanner will reward my searching.

When Harry was elderly and crippled with arthritis, one day a hunter's dogs bailed up a wild pig on the rock-face above his driveway. Harry shot the animal, somehow managing to cart it back to his garage on his tractor. He'd just closed the door when the hunter turned up to ask him if he'd seen his quarry. Harry said he had no idea. For the next few months he and Noma lived on wild pork.

The Liddles lived well into their 80s, becoming so attached to their Karekare lifestyle that they could not bear to be parted from it. Now a third and fourth generation use the Karekare house with affection for the place and the memory of the first members of their family to live there.

### THE BROWNES AND THE GRIBBLES

If you couldn't afford to stay in the grand Winchelsea House in the 1930s, you would be directed over the little wooden footbridge, around the corner where the generous, hospitable Brownes ran the second but never second-rate accommodation. Trampers, sports lovers and members of the Manukau Amateur Cycling Club, who made Karekare their second home, were almost permanent residents. Brownes' was full every weekend.

The club organised weekend cycle races from Auckland to Karekare. The condition of the road would have made the trip gruelling for the riders. Their girlfriends came by boat from Onehunga to the Whatipu wharf and walked along the coast to meet up with them. Frank Casey was one of Auckland's champion cyclists, and would continue riding until well into his 80s. On the 60th anniversary of the Surf Club, the women members re-enacted the boat trip and beach walk to Karekare. At Brownes' the lodgings were reasonable and the food excellent. Later, when the Surf Club was founded by these same members of the Cycling Club, the success of the Brownes' business was assured. You could always find a home away from home at the Brownes.

In fact, photographs show that it was an earlier version of a camp village. They loved the informality of their guests, who slept in tents and swam at the beach without the ceremony that went on around the corner. The cookhouse was in what remained of the Karekau mill, Murdoch's enterprise. The stone and concrete mill blockhouse wall and part of the machinery was standing on the property by the large phoenix palm, and still is to this day.

The fishing was magnificent all year. The creek abounded in eels and in the 1930s toheroa and mussels were in abundance.

The property was originally owned by John Shaw. Ted Browne had bought it from Maria Mary Farley in 1923. It had a small kauri cottage on it and a lean-to on the back. It was a large, triangular piece, which went right up to the Cave Rock which in those days was called Black Rock, as it was often burnt off in summer. The Lone Kauri Road had not yet gone through the property.

Ted was fit and wiry, enormously strong and seemed to be able to do anything in the bush. He had enlisted in World War One with his four brothers, who were all killed. The sole survivor was sent home as a small comfort to his parents. On the way back to New Zealand, Ted met Stella Jackson. This led to a long and happy marriage at Karekare and at Piha. Their friendship with guests "at the waterfall" is still spoken of by the old-timers who are hosted by the Gribble family on the lawn at the occasional reunion.

(ABOVE) **TED BROWNE WITH FRIEND RALPH AT BROWNES' BOARDING HOUSE, 1923. THE COTTAGE WAS ALMOST CERTAINLY BUILT OF TIMBER FROM THE KAKARE MILL THAT STOOD NEARBY.** (BELOW) **TED AND THE BOARDING HOUSE COW, 1932.** (OPPOSITE) **GROWING UP AT KAREKARE: FROM THE BROWNE FAMILY ALBUM.**

Fishing under Big Bridge

The ducks in the stream

"Timmy". My dog

Bill, Bob, me, Archie.

Just a Crowd.

Their children Bill and Margaret were born in the years following their move to Karekare. This family made their living with a few cows, some bees, and the hospitality offered in their boarding house. The encampment – for that was what the Brownes' boarding house really was – consisted of accommodation in tents and in lean-tos, but it worked. If you wanted to rough it and enjoy the weekend, then the Brownes suited you well. In 1930-31, Ted and Stella made a serious bid to compete with Winchelsea, erecting two bunkhouses, the frames of which consisted entirely of kauri rickers while the walls and roof were of corrugated iron. The Brownes provided three good meals a day, but there were no luxuries like bathrooms – the stream flowed outside. At Christmas, Ted opened up the area between his boundary and the waterfall for campers. His daughter Margaret remembers those years well. "My father's prices were ridiculously low," she recalls, "and everyone seemed to help with cooking and cleaning up." She remembers one New Year's Day when over one hundred meals were cooked and served, all on two wood stoves.

In the Depression, most of the relief workers at Karekare stayed at the Brownes' in semi-tents. These had a wooden floor and wooden walls, up to two metres high, and then a canvas top for a roof. When the Depression was over, Ted acquired a new tent village from the workers. This increased his accommodation and his business flourished. So did his beekeeping – the hives were scattered along the valley floor and he built what was known as the Honey House.

Brownes' survived the great flood of 1927. The entire Karekare Valley was flooded by a cloudburst, which swept a wall of water through the valley, lifting the former schoolhouse off its foundations and floating it down the beach where it was entangled in the girders of the bush tramline.

In 1936 these two popular hosts moved over the hill to the Piha Boarding House. They retained ownership of the Karekare property until 1944, when Stella rang old friends Joy and Ray Gribble and offered to sell it to them for £600. They

Kare Kare.

bought it on the spot. The most recent occupants had been possum trappers and the floor was covered in fat, which the Gribbles scraped by spade. Ray had first visited Karekare in 1928 and after their marriage they spent many holidays camped under a large puriri tree by the waterfall, or stayed with the Brownes. The property is still in the Gribble family today. Now with a third generation, they have restored the main house. The original doorstep was a slab of teak from the wreck of the *Orpheus*.

(TOP) THE NEWLY-FORMED LONE KAURI ROAD, 1947, CUT THROUGH BROWNES' PROPERTY, SHOWN LOWER RIGHT OF THE PHOTOGRAPH. IN 2000 LOCAL RESIDENTS ACQUIRED AND PLANTED THE SECTION ABOVE THE ROAD. (ABOVE) BROWNES BOARDING HOUSE 'TOURER' STUCK IN THE STREAM. (LEFT) MANUKAU CYCLING CLUB RELAXING AFTER RACE TO KAREKARE. (OPPOSITE FROM TOP) AGAINST THE ROAR OF WATERFALL IN FULL FLOOD, ONE OF TED BROWNE'S MANY BEEHIVES; THE MAIN HOUSE; IN 1935 BROWNES' FLOURISHED, AS DID THEIR BEES. (OPP. TOP RIGHT) BROWNES SUMMER ENCAMPMENT EXTENDED ACROSS THE CREEK.

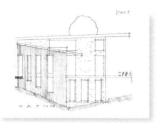

# THE ORIGINALS

### TE AO HOU: NATURAL BORN HEALER

Most mornings Te Ao Hou goes to the beach and stands on the sandhills waiting for the sun to rise behind the hills. As the rays warm his body, he focuses on stillness and begins tai-chi, using the ancient martial art to find his centre and enhance the connections he has with Papatuanuku and Rangi, the land and the sky. Behind him, the rise and fall of the waves seems to harmonise with his body. A surfer, healer and spiritual voyager, he has come here to find a soul existence and to understand the purpose of all. I enjoy his company, his quietness and his strength.

His Nga Ruahine forebears bequeathed the majestic Mt Taranaki to the nation. It can be glimpsed from where he stands, on a crisp winter morning, a tiny white dot across the Tasman Sea to the south. His mountain connects with him across the water as he moves through his morning exercises, drawing the energy he needs from a source greater than himself. After all, the stretch of coast on which he walks is called by the old name Taranaki Bay, named on the early maps by Maori who moved north after the Musket Wars and grieved for their homeland peak glimpsed across the bay on winter mornings. Once the sea mist rises, the mountain disappears from view.

Sitting by his fire in his house on Lone Kauri Road, he says that he feels he's been here before. Some people believe in previous lives, and out here it's not hard to feel that the bond and attraction you have for this place is special. But he believes in his very being that he has lived here, and I have no reason to scorn his claim.

Te Ao Hou completed a marketing degree at Otago before moving north to Auckland to work as a personal trainer at Les Mills World of Fitness, assisting many athletes to reach their potential. Lee Parore took him under his wing and acted as a mentor. During this time Te Ao Hou's interest in naturopathy flourished. It's meant everything to him, and he spent four years studying complementary medicine and healing, living for a time at Satyavan House, the household of Phillip and Jenny Cottingham.

Karekare has long attracted alternative lifestylers and as the 21st century evolves, it will continue to enlighten more people like Te Ao Hou, drawing them away from the superficial attractions of the big city.

Te Ao Hou and I go swimming down in the ravine that runs down at the bottom of the property. The pools each seem to have their own temperature. Fluctuating in depth and in current, the myriad of waterfalls is breathtaking. Some gush in stages, others pour like mini Niagaras and you can stand under them, dive or jump, and we do it often. There's no limit on age or fitness, you just take your pick and enjoy.

"I couldn't think of any other place I'd rather be," Te Ao Hou says softly. "Everything I want is here; my learning and my life unfolds before me at Karekare. I'm truly happy. In fact, there's so much energy here, I'm abundantly charged," he adds, leaping off a waterfall.

## Painters with Surfboards

Karekare attracts surfer-painters who can find a bach and paint for a summer, exhibiting and finding a ready market for their art. Justin Summerton and Tony Ogle are two of this breed. They have both travelled extensively, living on boats, seeking inspiration wherever they find it, painting and moving on, but always drawn back to the coastline of the Waitakeres. Both painters believe that their travels have helped to focus their art here on the west coast.

(ABOVE) **TE AO HOU DRAWING THE ENERGY AT A POOL IN THE COMPANY STREAM.** (OPPOSITE TOP) **RICHARD PRIEST ARCHITECTURAL DRAWING.**

(ABOVE) **JUSTIN SUMMERTON,** *THE WATCHMAN,* 2000,
OIL ON CANVAS, 1080x1520MM; AND (BELOW) *MT ZION
AND THE ISLAND FROM THE CAULDRON,* 2000, OIL ON
CANVAS, 1000x1000MM. (OPPOSITE RIGHT) **JUSTIN
SUMMERTON: PAINTING TO SURF.** (OPP. LOWER)
**JUSTIN SUMMERTON;** *UNION BAY,* 2000, OIL ON
CANVAS, 1080x1520MM.

Justin Summerton is a brilliant painter of the Karekare landscape. He first heard of the beach from surfer mates at St Clair in Dunedin. He packed his meagre belongings, the draft of an impressive novel called *The Albatross Boy,* his canvases and paints and headed north. He was not disappointed.

His first painting was of Split Pin Rock in Union Bay, and with this one work, which he quickly sold, he had arrived as a painter of Karekare Beach. The canvas is evocative and full of mystery. "The landscape here is so large and multi-faceted, there is an immediate greatness to Karekare," Justin says. "I like to paint parts of the beach that are striking, like the towering Watchman, which looks so different depending on where you are standing. I do a lot of climbing around to find the most interesting perspective. For me, vaporous clouds have become an ongoing experiment, kind of ethereal symbols of the landscape."

He says it's a cathartic process. First he photographs the area; maybe 30 prints are then montaged on a board so he can define the parameters of the composition, and he starts from there.

He shoots with a 50mm lens on an old Olympus OM10 which he's had for years. His brushstrokes are thick, often straight out of the tube, mixed and applied to the canvas in small, thick daubs. The technical term is 'scumbling' – it means to drag the brush over layers already built up, often creating areas of broken colour and allowing previous layers to show through in places. This way, working in oils, you build colour and texture with every brushstroke.

At Karekare, his waking day rotates around the tide changes, the wind, the sandbanks and the seasons. "I've made the sea my art. I thought I might as well make my workplace where I spend most of my time, so when I'm waiting for waves I look around and make mental notes to assist my painting. Then I'll come back the following evening with my camera, so the whole adventure of surfing and art are linked. Sometimes I feel that waves and cliffs are all I paint."

This is not quite true, as he has painted cityscapes in California, Paris and New York. In fact, he says, "I did my apprenticeship as a pavement artist in those cities." His original, quirky art is sought after by collectors and dealers both in New Zealand and overseas, and hangs in hotels, corporate offices and private homes.

In his early 30s, Justin Summerton is one of New Zealand's surf painters, a small group of artists who mix new art with their love of surfing. He is honest enough to admit that he paints to surf, and each year, picking the favourable months to surf the giant Hawaiian pipeline boomers, selling some art in Hawaii or California and returning to Karekare where he networks with his friends for a bach to work from.

When I went to meet Tony Ogle in his studio up the coast at Te Henga, he was finishing a painting of Union Bay, catching the reflection of the Split Pin in the wet black sand. His beautiful Pacific colours give his work a distinctive Polynesian feel. He paints with the screenprinting process in mind, achieving a matt finish that sits comfortably with large strong areas of flat colour. He shows me a graded sky effect achieved by moving paint across the surface with a squeegee, blending the colours. His studio overlooking the Tasman Sea contains drying racks for the prints. Against the wall are large imposing canvases awaiting the next exhibition.

Tony lived and worked at Matapouri Bay in the early 1980s before heading off for foreign adventures. After sailing from the Seychelles down the east coast of Africa to Cape Town, where he surfed and painted, he returned to New Zealand to

seek fresh locations. "I needed to find those untouched niches of the land and the coastline that convey timelessness and a sense of place," he says, adding that his real desire is to capture that sense of place in his work. His Karekare works give him that opportunity, although the richness of the colour lifts the landscape into a more exotic, tropical location that is not normally associated with this part of the coast.

### The Cottinghams: A View of the Ocean

When Jenny Cottingham and her husband Phillip were in Southern India in 1995, they discovered that their destiny was written in scriptures on 5000-year-old palm leaves. It was foretold that they would build a universal temple and a small community at a "place of power". They felt their destiny would take them to Karekare. They returned to develop Satyavan on a property overlooking the sea, that includes their large timber home and a wonderful eight-sided temple named Savitri, surrounded by gardens, waterfalls and sculpture. It is a place of learning, refuge and peace. As Jenny tells me, they now live away from life's busyness where the soul can be nurtured and the true self experienced.

They are devotees of one of the planet's great teachers and spiritual leaders, Sri Sathya Sai Baba, whom they visit regularly at his ashram and hospital near Bangalore in Andhra Pradesh, Southern India. His robe was given to the Cottinghams, who placed it in the temple at Karekare. As I walk with Phillip and Jenny up the winding stairway, I am overwhelmed by the serenity of the temple. Hidden from the road, its design is exquisite and truly beautiful. Jenny rings a large temple bell, whose sound echoes down the valley and announces a visitor. The household rises each morning at 5 o'clock for chanting, meditation and yoga.

The temple is dedicated to all the faiths and welcomes anyone to worship and to meditate here. The great western windows look out over the Tasman and the building itself is perfectly positioned between the folds of the hills. The dome of the temple is centred over the altar. It represents the elements of space, the primary element of the universe and as Phillip says, it amplifies the sounds of the temple and hopefully carries the vibrations out to the world. Like Sai Baba, they believe that we should all aspire to merge with the ocean of divinity, just as all rivers merge with the ocean. Here at Karekare, the sky, the ocean and the earth meet, enfolding us in peace and light.

Sai Baba has built large, modern, free hospitals in India. The Cottinghams would like to emulate this some day in New Zealand with a free naturopathic hospital. They are directors of the Wellpark College of Natural Therapies, an organisation dedicated to training and teaching holistic health. Not everyone appreciated a golden-domed temple, albeit small, sitting on a New Zealand farmland hilltop. But Phillip was adamant that it would be opened and honoured appropriately, so Te Kawerau ā Maki were invited to invoke ancient gods, to call on ancestors long

(OPPOSITE TOP) TONY OGLE, *KAREKARE, WEST COAST*, LIMITED EDITION SCREENPRINT ON PAPER, 1997. COURTESY THE ARTIST. (OPP. FAR LEFT) TEMPLE SPIRE CATCHES EVENING LIGHT. (BELOW) SATYAVAN. (LOWER) TIBETAN BUDDHIST MONK LAMA SAMTEN WAS HONOURED GUEST ON A DAY CELEBRATING THE UNIVERSALITY OF RELIGIONS.

dead but ever-present, on this impressive occasion. Christians, Buddhists and Hindu came together to bless and to revere this place and the building. The dazzling stained-glass windows acknowledge the greatest of unity and eight symbols of various faiths are depicted.

A year after the opening, three massive stone statues were added, of Shiva, Buddha and the Christ, all carved by Matt King. The trees have grown, providing shelter from the road for the temple, whose welcoming lamp is never extinguished.

For all of us who were there at the opening ceremony, it was a majestic presence of light and learning and it showed that this community is linked not only by physical land-owning, rates and regulations, but of deeper thoughts and aspirations.

## Jonathan Hunt: Mr Speaker

Jonathan Hunt never talks to you; he tells you. He's a mentor, a minder and he's terribly bossy. He is also an icon of wisdom and hospitality and it was in his house on the Lone Kauri Road, with the wind whistling through the pine trees one winter's night in 1992, that he convinced me I should run for Mayor of Waitakere City.

Jonathan has been a part of the Karekare community for 40 years. His small, comfortable house sits somewhat forlorn on top of the ridge like something from the set of Vincent Ward's film *Vigil*. Here, Jonathan has held court to generations of young, loyal Labour Party dilettantes, including me. Affectionately known as the Minister of Wine and Cheese, Jonathan Hunt was at last appointed Speaker of the House in 1999. He is a parliamentary godfather, the oldest parliamentarian. I think he still treats me like a naughty teenager, chiding me for bad Surf Club behaviour and over-exuberance.

No one ever shortens Jonathan to Jon: he is always in character. The house reverberates with loud Mozart and even louder Labour Party friends. His love for wine is legendary. He is the Prime Minister's closest and most loyal friend and mentor, a mandarin at the Court of Clark. She has journeyed out to the winding, tortuous Lone Kauri Road to his famed Christmas barbecues. Jonathan's year, like the ancient Christian calendar, revolves round Christmas and Easter. His generosity to locals and to the community knows no bounds. It was under his patronage, for a bottle of wine, that the Lone Kauri School was given life.

In his teens, Jonathan was a celebrity quiz kid and his general knowledge is still extraordinary. With his quick, photographic memory and a cool and often biting wit, it's been said that he's never been a plotter, and that has probably kept his political career afloat for so long. He knows more about the prime ministers of New Zealand than most, but his Mona Lisa smile betrays no secrets.

We had worked together on election campaigns for Norman Kirk, Bill Rowling and David Lange. Somehow, no matter how complex and cloudy the world seemed, Jonathan would point to a ray of hope, a way forward to victory, and when it didn't come, he wouldn't miss a beat. "There will always be another chance," he

(OPPOSITE) **THE RIGHT HONOURABLE JONATHAN HUNT, FATHER OF THE HOUSE AND BROADCASTER OF MOZART TO WAITAKERES WILDLIFE.**

would say, and after 18 years of waiting, he achieved his lifetime ambition of becoming Speaker of the House of Representatives, "Father of the House".

Like Jonathan himself, his own house is a time capsule: a modest Lockwood, for which he saved for 20 years on a schoolteacher's salary. His house is a retreat from the world of politics. The walls are lined with books; guests come from all over the world to stay for what seems like forever. In the basement is a full-sized billiards table, which doubles as a feasting board during parties. Everything that Mozart ever penned is there, and Jonathan has always been fond of using his massive speakers to broadcast the music to the cows and the Pararaha Valley wildlife below.

Jonathan is a truly a one-off individual: single and single-mindedly, he devotes his life to others. I'll stop by for a glass of wine, to rant and rave against the world and the problems of a politician in the public eye. Jonathan was instrumental in convincing me with his persuasive charm that I should stand for the position of President of the New Zealand Labour Party on the death of Michael Hirschfeld. I remember thinking that if I did not seize this moment, Jonathan would be somewhat miffed, and I probably wouldn't want to risk that. The wine might not have tasted so good during future visits.

### Richard Priest and Sue Curtling: Pioneer Seeds

Richard Priest is one of New Zealand's best known architects. He lives with his partner Sue Curtling and their baby daughter Ava in their dramatic house just off the Lone Kauri Road. This house is a magnificent architectural response to the Karekare hills, a sanctuary in a wild place. The roof kicks the landscape forward, a metal butterfly held skyward by thick, earthy, plaster walls of rich red and long panels of glass.

The house seems both anchored and floating. This is because when you leave the massive paving stones of the path, you fly on a suspended wooden walkway, passing over a small bathing pool and a Terry Stringer bronze, towards the huge welcoming door. This entrance is surrounded by aluminium panelling and gives no hint, before it can swing open to reveal the house, of the airy space beneath high ceilings and clean, clear lines that throw you into a breathtaking view of the sea and sky beyond.

Some of the furnishings came from the Selby Shoe Factory when it closed in Great North Road. A massive shoe cabinet, wooden and aged, looks like it came from a Venetian palace. A Terry Stringer banner in pencil flows down the main wall. The kitchen, with its long terrazzo bench, creates what *Cuisine* magazine called "a private universe" which finishes with an Ann Robinson glass bowl. A row of Bombo stools set you up at a servery.

Richard says that the house has "quite a complexity" about it. "My ideas are now heading towards more simplification, in both materials and lines. Architecture is something where you're constantly learning from what you've done before and from what's happening around you."

Sue Curtling is renowned for the organic propagation and cultivation of

heriloom vegetables and for food-producing garden design. She buys seeds from Koanga Gardens near Kaiwaka, a centre for organic gardening and agriculture. She propagates the seeds in her glasshouse and sells the plants at local markets around the city.

In an age where we mass produce most of our food, Sue's company Organic Harvest describes itself as providing "a commitment to creating bold, dynamic gardens that are as strongly visual as they are functional. With an emphasis on smell, texture, colour and taste." Her work is leading to a fantastic rediscovery of our forebears' cuisine.

Sue becomes animated as we talk about the good earth. "The aim of every organic gardener is to grow the soil," she says. "Put your energy into that and the plants are almost a by-product. Plants like lupins do all the work, and the lovely structure from the plant breaks down and feeds the soil.

"Seeds will learn to adapt to local conditions. You never need to use toxic sprays. If you plant them with a companion they like, you build up guilds, groups of plants that help each other. The monoculture type of agriculture that relies on fertilisers is breaking down the planet's soil structure."

Sue adds that living at Karekare has inspired her to get close to the land. "The more you respect the soil, the more you care about what you put into your body." That sounds like something even a politician might find hard to debate.

Richard and Sue noted the prevailing winds before he designed their home. "We dug this house into the earth," Richard says. "The back wall literally wraps around, giving a sense of sanctuary and stability that is not only practical but anchors this house in the gales sweeping up from the beach in the winter months. It inspires me just being out here," he adds. But he also agrees that living at Karekare can be a distraction. He loves to surf, and his children are junior lifeguards at the Surf Club.

We sit looking out over the sea, talking about our shared passion for India, and his work on the design of Wildfire, one of Auckland's finest restaurants. The discussion ranges over his townhouse designs and private commissions. We agree that in this timber-obsessed country of ours, concrete is under-rated as a building material. Within minutes, a huge raincloud rolls overhead, followed by lightning, an opera of weather happening before us.

This is why Richard Priest, Sue Curtling and other gifted individuals have come to Karekare: it's a collective, unspoken response to landscape and place. There's a definite feel with these people that they are here on a mission. They're not aliens in a strange land; they are here because they chose this place. Perhaps Karekare chose them.

## OLIVIA FROM BOLIVIA

Olivia Sheehan hails from a small town in Maryland, USA. This remarkable woman has been a fashion model, a professional photographer, a pilot, a skipper, and a psychiatric nurse. She has sailed the Caribbean and the Pacific, she has

(TOP) **RICHARD PRIEST, SUE CURTLING WITH BABY AVA AND SHED THE DOG.** (ABOVE) **SUE CURTLING: FEEDING THE SOIL WITH GUILDS OF PLANTS.** (OPPOSITE TOP) **VIEW OVER ZION HILL AND TASMAN SEA FROM DECK STRUCTURE OF PRIEST HOUSE.**

painted yachts and houses for a living, surfed in Hawaii and skied in the Swiss Alps. She sailed from California to New Zealand on an 18m ketch as a deckhand, navigator and cook. Living alone at Karekare for more than two decades, Olivia typifies the kind of person who is accepted as she is in this tiny community. Back in the suburbs she might be regarded as eccentric, but out here she fits right in. Perhaps because the land and nature looms so large at Karekare, people's regard for one another is inclined to be more tolerant and respectful of originality.

Even so, Olivia made an immediate impact when she first came to the valley. She sanded her house on the Watchman, sans clothes, which even for Karekare became somewhat of a legend. "I don't see why I should add to the laundry," she says matter-of-factly. Her working garb has inspired a number of stories. There is a missionary who will never forget encountering Olivia mowing her lawns in "gardening clothes" – just a pair of gumboots and a veil of hair.

She seems to have been to every party and grand occasion for as long as I can remember. With her sense of fun and *joie de vivre*, she was courted by local men who saw her as a prize catch, but Olivia seems to have escaped the net, preferring to travel to exotic parts of the world each year.

She visited Bolivia, hence her nickname. She cruised the Nile, where rumour has it she fell under the spell of a sultan's charms. Her souvenir of this experience is a complete set of harem clothes. Photographs of her performing what appears to be the Dance of the Seven Veils are pinned to painter Dean Buchanan's studio wall. She's a dear friend of the art community. They love her sense of humour, her irreverence for all things and her great love of the environment in which she lives.

Artist Barry Miller has painted her as a classic Victorian beauty on the beach, noble and regal, which she is also. She's a stunning looking woman, always tanned and with her hair in a long plait or coiled high into a crown. If ever I had the need for counselling services, I would turn to Olivia from Karekare. Her refreshingly honest approach to life is itself a kind of therapy for those whose lives she touches.

As we sit and talk, taking a strange and mystic tea, she recalls the first time she came out to this place. "I came here with architect Harry Turbott, who lives nearby on the Watchman. I knew then that I had at last found the one place where I wanted to live."

She first rented the old hall, a place I had been given a few years before for a mere $1300. From the hall, Olivia found her special cottage on the flank of the hill and she stayed, gradually transforming her three rooms into a cottage that glows with warmth and colour, and is embellished with mementos of her travels. Every year she sets off to encounter another dangerous place on a distant continent, and when she gets there she often realises she has lived there in a previous lifetime. Visiting Tibet, she felt she knew the layout of the rooms and doors of the Great Monastery in Lhasa. She sensed that those doors had once opened for her. She had similar experiences in Egypt and on the Inca Trail of Machu Picchu. Climbing through the Andes, she felt she was walking just above the ground. She smiles and adds that there is a simple explanation: when she was last here, in another time, the track was that much higher.

It all figures, she says; she's been around a long time, and as she tells it, you can't help but agree. Once off the Hawaiian coast she came close to drowning. Swept from her board, she drifted beneath the surface and felt herself giving up on life. In those final moments before what seemed like certain death, she felt a hand pulling her to the surface, then a strong pair of arms placing her on a long wooden board. She remembers little except for the texture and feel of the surfboard.

After recovering from her near-death experience, she says that a few days later she recognised the same board in Honolulu's Bishop Museum. It was the precious surfboard of the fabled Duke Kahanamoku; without a blink, she tells me she knows it was Duke who rescued her.

(LEFT AND OPPOSITE) **OLIVIA SHEEHAN ENJOYED A GLAMOROUS CAREER AS A NEW YORK FASHION MODEL IN THE 1950S BEFORE TRAVELLING THE WORLD TO ARRIVE AT KAREKARE.**

In full flight now, she tells me that on many nights throughout the years, but never on a full moon, she hears the unmistakable sound of birds crying high on the Watchman. "They fly at night, yet I have never been able to see them," she adds wistfully. "I guess they are the spirits of those who died up on that rock. I know that's what they are."

I listen to her story intently, and have no inclination to challenge her. Outside the light begins to fade from her long window. The beach is framed like a Siddell painting and even the surf seems to have stopped moving for a moment. "Where next?" I ask her. She sidesteps the question; there are perhaps too many possibilities. As I walk back down her steep path, bowing low under a huge pohutukawa trunk, night has already fallen. The stars are bright and the air crisp. I pause, straining my ears to listen for the birds. They do not call for me tonight, but then it is still early.

## NIKI CARO AND ANDREW LISTER: TRANSFORMING SPACE

Filmmaker Niki Caro is one of New Zealand's most exciting directors. Her film *Memory and Desire*, shot on this coastline, gained critical success. By the time Niki and partner Andrew Lister, an architect, bought their Karekare house, they had stayed at some of the best houses at the beach. What they settled for was a little different – what they call the Taj Mahal of Fibrolite baches – and they transformed it, revealing a wonderful sense of space.

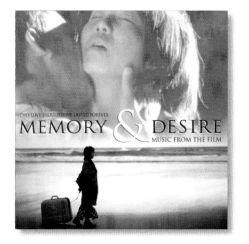

Bill and Mary Tonkin had bought a half-acre from Tom McGuire on the beach road. The creek ran through the middle of their section. First they built a house and then they planted a garden. And what a garden it is. After he retired, they worked from dawn to dusk, devoting 30 years to the cultivation of exotic plants and succulents. It seemed that everything would grow at Mary's touch in the fertile valley soil. The couple were loved by the people of the valley.

After Bill and Mary died in the mid-1990s, Niki and Andrew became the owners of the Tonkin home. These two innovative designers took over a 1950s-style box and taking their cue from Japanese and Pacific minimalism, they covered the sloping roof with sheets of bamboo plywood, echoing Samoan and other Pacific influences. Shiny black fibreglass on the doors and a Japanese screen evokes images from her film, which moves from Tokyo to Auckland's west coast.

Andrew was formerly with Richard Priest before he started his own consultancy, so he was already familiar with the Karekare landscape of lush surrounding hills, of lifting mist with sunlight filtering and changing throughout the day. The house has no clutter, and seems free of references to the past. They have created their own architectural mission, adding their own preferences for pure and simple design solution, and it works.

When I asked them what was the best thing about Karekare and what had brought them to the place, Niki said: "Well, it certainly wasn't about commuting. Karekare is a long way if you drive here after a long, hard film shoot, but when you get here, it's a small price to pay for swimming well after sunset on summer nights."

(ABOVE AND OPPOSITE) **ANDREW LISTER AND NIKI CARO: TRANSFORMING SPACE.**

# THE ARTISTS

AT GALLERIES and exhibitions, it seems to me that wherever New Zealand landscapes are showing, Karekare almost inevitably features. In the 1990s, the place became a statement of the New Zealand beach, probably more so than any other rugged stretch of coastline. Karekare bay has a quality of infinite light that has demanded attention from some of this country's foremost painters, as well as from hundreds of weekend enthusiasts with a palette and brush.

Ellen La Trobe was the teacher at the Henderson District School in 1885. Her paintings of Karekare with their soft, almost surreal light, reveal what a superb landscape painter she was. Unfortunately, only three of her works have survived. You can see her influence today in the work of Ruth Cole, who paints the area around the sand dunes after rain, with great sensitivity. Ruth says she is haunted by this landscape, as Ellen La Trobe must have been before her. Both these painters have brought a feminine response to a place which seems to mainly attract male painters to its rugged edges.

## MARTIN HILL AND PHILIPPA JONES: NATURE WORKS

Martin Hill and Philippa Jones create environmental sculptures in natural landscapes around the world. Their works are made from nature's materials found at the sites they journey to, which are often reached by rock climbing. The results are captured on film and the work is left to be dispersed by the elements and absorbed harmlessly back from where it came.

The process, they say, reflects nature's cyclical system on which all life forms depend. It is a metaphor for the way we need to redesign our lives and businesses to become sustainable.

Martin uses his photographs in the design of products such as cards, calendars, prints and books, which are distributed internationally and have a large following in New Zealand.

In order to confront the global impact we are making on the environment, Martin and Philippa are creating The Fine Line Project, a series of 12 climbs to make sculptures on 12 high points around the earth linked by a symbolic line starting and finishing on the summit of Mt Ngaruhoe in Tongariro National Park.

Their work has been featured in magazines and on television, and they have visited Japan several times to give lectures and workshops. Passionate about their work, these two artists wish to share their convictions and creations with as wide an audience as possible. Their intention is to help effect a radical shift in thinking towards sustainable environmental practices.

It was at Karekare that Martin first explored making environmental sculptures. He dreamed and planned on long walks up the Pararaha Gorge in all weathers, peering in streams and searching among the dunes for answers to the questions that troubled him. His goal was and is nothing less than "how to get a global shift in industrial practice, from the linear take-make-and-waste model to the cyclical, renewable processes found in nature, where all waste is food or energy for another

(ABOVE) *BALANCED STONES.* IN AN EARLY EFFORT TO COMMUNICATE ABOUT SUSTAINABLE DESIGN, MARTIN HILL BALANCED THESE HEAVY SEA-WORN STONES ON A BEACHED LOG. (BELOW) WITH THE BLACK SAND OF KAREKARE AS A CANVAS, MARTIN HILL AND PHILIPPA JONES WORK WITH THE RAMS HORN SHELLS THEY FIND THERE. (OPPOSITE) *2000 SHELLS* (FROM THE MILLENNIUM SERIES).

species or process, and poisons are degraded by natural processes." This is the most important design problem of our time, he tells me.

Martin decided to work for nature rather than against it, by combining all the things he loved: travelling in wild places, photography and design, climbing and making sculptures in the natural world. He continues to visit Karekare whenever he can to refresh his soul in the place where he was first inspired. With Philippa he makes a sculpture on each visit. There is an environment here that liberates the creative energies. The cycle continues unbroken.

## PETER AND SYLVIA SIDDELL: TWILIGHT ZONE

Although they had earlier felt the call of the Coromandel, Peter and Syliva Siddell decided to seek somewhere closer to their Auckland home. They wanted a small, secluded section with a waterfall nearby. They drove out to Karekare in 1971 and bought the last section from Tom McGuire, in the small corner that had once housed Murdoch's flax mill. The requisite waterfall cascaded from the hill behind.

Peter, who was just beginning his career as a fulltime painter, was enthralled by Karekare. Like me, he had grown up in the heart of the city and had been exposed to early New Zealand landscapes in the Auckland City Art Gallery. He remembers the thrill of discovering W.A. Sutton's *Nor'wester in the Cemetery*. In the early 1960s, he began painting as a hobby, and apart from one term at a night school, he is self-taught.

A life-long tramper and climber, he fell under the spell of a place of light, textures and brooding headlands. His first paintings combined colonial houses with west

(ABOVE) **PETER SIDDELL,** *NORTH BEACH;* 1995. OIL ON CANVAS; 710x1370MM. COLLECTION OF THE ARTIST. (OPPOSITE) **PETER SIDDELL,** *GOVERNOR'S ROCK;* 1995. OIL ON CANVAS; 900x600MM. COLLECTION OF THE ARTIST.

coast landforms, glimpsed in windows, mirrors and edging the canvas. His simplifed, hard-edge forms offered super-realism, finite detail, with images that Peter wanted to be still and clear. Not a single leaf flutters in the wind. Voluminous clouds are always static and there are frozen moments in a twilight zone. Peter's paintings are suffused with nostalgia and tranquil potency. With his wife Sylvia, he has become one of New Zealand's most successful exhibition artists. New work sells out within minutes of an exhibition's opening. His early paintings of the face of the Watchman bring the rock to life. His rendition of the skin of a tuatara is detailed and eerily still.

Peter has never favoured the use of people in his landscapes, houses or buildings. More than most artists, he is able to forcefully convey physical and psychological truth through paint. He simply imposes his order on the landscape.

Sylvia became a kitchen artist – with a difference. Her tortured, twisted utensils offer a dazzling, colourful and bizarre array of food implements. Her art, which is anything but safely domestic, started out as pencil sketches of household objects and became a fantastic voyage of the imagination.

At Karekare, their small house, virtually unchanged since they built it, is a haven as much as a studio. This is a summer and winter weekend retreat where they come to paint, spend time with the family, walk the bush tracks and sketch the headlands for future reference.

(ABOVE) **BARRY MILLER**, *PORTRAIT OF NATARANI THEOBALD*, 2001, OIL ON CANVAS, 420x320MM. COURTESY THE ARTIST.

## BARRY MILLER: PORTRAITS OF THE ARTIST

I first met Barry Miller when he lived in Ponsonby in the 1960s. He and his former wife Diana used to throw unbelievably great parties. Although I enjoyed the endless evenings with his interesting friends, it was his art that fascinated me. I considered him one of the best portrait painters in New Zealand, and I still do. Over the years he has simply got better.

He has a remarkable eye for capturing the beauty of women. When visiting him to discuss his painting, I was impressed with his absolute commitment to his art and to rendering the complexities of the female form. For Barry seems to have spent his life adoring women and painting them in settings that are both part of their lives and romantically juxtapositioned in different times and spaces. I recognised on his easel a woman from the Karekare Valley in a medieval Venetian setting, and the extraordinary Olivia Sheehan, who appears almost as a Victorian woman on the beach, with Paratahi Island as a backdrop.

His technique has been influenced by the great American painter Andrew Wyeth, although Miller's palette is softer. He was born in 1933 and educated at Canterbury College where his interest in art germinated. He trained as an artist in Christchurch and later joined the advertising agency J. Walter Thompson. He worked for Thompsons in the 1950s during the great age of advertising art in New Zealand, before television was established here.

When he left the advertising business in the 1960s to paint fulltime, interspersed with stints at local colleges tutoring art, he quickly built up a wide group of clients who commissioned his portraits. He's not a fast painter, so a work will take six months or more, but the skin and facial features seem to come alive. His studio at Karekare is in the tower of the rustic baronial mansion of lawyer Alex Witten-Hannah.

Alex, with his first wife Margie and son Sasha, lived in a small cottage on what was the Odlin farm. The house started to take shape and simply grew. New ideas came to Alex and he added on. In the 1990s, with his second wife Amanda Ace, his home took on a new dimension. It became a place for memorable evenings around the massive fireplace. With her taste for the grand life, Amanda now resides in a 15th century château in the Loire. She is fondly missed by the locals.

This is one of the most amazing houses on the west coast. It is vast by any standards and medieval, not only in its design and appearance but in its furnishings. A five-metre table, braced with church pews, forms the centrepiece of the main room. Cobwebbed candelabras hang from the high vaulted wooden ceiling. The house is crowded with memorabilia from Alex's extraordinary travels, to Everest, Africa and beyond. Books, mementos, skulls and animal heads line the walls. There are two massive rocking chairs in the shape of women on either side of the fireplace. Barry and Alex will often roast a suckling pig over the fire.

These two incorrigible old bachelors have linked up with local ranger Andy

(ABOVE) **BARRY MILLER**, *PORTRAIT OF OLIVIA SHEEHAN*, 2001, OIL ON BOARD, 420x320MM. COURTESY THE ARTIST.

Pedersen. Together, the three of them throw jazz parties on a Sunday afternoon. It's a way of getting a wide variety of new friends interested in their obsessions. You can't help but admire their dedication to enjoyment of life and their continuing admiration of women. This house carries its age with pride: there is a great deal of dust, a sunken bath, a waterbed and a profusion of tiger and leopard skins, as well as a giant boa constrictor skin which snakes its way around the great smokey beams. The house goes on forever.

The walls in Barry's upstairs turret studio are pincushioned with photographs of local women who have sat for his portraits. The working drawings fill the available floor space and one wall contains completed and half-finished paintings. The large canvases shimmer with life. They are a tribute to his skill, technique, and I am sure, the patience of his sitters.

Barry has lived alone in a wing of the mansion since coming over from Huia, where he was the local ranger for 11 years. As we talked of our long friendship and my admiration for his commitment to portraiture, the years seemed to roll away. I remembered many of the canvases that I had seen as a young man at his house in Ponsonby and now, over a glass of wine on a damp winter afternoon, we discuss his autumn years at Karekare and the subjects who he somehow managed to talk out of their clothes so that this kind-hearted and hugely talented painter of the human form could capture their beauty for posterity.

## DEAN BUCHANAN: WILD NATURE

Dean Buchanan has been called as the wild beast of New Zealand art, and in a way, he fits the description. He walks and runs incredible distances throughout the ranges. There's scarcely a valley or rock-face he doesn't know intimately. I don't think there's anyone I know with more energy – he exudes raw electrical charge, a creativity that flows from him into his paintings. Most are large by contemporary standards, but even when his canvas is smaller, the image leaps at your senses.

Buchanan is one of the most prolific painters in the country. He works from his Farm Road studio below the home he built in 1994. It overlooks Union Bay far below and has an expansive view across the Tasman. He's been painting for more than two decades now, exhibiting in New Zealand, Japan and the USA. His subject matter seems always to return to the west coast. His short, stabbing brushstrokes flicker light through the kauri. Primrose yellow and viridian green carve out the contours of a hillside. Indigo blue, silver and vermilion red shimmer on the scales of a fish.

His studio is crammed with interesting objects, for he has an amazing ability to uncover hidden treasures, whether it be an adze in a creek bed or the remains of a settler's pipe. The shelves are crowded with both found and acquired artifacts – pieces of Dutch tile, Japanese lacquer uncovered in junk shops or given to him along the way. There are always around 20 canvases drying, hanging ready for frames or rolling for exhibition.

When I first met Dean, he lived in the valley and painted in Jocelyn Strewe's garage. It was small and cramped and he painted large 4m canvases stretched around the room. The locals would stop by at weekends to see a work in progress, to have a beer and rave. For Dean does indeed rave: if a subject is close to him, without a moment of small talk, he will engage you with complex, intense ranting. For many, it's off-putting as he insists on immediate attention to the subject. Dean has never wasted a breath on smalltalk, and his paintings are a statement too of how he sees the world: a combination of intense light and impenetrable bush.

I did a long interview with him which was later turned into a television documentary. It shocked many people, revealing his fascination with German war memorabilia, flags, uniforms and Japanese death rituals. This dark side of Dean is both complex and revealing. He can be obsessed, ritualistic and macho. His critics

(ABOVE) **DEAN BUCHANAN,** *WATERFALL;* **OIL ON HESSIAN, 1700x2000MM.** (OPPOSITE) **DEAN IN HIS CAMOUFLAGE OUTFIT: ADDDRESSING A CANVAS WITH TOTAL COMMITMENT.** (OVERLEAF) **DEAN BUCHANAN,** *NIKAU AND SUPPLEJACK;* **OIL ON HESSIAN. 2100x 3000MM.**

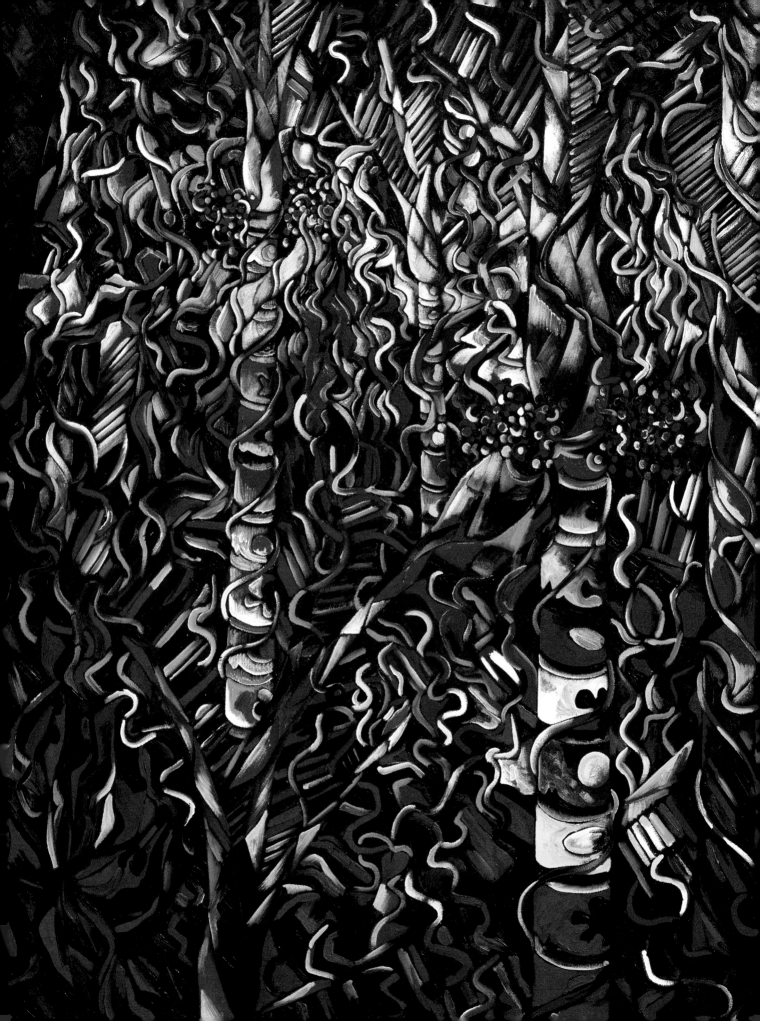

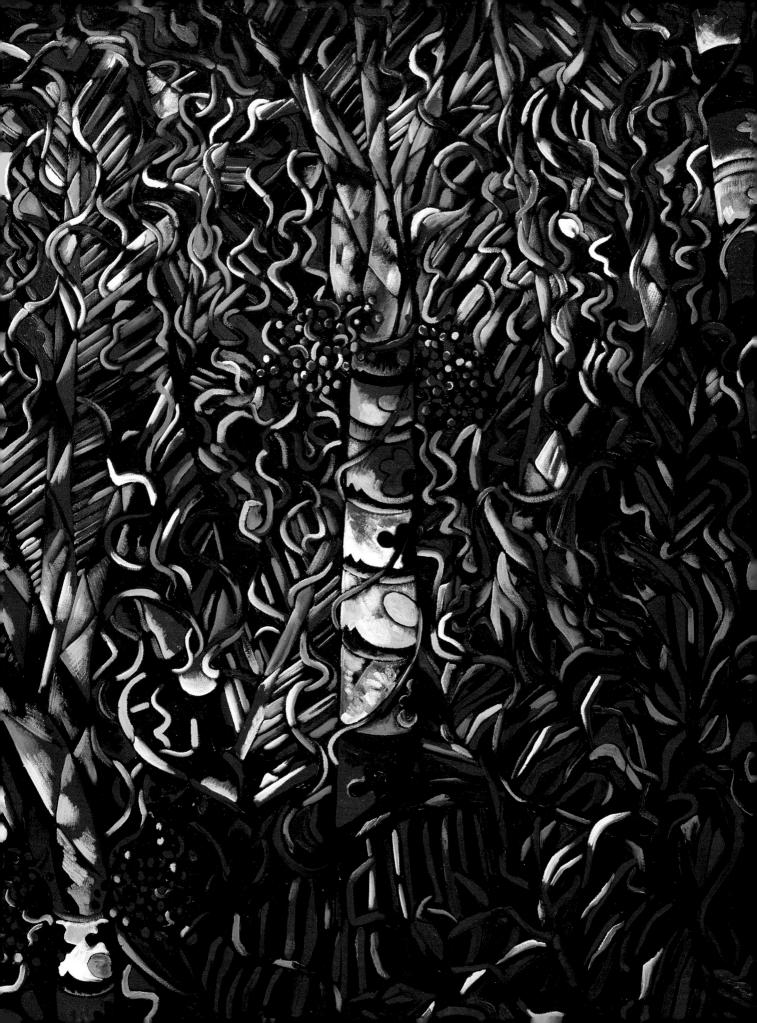

Wendy & Lisa

find this part of his life the most difficult and frequently comment on the complexities of his wild nature.

There seems to be an aversion to prolific painters in New Zealand, and Dean could never be accused of laziness when it comes to his art. He is always working on new concepts, yet trees, leaves and rock always seem to dominate his canvas; people rarely, if ever, are his subject.

Without a doubt, he thrives on the *enfant terrible* tag. He will often paint in his underpants, sweating and throwing his everything onto a canvas. When finished, he's exhausted, and the painting is complete and powerful. Even his critics have to admit that he addresses his canvas with the total commitment of his creative power.

During winter, he lights a stove and we sit and talk about planned exhibitions and his weekly bicycle tours to distant parts of the North Island. He sets off on a Monday and by Tuesday will be in Taumaranui. Along the way he absorbs the landscape, the shape and sharpness of our hills and light. The remainder of the week he devotes to expressing it on canvas. His partner Helga and their children Rudi and Celeste share his mountaintop life. Their spacious house seems always to be hosting guests of like mind and passion. Dean has a powerful effect on people, drawing many into his vortex of life, art and the sheer joy of living.

### John Edgar and Ann Robinson: Living on a Ridge

I'm walking up the Opal Pools Stream with John Edgar, one of New Zealand's finest sculptors. We're looking at the boulders dynamited down when the road through the gorge was cut into Karekare in 1948. We agree that given some heavy machinery and an army of volunteers, we could actually restore the 40 or so pools that connected the waterfalls of the Opal Pools, one of the wonders of the coast. We come upon a deserted house that was an early showhome for the Lone Kauri Estate, a dream of timber tycoon Jack Odlin. Following the blasting of the road, the Odlins subdivided sections, but nothing came of their grand scheme. The home of John Edgar and his partner, the glass sculptor Ann Robinson, is the only inhabited one on the property.

High above the Opal Pools, John and Ann, daughter of Auckland's most famous mayor, the visionary Sir Dove-Myer Robinson, work together, producing elegant objects that enrich our lives. Their property is called Te Rau Mako (the Fingers of the Lizard), a four-hectare block of steep ridges and gullies. The place was almost inaccessible when they bought it. Located on a high ridge overlooking the beach, its importance in Māori history was sufficient for John and Ann to invite Te Kawerau ā Maki to come and bless their venture, for here many paths converge, leading from the pa sites into the interior of the ranges. They say that they have since been blessed with harmony in their artistic endeavours.

John established his first stone carving workshop in 1979. He mounted prospecting expeditions to other parts of New Zealand, as well as to Australia, China and Korea, finding stone to insert and layer into his sculpture. His workshop at

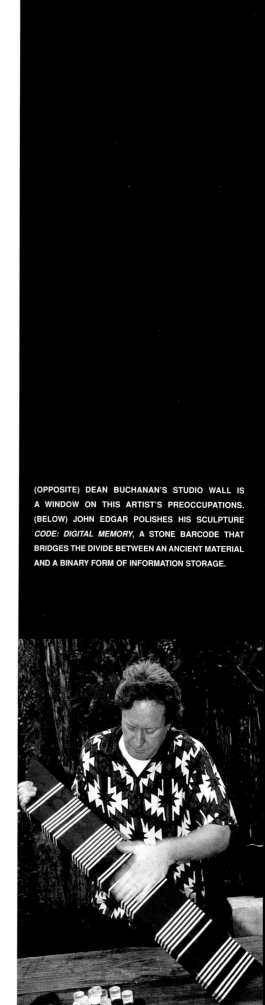

(OPPOSITE) DEAN BUCHANAN'S STUDIO WALL IS A WINDOW ON THIS ARTIST'S PREOCCUPATIONS. (BELOW) JOHN EDGAR POLISHES HIS SCULPTURE *CODE: DIGITAL MEMORY*, A STONE BARCODE THAT BRIDGES THE DIVIDE BETWEEN AN ANCIENT MATERIAL AND A BINARY FORM OF INFORMATION STORAGE.

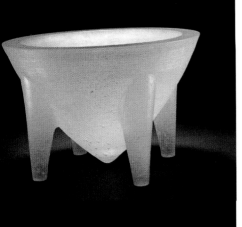

Karekare was built in 1991, and since that time, he has worked with granite, glass and metal. Many of his pieces are responses to the Karekare landscape. Each object describes a special space; sometimes it's a horizon, defined in granite inserted into marble. In his impressive piece *Vent*, a red plug seems to be forcing two black granite sections apart, welling to the surface, playing darkness and light in a volcanic theme.

John's exhibitions often include small riverstones, beautifully segmented with smoothed and polished glass. His larger pieces in exhibitions such as *Digit 1999*, feature large slabs of rock interlaid with star motifs, crosses of blood and marble. John evokes something very ancient in both his talisman pieces and his icon granite monoliths that give us a sense of worlds unknown. He is a brave artist: in his work *Badge* John turned the New Zealand flag into stone, using the imagery of our national symbol to re-appraise its purpose as a sign of hope.

Ann has a separate studio. In my opinion, her work is among the most beautiful of any art being produced in New Zealand. From an early knowledge of casting in bronze, her refinement of the lost wax process (ciré perdu) has brought her recognition as a world leader in glass casting. Everything she produces and exhibits is stunning. She is considered to be the finest glass artist working in New Zealand. For many, this country has been a painters' land, while the history of glass as an artform is more recent, and follows closely Ann's own career.

Ann takes a holistic approach to both her career and her art, and produces work that is culturally and historically important. Karekare offers her the freedom and the sense of place to soar with her craft. Her pieces are linked in colour and texture to the bush and the New Zealand landscape. With Gary Nash and John Croucher, Ann was a partner of the Sunbeam Glassworks that focused attention on studio glass in an exciting nine-year period to 1989. As well as producing a wide range of massive bowls and exhibition pieces, she has also taken her skills overseas, teaching glassmakers in Canberra and the Pilchuck glass school on the U.S. west coast. Glass is a particularly unforgiving medium. It demands the highest technical expertise to achieve colour and form. The clearest description of what she does with her lost wax method of casting known as the comes from Ann herself:

> The lost wax technique is a modified version of bronze casting. A wax blank is formed by pouring molten wax into a plaster base mould. This wax blank is then modified and re-invested in a second mould, made of refractory materials – that is material that can withstand a long period in the kiln at high temperatures. After the wax is burnt out, the cavity is filled with molten glass. The glass-filled mould is then slowly cooled to room temperature. Large pieces require up to three weeks cooling and one week finishing. Casting up to 50 kilos of glass is extemely challenging, pushing the technique to its limits.

Over the years, she has continued to experiment with glass and other materials. As I wander through the studio with Ann, her new flax and nikau forms are emerging in rich greens, reds and sumptuous golden hues.

Later that day, down at the Surf Club, we talk about planting the hillside by the cave. This talented woman doesn't hesitate to volunteer to plant the new trees. As we dig together, we talk about her father. I worked for him in his political campaigns and learned much. We remember his visionary commitment to soil conservation, drainage and transport. In our own separate ways, Ann and I are continuing his vision at Karekare, her with her art and me with policies promoting sustainability.

When the planting is finished, she will return to her studio to finish a bowl that tomorrow will go to a collector in Germany. With care, it may last a thousand years. We both hope the Karekare Valley will remain unspoiled for that long too.

# KAREKARE
# ON LOCATION

I'M WALKING the endless aisles of the Locations Expo in the vast pavilions of the Exhibition Center in Los Angeles. Here, the world's directors and producers scout for the best places to shoot their upcoming projects. In the world of film, location is everything. It seems to me that Karekare and our untamed coast of the Waitakeres are as exciting and enticing as any of the locations that are being promoted.

New Zealand has a small but strategically-positioned stand. Lush bush and burnished beaches are presented as locations that are safe and relatively inexpensive. The Piano beach, as Karekare is known internationally, is always a hot topic. That one film, released in 1993, conveyed a sense of dramatic place and versatile context that tipped off industry insiders to the possibilities Down Under.

While Jane Campion's masterpiece made Karekare famous, the beach had been discovered long before by New Zealand film and documentary makers. The coast, with its rugged backdrops and proximity to studios in Waitakere City, make for what is known in the trade as a "workable location". Yet it's not just convenient – it has a powerful and clear light for film, partly due to the closeness of the surf. It is timeless, as few buildings can be seen from the beach and none break the ridgeline.

Jane Campion's most celebrated film was set almost entirely on Auckland's west coast, with filming based at Karekare. With an ensemble cast of Holly Hunter, Harvey Keitel, Sam Neill and Anna Paquin, the film won two Oscars – best original screenplay for Jane Campion, and best supporting actress for Anna Paquin.

Recognised immediately as a major work and a potential classic, *The Piano* is set in 19th century colonial New Zealand. It opens with a group of settlers arriving amid massive surf. If the credibility is stretched by those who know surf, that any longboat could make it through such waves to shore, so too was the patience of

(TOP LFT AND OPPOSITE) **GORDON HADFIELD IN THE PROMOTIONAL VIDEO MADE TO ATTRACT INTERNATIONAL FUNDING FOR NEW ZEALAND-PRODUCED TELEVISION DRAMA SERIES** *GREENSTONE.* (MIDDLE AND LOWER) **BARRY BARCLAY'S FEATURE FILM** *FEATHERS OF PEACE* **WAS SET ON THE CHATHAM ISLANDS BUT MANY OUTDOOR SCENES WERE FILMED AT KAREKARE.**

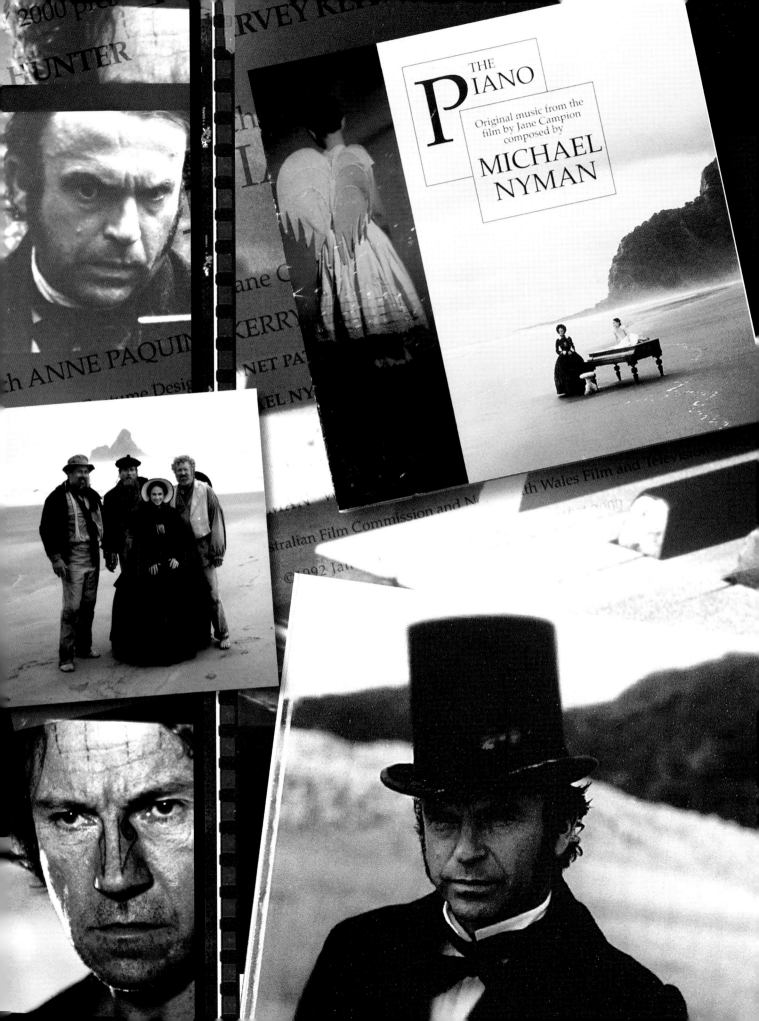

locals, as the meticulous director ordered countless retakes over a 12-week period. There were long periods when the beach had to be kept free of walkers and surfers. Sweepers were employed to keep the sand pristine. The real-life drama came to a head when someone slashed the ropes used for pulling the craft ashore, resulting in hundreds of dollars worth of props being lost in the waves.

Not all locals felt annoyed. The crew and cast rented Karekare houses and baches, while men with beards were enlisted to play settlers and sailors alongside the stars. I was seconded to provide Surf Club back-up in the form of rescue craft to ensure that any surf emergency was quickly dealt with. The Surf Club also became a base for the production company.

Although this film was an Australian and French co-production, it was with some justification widely regarded as a New Zealand work. The worldwide success of *The Piano* was a milestone in New Zealand film history, setting new standards of excellence in direction, acting and production. The film unashamedly shows a bleak, comfortless colonial New Zealand where emotion and sexuality seethe beneath the surface. It was the first major film to look beyond the surface splendour of the landscape and take cameras deep within the New Zealand bush in winter.

As a result of tensions between the film crew and the local community, regional authorities subsequently developed a film policy, requiring permission to be granted and fees paid for film and television production shoots on location. The Waitakere City Council and the Auckland Regional Council are pro-active in encouraging filmmakers to use wilderness areas for their shoots. Because of the demand, and the fragility of the environment here, the fees are higher for location work at Karekare, and are set aside for local community projects such as tree planting.

Within months of the release of *The Piano*, Cybill Shepherd and Elle Macpherson were strutting the beach in mini-features and fashion shoots. In advertisements for shirts, computers, bread and even life insurance, Karekare became the first choice of art directors and designers. The lure of this beach shows no sign of abating. In a Tokyo bar I catch a glimpse of Karekare in a karaoke video and later in a lavishly-produced commercial for a liqueur featuring a white piano.

In the television series *The Homecoming*, a homage to successful New Zealanders returning to their favourite places, one of my oldest friends, the Hollywood-based director Roger Donaldson, reminisced with me about what this beach had meant to us in our early years. Roger remembered that when both us were newly married with young children, and somewhat poorer, we would take a chainsaw and gather firewood on the beach for our winter fires. A stills photographer at the time, Roger brought his first Bolex camera to this beach to experiment with filming

(OPPOSITE AND RIGHT) **JANE CAMPION'S MASTERPIECE** *THE PIANO* **BECAME ONE OF THE MOST ACCLAIMED FILMS OF 1993, WINNING TWO OSCARS. KAREKARE AND THE WAITAKERE RANGES PROVIDED A MOODY, MISTY SETTING FOR THIS EMOTIONALLY-CHARGED DRAMA OF COLONIAL DAYS.**

techniques. From this morning came his first 16mm reel, a three-minute gem of moody coastal light and sea, with a karakia spoken on the soundtrack by poet Hone Tuwhare. It is now in the National Film Archive. He would later go on to direct the pioneering New Zealand films *Sleeping Dogs* and *Smash Palace* before moving to Hollywood and success in films like *Mutiny On The Bounty*, *No Way Out*, *Cocktail*, *Dante's Peak and 13 Days*.

Like Roger Donaldson, Rodney Charters, a young filmmaker from Elam Art School at Auckland University, made a short, brilliant film on this coast, as his final year project. With a soundtrack by 1960s New Zealand rock legends the La De Dahs, *Film Exercise* has become a small archival masterpiece. Now a much sought-after cinematographer who has moved on to directing, with credits for multiple episodes of *The Pretender* and *Roswell*, Rodney looks back with pride on his early work, remembering the filming at the beach was "all very heady and exciting."

*Film Exercise* was screened at the Sydney and Melbourne film festivals, and it got him into the Royal College of Art in London in 1968. "Essentially it was an early rock video," he says, "but it was ahead of its time. I shot it on my dad's Bolex. The story is a little dated, a little simplistic, but otherwise I think it holds up well."

FINESSE KAIRU (LEFT) **AND TEMUERA MORRISON** (ABOVE) **BEFORE THE CAMERAS FOR A FUNDING VIDEO MADE PRIOR TO PRODUCTION OF** *GREENSTONE* **TELEVISION DRAMA SERIES.** (RIGHT, FROM TOP) **CLIFF CURTIS AND VANESS RARE STAR IN** *KAHU & MAIA*, **A SHORT FILM MADE BY HE TAONGA FILMS AS PART OF NGA PUNA MAORI DRAMA SERIES; SCENES FROM** *KAHU AND MAIA*.

100% PURE NEW ZEALAND

A short drive out of Auckland and you're staring at one of the most beautiful beaches in the world. The sands are volcanic and the view is unforgettable. People come here for the surf, the solitude and to make the occasional movie. If you haven't seen 'The Piano' it's time you did. If you haven't been to New Zealand, what are you waiting for? **100% PURE NEW ZEALAND** purenz.com

(ABOVE) **TOURISM NEW ZEALAND'S FLAGSHIP BRAND CAMPAIGN '100% PURE NEW ZEALAND' UNDERSCORES CONTINUING WORLDWIDE INTEREST IN JANE CAMPION'S FILM *THE PIANO*.** (BELOW AND OPPOSITE LOWER) **AGENCY COLENSO BBDO TEAMED WITH ROLLING FILMS TO SHOOT THIS MOLENBERG BREAD TV COMMERCIAL WITH A TROOP OF EXTRAS AT KAREKARE.**

Years of exposure to the bright lights of Hollywood have failed to dim the flame Rodney Charters holds for the coastline of the Waitakeres. He has written an intriguing filmscript whose major location is Karekare. He tells me that he has been visualising and dreaming of such a film since his art school days.

With a working title of *Blacksand*, the film opens on a stormy morning at Kare-kare with a blind Cambodian woman drowning in the surf. Her suicide attempt is foiled by a young American surfer who later persuades her to journey back to her homeland to revisit the site of her parents' execution by the Khmer Rouge.

"Many Cambodian women actually went blind during the Khmer Rouge reign of terror," Charters explains. "I took this idea and dramatised it in the character of this woman who is a refugee in New Zealand, with no family left. Ultimately though, it is a love story, set against the horrors of the Pol Pot regime."

"I grew up in New Plymouth on the beach, so it was west coast beaches and black sand for me from the start. When I moved to Auckland, I went out to Karekare and stayed for three days in the Surf Club. I walked the beach, looked at

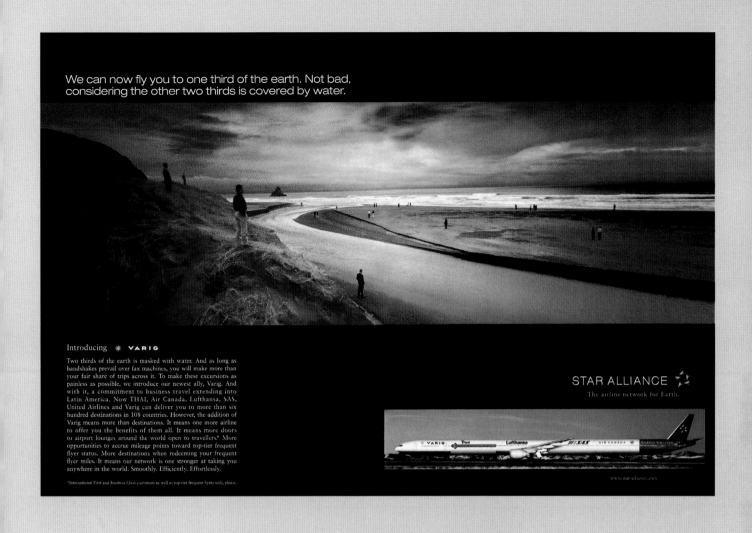

the waves, saw no one at all. The rocks, the cliffs, the way the stream meanders out to the sea – it's strong imagery. I took my dad out there the year before he died and he told me he'd swum there as a young man in the 1940s.

"Every time I return to New Zealand, one of the first things I have to do is to go out to Karekare. The beach has a power that no one can fully explain."

When the historical epic television series *Greenstone* was being scoped for international funding, a promotional video was first made at Karekare. This involved building a Māori village, and bringing together the cast to dramatise a part of the story about 19th century conflicts in New Zealand. Producer Robin Scholes was enthusiastic about the possibilities offered by Karekare. The multi-million dollar BBC co-production was based over the ranges at the Waikaukau Road Studios in Glen Eden, while the coast became the bloody battleground.

Most weeks an amateur or professional group will be making a video or film somewhere at Karekare. Polytech students use the beach for experimental videos in their final year assignment. These projects often contain highly imaginative

(ABOVE) INTERNATIONAL AIRLINE CONSORTIUM STAR ALLIANCE CREATED DOUBLE-PAGE ADVERTISEMENT USING IMAGERY OF KAREKARE BEACH TO LAUNCH ITS INTERNATIONAL PRINT MEDIA CAMPAIGNS.

work and some of their creators, like Roger Donaldson and Rodney Charters, may return later in their careers with more ambitious and expensive projects. The demands of productions, at times two or three a week, can prove frustrating for Karekare people. An international crew filming a television commercial for a new Peugeot release had done everything right in notifying locals of closure of the Cutting road. Everything was proceeding to plan, with helicopter aloft, when a resident suddenly needed to get his wife to hospital. The frantic husband was on a collision course with a rally driver and neither was willing to give way.

Fashion photographers also love to take their models out to Karekare for a stylish romp on the beach or dunes. You may think they'd be tiring of it by now, but this place has so many faces and moods that finding a fresh perspective is not difficult.

New Zealand's long-running sitcom success story *Shortland Street* celebrated its 2000th episode with the wedding of lead characters Rangi and Stephanie on the beach at Karekare and at the waterfall. This was the most-watched episode in the programme's history. The producers, South Pacific Pictures, have set their other top-rated television series *Jacksons Wharf* here, using local hillside houses as interiors, and the beach as a setting for rural dramas.

The cutting edge of the music industry for the last two decades has been the short video clip, in which image and music are dynamically synchronised to sell the package. Of all New Zealand beaches, Karekare has without doubt been the first choice for video shoots. Groups like the phenomenally successful Polynesian rhythm and rock group Te Vaka filmed their American tour video in Union Bay. As dusk fell, the 14-strong group of Niuean, Tongan, Tokelauan and Māori performers began drumming and dancing around a huge driftwood bonfire. The video helped pack American audiences into auditoriums to experience these exciting performers.

Although Karekare is much better known as a film location, its influence in the world of recorded music is possibly just as impressive.

On his 25th birthday, Nigel Horrocks made a decisive move that would change his life, and eventually enrich the lives of music lovers and performance artists around the world. He bought a bare section at Karekare from Sir Edmund Hillary. It was a move that would eventually lead to the young adventurer climbing some formidable mountains of his own.

As a base camp, its location was sensational. Horrocks had been going out to Karekare since he was a boy and says that somehow he always knew he'd build a house there. He'd met friends in the music industry during the 1970s and 80s, and he'd paid his dues, running successful businesses in Kathmandu and Europe and leading the kind of life you'd expect of a young man moving in high circles.

He came back to New Zealand with the rhythm of Karekare pounding in his veins. If you really listen to nature instead of just taking it in visually, you'll notice

(LEFT) AUSTRIAN MODEL NATALJIA BAJRIC ON LOCATION AT KAREKARE STREAM, 2001, FOR PHOTOGRAPHER CRAIG OWEN ON ASSIGNMENT FOR *PAVEMENT* MAGAZINE. (RIGHT) NEW ZEALAND SINGER-SONGWRITER CLAIRE PRICE IN A DEREK HENDERSON SHOOT FOR *PAVEMENT*.

that there's a lot going on out here on the edge of the island, where the Tasman rollers boom and dump their fury on the ironsands and the wind stirs branches high in the trees. For someone whose life revolves around sound, that's music to the ears.

Nigel Horrocks decided to build his house here, facing south towards the beach. His intention was to develop a multi-purpose structure that could be used as a performance space. He contacted young Auckland University architectural student Andrew Patterson and over the next two years they worked together on designs.

Horrocks brings a measured intensity to his view of the world. "I had fairly grandiose ideas for a 25-year-old." he says. "I thought New Zealand architecture was incoherent. It was a little bit of this and a little bit of that, not necessarily related to the environment in which we live."

The house was completed in October 1986, and the following year it won for Andrew Patterson the Young Architect of the Year Award. For the next seven years, Horrocks concentrated his energies around the property, planting out some 14,000 native trees, mainly kauri, puriri, pohutukawa and totara. He studied the forest around Karekare and tried to recreate it in his planting patterns.

There were other things germinating while he was preparing his special place. When the time was right they simply thrust into the daylight and his house became the centre of some creative eruptions that would open many minds.

"In 1991 I had a change of lifestyle and went to East Cape to run a mountain bike business with Mangatu Corporation, the local iwi," he recalls. "When I returned to Auckland in 1993, I was asked if I'd like to rent a house to the American actor Harvey Keitel. He was a good person to have around, and the interesting thing was that he envied the way I lived.

"When he left after the filming of *The Piano* had finished, Neil Finn turned up one day. We knew each other through mutual friends. At the time, Neil wanted to return to New Zealand to live and record. During Christmas 1993 and January 1994, Crowded House recorded their *Together Alone* album at the house. It was their last major album. Personally, it was good for me as it connected me back with people I'd known from the music business in Europe. People like Youth, who produced the album."

*Together Alone* carried the sound of Karekare to the widest audience. Listen to the opening track 'Kare Kare', with its surging waves bursting from the speakers, pure, airy, floating guitars soaring like seabirds above a powerful, pounding surf. Neil Finn sings of "a valley lit by the moon". The words and the musical language are unmistakably, authentically Aotearoa. The title track 'Together Alone' is a successful blending of traditional Maori and Polynesian music, wrapped in a western rock idiom. The chorus or waiata is underpinned by Cook Island drums. It's blood-stirring, passionate stuff, rousing and emotional for those who care about this land, our people, the South Pacific. Neil Finn's music pays homage while threading these apparently disparate musical traditions into a new cloth.

The two months of recording mainly involved just eight people, but on the last

(OPPOSITE) **IF JANE CAMPION PUT KAREKARE BEACH ON THE INTERNATIONAL FILM MAP, AUSTRALASIAN ROCK GROUP CROWDED HOUSE TOOK THE SPIRIT OF KAREKARE TO A WORLDWIDE MUSIC AUDIENCE WITH 1993 ALBUM *TOGETHER ALONE*, RECORDED AT NIGEL HORROCKS' VALLEY HOUSE (ABOVE) WHICH ALSO APPEARED IN THE MEMORABLE VIDEO. ALBUM COVER (OPPOSITE, MIDDLE-TOP) FEATURED ARTWORK BY SINGER-SONGWRITER NEIL FINN'S YOUNG SON LIAM, WHILE THE CREDITS INCLUDED THANKS TO "ALL THE PEOPLE OF KARE KARE".**

Drummers on Together Alone, Private Universe: Joe, Tereo, Martin, James,
Benjamin • Brass Band on In My Command, Together Alone: Clyde Dixon,
Stephen Bremner, Lauren Astridge, David Bremner, Skaun Jarret • All
tracks engineered by Greg Hunter • Additional engineering: Nick Morgan,
Graeme Myre, Angus Davidson, Chris Corr, Kaiju Tonuma • Equipment and
assistant engineering – Dugald McAndrew • Programming: Matt Austin •
Special thanks to: Grant Thomas, Brent Thomas & Bill Cullen • Gary
Stamler, Monica Danner & Eva Leletzopoulos • Peter Green • David Field,
Camilla Tuckey • Dugald McAndrew • Crowded House Club: P.O. Box 333
2181 Australia (Please include a stamped self-addressed
— Management, Sydney • Gary

weekend when they laid down the title track, there were 50 musicians in the studio and a Pacific Island-size group of some 250 friends, family and locals gathered on the lawn in front of the house. Neil Finn had invited the dance group Pacific Tamure, a 30-voice choir from Te Waka Huia and the horn section of the Continental Brass Band to add colour and texture to the track. After the session everyone got together for a huge party at the late Marty Clark's farmhouse up Lone Kauri.

Nigel Horrocks is a gifted producer and performance facilitator who commands respect across several genres. If pressed, he will tell you who he turned down. "After the Crowded House album, I got a lot of offers to do work with overseas artists like Madonna, Whitney Houston and Paul McCartney. I turned them down as I didn't build at Karekare for me to be a doorman to others. Instead I got a job with the Auckland City Council writing a play."

He had no wish to see his beloved Karekare turn into a tourist destination with the access roads blocked with stargazers looking for the second coming of The Beatles, helicopters spooking the wading birds and the drone of rotors drowning out the surf. That was the celebrity business, not music. But it's not easy to walk away from where your talents rest, and he soon immersed himself in music once again. "Since 1994, I've been seven days a week recording music, some of it in the studio in my house. I never advertise it; I just stick to doing my own projects."

The projects have included the Hungarian Modern Dance Troupe, who came out to Karekare to create a new dance piece and stayed a month. Ema Paki, who has won many New Zealand music and video awards, reached back to her roots under Horrocks' direction and recorded an album of contemporary Māori music in

(TOP AND LEFT) POWERFUL POLYNESIAN PERCUSSION SOUND OF TE VAKA CONSTANTLY TOURS OVERSEAS. PRIOR TO THEIR FIRST NORTH AMERICAN TOUR THE GROUP FILMED A PROMOTIONAL VIDEO AT UNION BAY. (OPPOSITE, TOP) JUSTINE FRISCHMAN AND DONNA MATTHEWS OF ENGLISH ROCK GROUP ELASTICA ON A *PAVEMENT* SHOOT IN KAREKARE STREAM. (OPP., LOWER) MARGARET URLICH'S 1999 ALBUM *SECOND NATURE* WAS PACKAGED WITH A BOOKLET OF PAINTINGS BY JUSTIN BURROUGHS, INCLUDING *PARATAHI ISLAND, KAREKARE*.

his studio. Che Fu, one of New Zealand's biggest selling artists, loved the atmosphere in the valley studio and laid down numerous tracks. Hinewehi Mohi, who hit the headlines when she scandalised one-eyed rugby fans by singing the national anthem in Māori, recorded an album here.

Neil Finn returned to record some of his solo work. English group Killing Joke stopped by. Grunge rockers Pearl Jam from Seattle played at the studio with Tim, Neil and Liam Finn. There are no plans to release the 'Finn-Jam' recordings.

What matters more to Nigel Horrocks is not this week's *Billboard* Top One Hundred but what is called World Music, especially the Polynesian variety. "I've recorded for the United Nations and UNICEF and other organisations," Horrocks says. "I've worked a lot with Tongan and Cook Island groups, and done traditional instrumentation of Māori music. That sort of music, and the evolution of it, is much more in my heart. I truly believe I'm a white Polynesian. That's why I've felt safe to involve myself in Māori and Pacific Island music."

What better place to introduce these streams to the ocean of world music than at Karekare Beach. Nigel Horrocks has given a lot of thought to the meaning of place, which is of such importance in Aotearoa New Zealand. "I personally like the privacy out there and I keep to myself. Karekare is a strange combination of extremely challenging and quite nurturing. You know it'll be reasonably kind to you, but it will always win.

"The house and the place forces respect on you. I won't necessarily continue recording there. I'm allowing New Zealand bands to come through this year, but we just do it week by week, not planning too far ahead. If you're the kind of person who wants to record at Karekare, there isn't another studio in the world like this. You walk on the beach in the morning, and start recording in the afternoon. I want to keep people creating there."

Already past his 40th birthday, Nigel Horrocks burns with an inner fire that ignites other creative talents. Just as we finish our conversation, he suddenly asks: "Did you see the movie *Repo Man*? You know how they had the Code of the Repo Man? Well an old friend and I have the Code of the Karekare Man: *A Karekare man should spend his life getting into intense situations.*

"Karekare is a place where the energy is always greater than yourself, and I don't want to feel at ease; I want to feel inspired. I'm trying to live a peaceful, constructive life out there. To me, Karekare is the essence of everything about New Zealand, and about how to live."

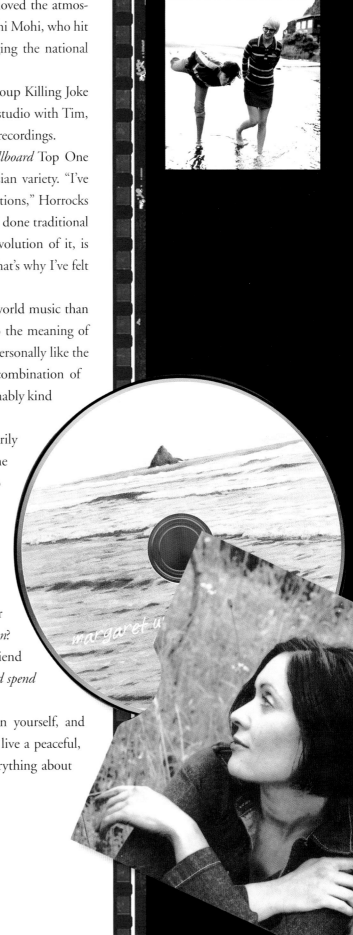

# THE GUARDIANS

THE KAREKARE ENVIRONMENT is fragile. When it comes to sustainability, there are now plenty of people willing to support a system to ensure that both the sea and land ecosystems are protected.

There is no more passionate community than Karekare, where locals are anxious to ensure there is no repetition of the Waitemata Council's decision to unwittingly allow the destruction of the beautiful Opal Pools. The pools were one of the main attractions of Karekare and indeed the coast. A series of deep pools were linked by 40 waterfalls flowing down the side of the farm road known as Lone Kauri.

This road had been cut by the Lang Freeth Company to extract kauri from the plateau country above the beach. The road down towards the beach past the farm-house had been cut by relief workers in the 1930s, but it stopped short of the bluff close to the beach. The new owners of the block, the Wellington-based Odlin Timber Company, took out the remaining timber and the family became Karekare enthusiasts. They built small holiday homes down the track and dreamt of a subdivision above the Opal Pools. The only problem was access. One of the more enthusiastic members of the family was Jack Odlin. With a bulldozer and some dynamite he took the road around the bluff and down to the beach. Although the Lone Kauri Road had been pushed through, the pools were filled with debris, massive boulders and slips.

It was not until the work was completed and the realisation dawned of the destruction of the pools that the Waitemata County Council was held accountable for allowing this to happen. If there was anything positive to be salvaged from this sorry affair it was that the veteran campaigner William Roy Macgregor, the president of the Auckland Forest and Bird Protection Society and a sworn enemy of the Council, brought together a group that would be known as the Waitakere Protection Society. This group remains a watchdog of the ranges.

When I walk up the Lone Kauri Road for a swim in one of the remaining Opal Pools, I am mindful of the support that now exists to safeguard the environment for

(ABOVE AND OPPOSITE LOWER) SEA ANEMONES ARE PART OF A RICH FAUNA IN THE TIDAL ROCKPOOLS OF KAREKARE. (TOP) THIS POD OF THE ENDANGERED HECTORS DOLPHIN WAS PHOTOGRAPHED CLOSE IN TO COAST BETWEEN KAREKARE AND MANUKAU HEADS. (OPP. TOP) STARK PROFILE OF PARATAHI APPEARS DECEPTIVELY NEAR, BUT MANY SWIMMERS HAVE RISKED DROWNING WHILE ATTEMPTING ACTS OF BRAVADO.

future generations. This wake-up call at Karekare heralded the eventual passing of the landmark Resource Management Act, one of the most innovative planning policy acts in the world. It established New Zealand as a trailblazer in this field. A narrow, winding, dusty country road and an insensitive county council were the catalysts for this change.

In the 1990s new waves of migrants arriving in the Auckland region found the west coast beaches a handy source of shellfish which were apparently free for the taking. The local communities were outraged by the huge and often irresponsible collection of shellfish and at Karekare it was decided to enlist a wide range of interested groups to endeavour to reduce or even halt the taking of shellfish. Led by Te Kawerau ā Maki, it was decided to bring a rahui to the beach. This was a traditional tapu placed by elders to avoid contamination following a drowning or tragedy.

In May 1993 the local residents and the Ministry of Agriculture and Fisheries put legal restrictions on the taking of all marine life except finfish from Karekare. Karekare was the first west coast beach to have such a closure and one of the few to continue the Polynesian tradition of rahui. This brought a sense of appropriateness and unification to the closure, which became legal under the Fisheries Act (1996). The rahui has now been extended past its original five years. Signs in three languages near the beach entrances state clearly that the taking of shellfish and crabs is strictly forbidden. It appears that most people are willing to observe the restrictions. However recovery has been slow, due to both natural factors and the poor state of the environment when the closure was effected.

A number of honorary Fisheries Officers have come from the community and although it is impossible to police the rocks all the time, there is now a partnership between the beach users and the community that is working.

The rahui will continue, with community support, probably throughout the 21st century, as Karekare now has a permanent legal closure under the Fisheries Act (1996). It may be extended south towards the Pararaha and even as far as Whatipu. This will support the conservation of a sustainable coastline and form the basis for a marine park.

The local people of Karekare have formed a landcare group, one of at least 200 nationwide. "We are passionate advocates for preservation and restoration of the environment," according to Rob Taylor, Ella Barker and Mary Gardiner, the driving force

behind the Karekare group. The organisation brings together people interested in community landcare activities, an effective vehicle that the Karekare group believes is essential to meet the needs of future generations. "We are a unique blend of land-use conservation and recreation," Taylor comments. If you're interested in their activities, visit the Karekare website at: www.karekare.org.nz

In the late 1980s, retired architect Bill Witten-Hannah brought together the local Residents and the Ratepayers Association to think through a management plan for the area. The original plan made 32 recommendations to local authorities. The objective was conservation of the natural landscape; from it grew the West Coast Plan, the Council initiative to protect the entire coast, to manage it and ensure its sustainability during the 21st century. Every decade, the Karekare Management Plan is updated, again with consultation that takes in the democracy issues, the relationship between the community, the City Council and the Regional Council. The plan recognises Te Kawerau ā Maki as the mana whenua, and their input is the underpinning factor that allows the Plan to grow and operate.

Each decade, the plan is to be fine-tuned to enhance eco-structure protection and monitoring. The seven neighbourhoods which make up the plan are recognised under one vision, the Karekare Catchment: The Valley, the Seaside Village, the Lone Kauri Road, Farm Road, La Trobe, Parkland, and the Beach Zone.

In 1954 the Gribble property was cut in half by the construction of the Lone

(ABOVE AND BELOW) **DEPARTMENT OF CONSERVATION OFFICERS BAND DOTTEREL CHICKS AND RECORD VITAL DETAILS OF THIS SPECIES ON WHATIPU SANDS.** (OPPOSITE, FAR LEFT) **DOTTEREL TRACKS.** (OPP., TOP) **DOGS ARE ALLOWED ON KAREKARE BEACH BUT ARE PROHIBITED SOUTH OF THIS SIGN ON WINDY POINT, WHAKARURO BAY.** (OPP., LOWER) **A DAY'S SNAPPER CATCH OFF THE CAULDRON ROCKS.**

Kauri Road. At the bottom of the hill, a new bridge was built and for the first time, the Gribbles were able to drive a vehicle onto their property. Ray Gribble had been greatly disturbed by the construction of the road. He told me before he died, "One man and a box of gelignite blasted his way around the bluff." The northern part, sloping up to the great cave Wharengarahi, was offered for sale to the local community by the Gribble family in 1996. It was a strategic and important parcel of land for the Karekare Valley. Timing was critical. The locals were alarmed: if this section was put onto the open market it would be snapped up and a magnificent archaeological site would be lost. With the help of the ARC and the Waitakere Council, the community decided to buy the land and forming an original land banking trust, they decided to hold an auction of local art to pay for a loan raised from the local council. The residents needed to find a quarter of the purchase price, $21,250, a considerable sum for a small group of ratepayers.

First there was a small investment from local people. A $10 pledge bought them five square metres while $100 bought 50 square metres with a pohutukawa. There was no shortage of donated art, which was brought together by Helga Strewe and Dianne Carter. They spent a year selecting art that would open the cheque books. Lopdell House in Titirangi, owned by the council, agreed to exhibit and assist with the auction. The line-up of artists included some of New Zealand's finest: Pat Hanly, Peter Siddell, Dean Buchanan, Ann Robinson and John Edgar.

The event was a great success. Over $27,000 was raised from the auction in half an hour and in the first month of the new millennium, the land was saved from development.

(ABOVE) **LOCALS TURNED OUT TO PLANT NATIVE SHRUBS AND TREES ON LAND NEWLY ACQUIRED BY COMMUNITY.** (LEFT) **PARARAHA SWAMP IS ONE OF THE LARGEST WETLAND AREAS ON WAITAKERES COASTLINE.** (OPPOSITE) **VIRGINIA KING INSTALLATION** *RAFT*, **1994, MADE FROM DEMOLITION KAURI, WAS FILMED AS A VIDEO ENTITLED** *STYX (STICKS)*, **AS AN ARTISTIC RESPONSE TO THE DESTRUCTION OF THE KAURI FOREST IN NEW ZEALAND.**

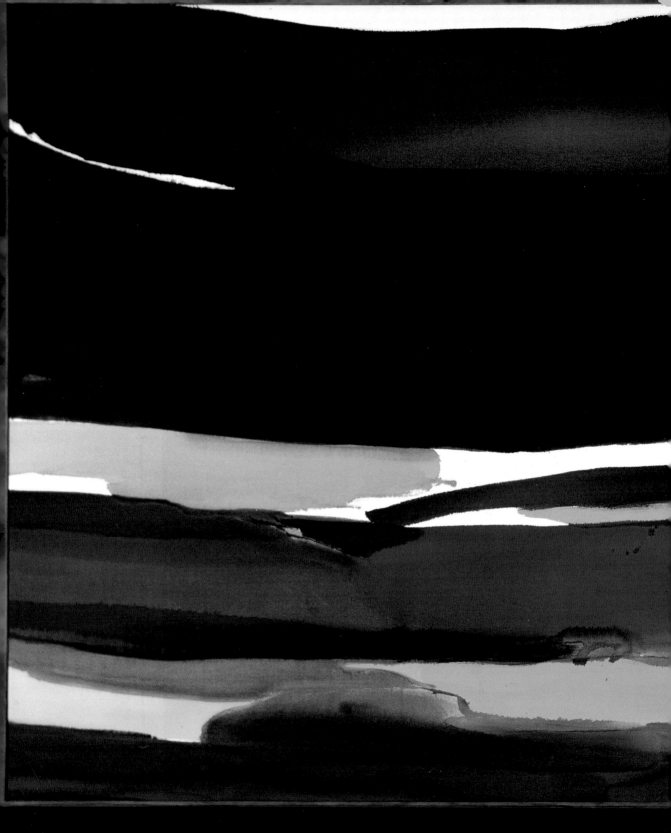

GRETCHEN ALBRECHT *KAREKARE 1* 1975 ACRYLIC ON CANVAS 1280x1785MM COURTESY THE ARTIST

## I. LONE KAURI ROAD

The first time I looked seaward, westward
it was looking back yellowly,
a dulling incandescence of the eye of day.
It was looking back over its raised hand.
Everything was backing away.

Read for a bit. It squinted between the lines.
Pages were backing away.
Print was busy with what print does,
trees with what trees do that time of day,
sun with what sun does, the sea
with one voice only, its own,
spoke no other language than that one.

There wasn't any track from which to hang
the black transparency that was travelling
south-away to the cold pole. It was cloud
browed over the yellow cornea which I called
an eyeball for want of another notion,
cloud above an ocean. It leaked.

Baldachin, black umbrella, bucket with a hole,
drizzled horizon, sleazy drape,
it hardly mattered which, or as much
what cometing bitchcraft, rocketed shitbags,
charred cherubim pocked and pitted the iceface
of space in time, the black traveller.
Everything was backing away.

The next time I looked seaward,
it was looking scooted red, a bloodshot cornea
browed with a shade that could be simulated
if the paint were thick enough, and audible,
to blow the coned noses of the young kauri,
the kettle spout sweating,
the hound snoring at my feet,
the taste of tobacco, the tacky fingers
on the pen, the paper from whose plane
the last time I looked seaward
would it be a mile, as the dust flies,
down the dulling valley, westward?
everything was backing away.

Allen Curnow
from *Trees, Effigies, Moving Objects*

INTO THE NIGHT

# THRESHOLD

*There are places in this world that are neither here nor
there, neither up nor down, neither real nor imaginary...*

Thomas Moore

ON MOONLIGHT NIGHTS, John Madden and Richard McWhannell walk south along the coast to the Pararaha, where they turn inland away from the booming surf. They are successful artists seeking new perspectives on the landscape. Their dark, eerie canvases suggest dimensions beyond the postcard beaches. John, who painted miners on the South Island's West Coast where he grew up, came to Karekare and began to paint complex, dark work on large canvases, embellished only with a streak of moonlight or a dying sun. Richard's landscapes of the Pararaha are lighter but just as unsettling.

I believe that what these painters are doing in their individual styles, is forcing us to confront the darkness within us. Both artists sketch and paint in the silence of the night, with only a dog and each other for company, returning home along the sands at dawn.

When the sun goes down and darkness descends at Karekare, others are drawn to this place for special rituals, a use of the beach that usually goes unnoticed. During the day, the beach is of course enjoyed by swimmers, sunbathers and walkers. But at either end of the beach, it's not unusual to see a wedding taking place, the bride in white skipping in the surf, the groom in bow tie and rolled trouser legs, wading in her wake.

Often at sunset a group will stand on Farley Point above the Cauldron huddled together against the wind and spray. As ashes are cast into the surf, a friend of the beach becomes part of the great surrounding ocean.

There's a sense of freedom and an unspoken tolerance here that defies easy explanation. Nude sunbathing is accepted at the southern end of the beach, where regulars return year after year to their favourite sand dune. And unlike many other New Zealand beaches, Karekare still tolerates dogs.

In the ancient world, there are places where for thousands of years ley lines have crossed; cathedrals and grottos have nourished pilgrims, the sick and the troubled.

(OPPOSITE AND OVERLEAF) **"BONFIRES SURROUNDED BY FIGURES DANCING TO THE RHYTHM OF DRUMS, PRIVATE RITUALS OF CELEBRATION AND PASSAGE."**

(ABOVE) **RICHARD McWHANNELL**, *WINTER MOON, PARARAHA*; 2000-2001. OIL ON CANVAS ON BOARD. 510x720MM. COURTESY THE ARTIST.

In Europe some of these special sites have become places of worship, and they have not lost their former significance. The Greeks had their groves of trees where mysterious life forces moved and became real. In New Zealand, we tend to scoff at this kind of thing. If we like a place, we seldom accord it any deeper significance. We may pass through on holiday once a year, but we are coy about admitting the healing powers of a particular area. It is my belief that Karekare is such a place. I have no material evidence to back up my theory, nor any to the contrary. I simply accept it, and I am surprised by the number of people who apparently concur.

The past is always present in a certain place. There's a kind of spiritual essence which we can take for our own use, or simply ignore. If you are inclined to a belief in a greater being that orders creation, then at Karekare you may sense the presence of that mighty and mysterious hand.

English writer John Hutton told me that he was sitting in a London cinema watching *The Piano*, when he experienced an overwhelming desire to find that beach and get married there. When the film ended, he phoned his fiancée and they booked a flight from London to Auckland and married on the south end of Karekare Beach. An Indian couple from Mumbai related a similar tale to me, as did

(ABOVE) **RICHARD McWHANNELL**, *HEADING SOUTH;* 2000-2001. **OIL ON CANVAS ON BOARD. 382x586MM. COURTESY THE ARTIST.**

an Israeli soldier and his Jordanian partner, whom I met on the beach and whose honeymoon base became my bach. Many Japanese people enquire about visiting "the Piano beach", and I sense that what they and others who come from afar are seeking is not so much the brooding landscapes shown on the screen, as that ineffable spiritual place that is sensed in the darkness of the cinema.

Sometimes when I'm walking back from the Pararaha, I see groups of people arriving, some with drums and other musical instruments, preparing for a private occasion. They cannot all be dismissed as New Agers heading for a secluded dune, or aging hippies on a new groove.

I remember being on the beach in the middle of a starlit winter's night when suddenly it became warm, as if a tropical wind were warming the sands. I doubt that the weather office could have explained such a shift.

At other times I have noticed bonfires surrounded by figures dancing to the rhythm of drums, private rituals of celebration and passage, the firelight casting giant human shadows high onto the cliffs. In the morning there would be little evidence to mark where women and men had come to find a wildness in themselves and explore the night.

(ABOVE) JOHN MADDEN DEEP IN CONCENTRATION IN HIS LONE KAURI ROAD STUDIO AFTER ANOTHER NIGHT EXCURSION TO THE PARARAHA. (BELOW LEFT) JOHN MADDEN PEERS INTO KILN PEEPHOLE DURING ANNUAL FIRING OF HIS POTTERY. (OPPOSITE) HAMILTON PHOTOGRAPHER JENNY SCOWN CAPTURED THIS IMAGE OF EXUBERANT OLYMPIC BOARDSAILING GOLD MEDALLIST BARBARA KENDALL KICKING UP HER HEELS IN THE KAREKARE SURF.

I have been told by friends that groups of men seeking a new meaning to shattered lives will play drums here, after workshops that try to heal their lives and to give them a second chance to be better human beings.

In our digital age, where everything is supposed to be able to be expressed by combinations of 1 and 0, I believe there are other dimensions beyond logic and reason. Ultimately, Karekare is a state of mind, in harmony with the rhythms of nature and life itself. Look closely and you'll notice that the beach and everything around you is constantly changing. Down at the tide where the wavelets slide around your feet, when the stars are out and the moon is late rising over the ranges, all your senses are amplified. This place will give you what you ask of it: peace for a quiet walk, a chance to clear your head, restful sleep in the dunes. You will awaken with a finer sense of your true self.

Let me invite you to go there now, to your own Karekare, and rediscover the flame within you.

# TEN GREAT
# SWIMS & WALKS

## THE SWIMS

### PARARAHA VALLEY AND GORGE

Walk either from Karekare or Whatipu to the mouth of the Pararaha Valley as far as the Muir rest shelter. You are halfway to a series of waterfalls and pools that are unsurpassed in the Waitakere Ranges. Follow the stream, crossing over it several times until you reach the logjam. To climb over the logs, you'll need to boulder-hop on the right hand side. Climb over the great kauri stumps with care and you will see your destination ahead. There's a 20-metre high cascade with a deep pool beneath. What a place for a refreshing dip on a summer's day, although by the time you have reached this spot, you may have already enjoyed some of the dozens of other small pools along the way. After heavy rainfall, the water level in this gorge can rise by over two metres, and within minutes, can become a raging torrent. If this happens, head for high ground and stay there.

### BLUE CANYON

Drive down the Lone Kauri Road to the carpark on the left, about 3 kilometres from the Piha road. Walk down the Odlin Track to the bottom. Continue over the stream south towards Huia. You will come to a major tributary and you are now in one of the great canyoning places in the ranges. This gorge contains beautiful waterfalls and pools, each one different in shape and size. Even the water itself feels softer here. Some of the pools are deep enough for you to be able to jump into, although of course you should always check the depth before risking your life from a high diving spot.

### THE OPAL POOLS

If you have swum in these before, you are already an authority on the great Waitakere swimming holes. If you haven't, go there by taking the track to the big Karekare falls and at the bottom of the track you will see the first of the pools. If you're afraid of eels, this is not the place to dangle your appendages. If you head up and around the hill, you'll discover more pools; each one seems to be better than the one before. A good way to explore the Opal Pools is to treat this adventure as a leisurely run, stopping at any pool that looks inviting, taking a cool plunge before running on to the next.

### UPPER PARARAHA

Just 50 metres from the carpark on the Lone Kauri Road, the Odlins Timber Track takes you down to the Pararaha Stream. Turn left at the

(LEFT) **PARARAHA GORGE BELOW THE LOGJAM.** (OPPOSITE) **DESCENDING INTO MERCER BAY DURING INAUGURAL AQUA-TERRA 24-HOUR ENDURANCE EVENT, APRIL 2000. COMPETITORS KAYAKED, WALKED, RAN, ABSEILED AND MOUNTAIN BIKED FROM WAINUI INLET ON KAIPARA HARBOUR TO FINISH AT PIHA.**

campsite at the bottom of the steep incline. To avoid getting lost, do not leave the stream. The waterfalls on the Upper Pararaha are high and truly magnificent. You can explore here all day. Each one cascades in a different way from any other. Some bounce and spray off luxuriant fern banks while others are like the Huka Falls in miniature. Above you, ancient kauri command the skyline. This walk is for experienced trampers only.

### THE COMPANY STREAM

To access the pools on this stream, you will need to walk down the La Trobe Track or the Taraire Track, then head towards the beach. The large pool below a cave, where prison escaper turned folk hero George Wilder hid out, is a real beauty. Wide and not very deep, it seems to be drenched in sun all day. Although there's a bit of bush-bashing required, it is advisable not to wander far from the track. You will be rewarded with a cool swim in one of the pools. Do not proceed further down the gorge, or you may face grave danger as there is a sudden drop over the Karekare Falls.

### THE KAREKARE STREAM

From the Piha Road, the Arthur Mead Track leads you to the headwaters of the Karekare Stream. This is a long walk and you will need to go around a large waterfall halfway down the track. You will see the wooden remains of the old dams from the milling days. The stream picks up more tributaries as it races towards the beach. It's always very cold, or refreshing to the hardy. It is not a safe and easy walk, but it's rewarding for the experienced tramper. The gorge below is private property, but there's plenty of public parkland to enjoy around here.

### WAIHUNA STREAM

After you've climbed the Zion Hill Track and you're dropping down to the Pararaha on the Buck Taylor Track, you'll find this stream in a dreamy glade. It's great place to rest and reflect. The pools are not deep enough to swim, but they are a wonderful place to soak your tired feet. The stream finally plunges into the Pararaha Valley. You can see the waterfall framed by the bush from the big sand dune on Taranaki Bay. I've always found it too difficult to access from the beach.

### A KAREKARE SECRET

At the bottom of the Cutting, McCready's Paddock and camping area (owned and operated by the Auckland Regional Council) leads to Skidmore, the old name for the kauri rail incline to the early mill. Keep to the stream, as the bush has now overgrown the track to the kauri, which fortunately are regenerating and are well worth seeking out. Your destination is a small waterfall and pool that is a hidden gem. It will take you 20 to 30 minutes to reach the steep flank of the Karekare Valley. Do not try to access this from the Horoeka Track, as this stream sits in an adjacent steep-sided valley.

### KAREKARE FALLS

This waterfall is a Karekare icon, much photographed and painted and a popular spot for wedding ceremonies. Below the shimmer of spray that in summer gives these falls additional appeal, is a fine shallow pool that is wonderful for children. Except when it is in flood, the waterfall is easily accessible from the picnic area via a short track that you can walk in a few minutes. The bottom of the pool is stony and you can swim or wade across it to the base of the cliff.

### KAREKARE BEACH

Finally, the beach itself. Karekare can be extremely dangerous and care must always be taken, even by the strongest swimmers. Always swim between the flags, as there are holes and fierce rips right along the beach. You will know the danger areas on a surf beach as these are the places where there is no surf. This is where large volumes of water are returning to the ocean, and the rip will quickly take you with it. If you are a keen surfer, Karekare offers wonderful waves. When swimming, always confront the surf head-on. Dive or duck

(LEFT AND OPPOSITE) **CANYONING IN THE RANGES HAS BECOME A POPULAR SPORT FOR THRILLSEEKERS.**

under all waves. The old rule, never turn your back on the surf, applies here, even on the calmest summer days. It can be dangerous to test your bravado beyond waist-deep water.

## THE WALKS

### HUIA RIDGE TRACK

This is one of my favourite long winter runs. If you're looking for a more demanding day's workout, this provides a round trip along the ridges all the way to Whatipu, then back along the beach to Karekare. A good place to start is from the Lone Kauri Road carpark 800m off the Piha Road, picking up the Huia Ridge Track here. At the junction of the Twin Peaks Track you can take a short detour to the highest point in the ranges, Te Toi o Kawharu (459m). Continue along the Huia Ridge Track under a lush fern canopy, to Karamatura Forks. Proceed to Orange Peel Corner, the junction of the Odlin Timber Track and the Walkers Ridge Track. The round trip will take you all day, so plan to set out early, take a good map, food and emergency supplies and tell a friend where you plan to go and when you expect to return.

### ZION HILL TRACK

Here's a fairly easy walk you can take up the hill behind the Pohutukawa Glade. The old fig tree at the start of the track was planted by John Bethell from a cutting taken from Samuel Marsden's Northland mission. The track itself follows the old Maori peacetime trail to the Pararaha. You'll find a few muddy spots during winter, but mostly the track is dry and although there are steps on the odd steep pinch, generally it's a comfortable grade. At the three lookouts, you can see how the wind has shaped the headlands. The bush not only bows to the ferocity of the winds, but lets itself be shaped, bent, twisted and bowed by it. The trees are stunted, clinging for life and to each other, daring not to stand upright. Maori called this phenomenon nga kaihau, the windeaters. At 262m you crest Mt Zion, where you can continue along the Zion Hill Track to the Pararaha or take the Zion Ridge Track that brings you out on Lone Kauri Road, or branches to the Pararaha via Buck Taylor Track (see map for options). Allow about three hours for the full round trip via the road or add an hour or so along the beach to the carpark.

### COMANS AND AHU AHU TRACKS

From the carpark, cross the old bridge by Winchelsea House and walk up Watchman Road to the end. There is a choice of a coastal

walk on Comans Track, or the inland Ahu Ahu Track, or simply combine them in a loop. My favourite is Comans, which is steep, dry and full of surprises. You will spot some locations from *The Piano* on the way. You can see all the way down the coast to the Manukau Heads. Below are the kelp beds of Union Bay. Along the ridge above the bay you reach Hikurangi (278m), the highest pa site on the west coast. Below you is where in Maori legend, Rangitoto was plucked from the sea. From here you can take the Mercer Bay Loop Walk which comes out on Log Race Road, or return to Karekare by turning right onto the easy and wide Ahu Ahu Track. Allow two and a half hours for the round trip. If you prefer more gentle uphill grades, take the Ahu Ahu Track first, returning via Comans. Fit runners could complete the loop in under an hour. Comans is not suitable for young children or nervous adults.

## MERCER BAY LOOP WALK

Allow at least an hour for this breezy invigorating winter walk. This track links from the Karekare carpark via Comans or Ahu Ahu tracks, or you can drive to the end of Log Race Road from the Piha Road and park at the site of the radar station. There are panoramic views up the coast towards the Kaipara. The well-maintained track follows the headland below the wartime radar station. Have a rest on the seat above the cliffs of Takatu Head. Continue around the northern clifftop of Mercer Bay. Easy for all ages and safe for children.

## HOROEKA TRACK

If you're starting the Horoeka from the bridge at the bottom of the Cutting by McCready's Paddock, don't be put off by the heart-stopping first 20 metres, as the track gets easier further up. Even so, it's a place for the fitter walker and is a fine training track for a marathoner or triathlete. Even at my fittest, I've never made it all the way up without stopping. The track at the top comes close to where the rollercoaster rail incline plunged into the Karekare Valley. The seaward valley below was known as Skidmore and was

extensively milled. At the top you can return via Ahu Ahu Track off Te Ahu Ahu Road, or the Piha Road and the Cutting. Schedule a recovery day after this one.

## CAVE ROCK TRACK

This is a good track to walk in summer or winter, sheltered from the howling southerly, but with breathtaking views of the valley and ranges and the beach. Start at the picnic area by the bridge, heading up through the trees on your left. At the lower end the track is steep, especially where it winds around a straggly old macrocarpa. This walk will bring you out on the rock buttress above the great cave where Ngapuhi invaders prepared the fire bundles that were used to drive out their victims. You can see where a jarrah channel took water to the power generator used by Winchelsea House. There is no safety fence, so extreme care must be taken at the top. Return by the same track for a round trip of about one hour. Not suitable for young children.

## LA TROBE AND TARAIRE TRACKS

This is a one-hour-plus return trip along an old linking route, possibly one of the oldest Maori peacetime tracks. Take the track opposite Winchelsea House. It leads from the lawn of the last house on the left going down the valley. It's well signposted. The first 10 minutes is quite steep, where the track is cut into the hillside with wooden steps. Below you, Winchelsea House looks splendid. Soon the track flattens out and you will come to an ancient puriri that's worth the effort of the climb. You pass a small inland pa site, crossing a tiny stream before climbing up to the junction with the Taraire Track. Stay on this track, and suddenly the vegetation changes to larger trees, giant rata vines and bulbous cliff-faces covered in moss and small ferns. Drop down to the Company Stream, crossing it near two kauri. This track will take you down to a water-fall, with spectacular views of the southern end of the beach on the way, allowing you to peer directly in to the big cave. Allow two hours. It is safe and ideal for children accompanied by adults.

### Odlin Timber Track

Park in the Lone Kauri carpark halfway down the road and walk back up the hill about 100 metres. You will see a signpost marking where the track enters the bush. From here it drops down to the Pararaha Stream. Well-maintained, with wooden steps, the track drops down gently to a small campsite at the junction of the Pararaha Stream and tributaries. It's a beautiful, peaceful spot, but you'll need a permit to camp there. This can be obtained at the Arataki Visitor Centre on Scenic Drive. A great adventure for children; 20 minutes there, or 45 minutes back.

### Muir Track

Named after Farmer Muir, whose shearing hut became overnight accommodation for generations of trampers, this goat track up the south side of the Pararaha will test you before rewarding with a view of the massive rock monolith that forms the entrance to the Pararaha gorge. The goats have gone now but the track is rocky and tight. Although safe, it's not recommended for young children. The Muir Track leads to the Gibbons Track, following the high cliff to Whatipu. In the early 20th century there was a perilous track out to a signal above Windy Point. The walkway has disappeared.

It's best to allow a full day for the round trip from Karekare. Take food, water, a map and emergency supplies, as it is a long walk back to Karekare.

### Coast Walk to Whatipu

Set out from Karekare on an outgoing tide and allow a full day for the return journey; or arrange with a friend to walk from the Whatipu end and swap cars later. This walk gives you nature in the raw: the roaring surf, the wind in your face, the endless expanse of sand, sky and sea. You'll probably feel like fossicking for shells, running over the dunes, or exploring the nooks and crannies of the headlands. It's a great place to take children, but dogs are prohibited as this is a breeding ground for dotterel and oystercatchers. In summer, the stretch of coast to the Pararaha Stream seems to shimmer in the heat and sometimes you can see mirages, images of water floating in the hazy distance. Out at the tideline the sand is flecked with beautiful patterns left by receding waves. You can get through a lot of film here if you're toting a camera. I'm always looking for relics of the *Orpheus* wreck along this coastline. Stay alert, because from time to time the coast reveals a secret from its history. Take food, water, map and emergency supplies.

(OPPOSITE) **WALKS IN THE WAITAKERE RANGES ARE WELL SIGNPOSTED; TAKE A MAP AND EMERGENCY SUPPLIES; KEEP TO THE TRACK AND YOU ARE UNLIKELY TO GET LOST.**

# PHOTOCREDITS

*All photographs are © Copyright the photographers, families, artists, magazines, companies or organisations credited here. Credits for photographs on text pages are listed clockwise from top left, unless otherwise stated.*

**COVER SECTION**
Front Cover: CPL, *New Zealand Surfing* magazine; Back Cover: Ted Scott Fotofile. Bob Harvey portait: Jane Ussher, *The Listener*. Inside Front Cover: Arne Loot, courtesy Don Binney (Private collection). Background photographs: Miles G. Hargest.

**CREDITS AND CONTENTS:**
Title Page: CPL, *New Zealand Surfing*. Page 2: Phil Morton. pp.3-8 Peter Siddell. pp.8-9; 10-11: CPL, *New Zealand Surfing*.

**APPROACHING KAREKARE**
pp.12-13: Phil Morton. p.14: Rex McLeod (b&w); Ted Scott Fotofile. p.15: Ted Scott Fotofile. p.16. Rex McLeod; David Galbraith; Colin Callan. p.18: Phil Morton; Phil Morton. p.19: Phil Morton; Ted Scott Fotofile. p.20: Rachel Mooney. p.21: Neil Roberts; Tim Chamberlain. p.22: Ted Scott Fotofile. p.23: Auckland Art Gallery Toi o Tamaki. p.24: Auckland Art Gallery Toi o Tamaki. p.25: Courtesy Mr & Mrs Pat Murphy; photograph Ted Scott Fotofile. pp.26-27: pp.22-23: Courtesy Stanley Palmer.

**THE LIVING PAST**
pp.28-29: Antoine Millett. p.30: Antoine Millett. p.31: Antoine Millett. p.32: Ted Scott Fotofile; Antoine Millett. p.33: Ted Scott Fotofile. p.34: all Ted Scott Fotofile. p.35: Antoine Millett. p.36: Antoine Millett. p.37: Antoine Millett; Ted Scott Fotofile. p.38: Ted Scott Fotofile. p.39: Ted Scott Fotofile. p.40: Ted Scott Fotofile; Bernard Makora. p.41: Bob Harvey. p.42: Ted Scott Fotofile; Auckland Central Library. p.43: Waitakere City Council albums; crinoline lifter: Vinod Patel. p.44: Waitakere City Council albums; Shaw family collection. p.45: Murdoch family album; Shaw family collection; Shaw family. Background: Bob Harvey. p.46: Shaw family collection; Badham album; Mudoch family album. p.47: Alexander Turnbull Library; Murdoch family album. p.48: Waitakere City Council albums; Murdoch family album. p.49: Auckland City Council. p.50: medals: Bill Haigh; crest: Vinod Patel. Foote: Vinod Patel. Small photograph r.h. side: author's archive. p.51: Murdoch family album (3 small images); Goodbear album (Alexander Turnbull Library). p.52: Vinod Patel; Gribble album (courtesy Robyn Agnew). p.53: both Murdoch family album. p.54: all Murdoch family album. p.55: Waitakere City Council albums; WCC; Alexander Turnbull Library; Casey family; courtesy Graham Stewart. p.56: Waitakere City Council albums; Margaret Clarke. p.57: Waitakere City Council albums; Bob Harvey; Ted Scott Fotofile. p.58: Waitakere City Council albums. p59: Dorothy Butler. p.60: Dorothy Butler; Oratia School; Dorothy Butler. p.61: Gribble album; Alexander Turnbull Library. p.62: Wally Badham, courtesy Lisa Fallow. p.63: Wally Badham; Waitakere City Council albums. p.64: Karekare Surf Club archives, courtesy Jim Ferguson. p65: Marge Wales, Karekare Surf Club archives, courtesy Jim Ferguson.

**NOSTALGIA TRACKS**
pp.66-67: Herbert Arthur, Waitakere City Council albums. p.68: Top: Dorothy Butler. Hatbox: Ted Scott Fotofile. Destination roll: Ted Scott Fotofile. p69: May family glass slide collection. Lower:

Murdoch family album. pp70-71: Dorothy Butler. p.72: portraits are all Badham family album, courtesy Lisa Fallow; vases and tapestry: Ted Scott Fotofile; p73: Sampler & album: Ted Scott Fotofile; courtesy Lisa Fallow. pp.74-75: Badham album courtesy Lisa Fallow (except seal, courtesy Dorothy Butler). p.76: all Badham family album courtesy Lisa Fallow. p.77: Badham family album, Lisa Fallow. Songbook: Ted Scott Fotofile. p.78: Badham family album, Lisa Fallow; Bob Harvey. p.79: Littlewood family. pp.80-81: Dorothy Butler. p.82: courtesy John Gow Galleries; p.83: Lithograph, Grove family; photograph and autograph album, courtesy June Fletcher (nee Farley). pp.84-85: Ted Scott Fotofile. p.86: Margaret Clarke collection. Clock: Ted Scott Fotofile. p.87: *New Zealand Herald*. p.88: Ted Scott Fotofile. p.89: Ted Scott Fotofile; Antoine Millett. p.90: Auckland War Memorial Museum; courtesy Auckland Art Gallery. p.91: Auckland Art Gallery Toi o Tamaki. p.92: Private collection, photograph courtesy Peter Webb Galleries. p93: all courtesy Baptist Tabernacle Archive. p.94: Blomfield painting reproduced from a printed copy. p.94-95: small Blomfield photographs and plaque: author's collection. p.96: portrait, courtesy Bruce Mai; Blomfield photographs. p.96-101: Waitakere City Council albums, except Rhoda photograph. p.98: courtesy Bruce Mai. p.102: Badham family album; Alexander Turnbull Library. p.103: Phil Morton; RNZAF Photographic Archive WH TIN 207, Frame 3131; p.104: Alexander Turnbull Library; RNZAF Photographic Archive WH TIN 207, Frame J5098; Ted Scott Fotofile. p.105: Jocelyn Carlin; Jocelyn Carlin; Ted Scott Fotofile.

**THE ENERGY OF WAVES**
pp.106-107: Ted Scott Fotofile. P.108: Medals are courtesy John Eden Badham. Badge is courtesy Karekare surf club archives. p.109: Oliver Strewe. p.110 top: Les Reed collection; rest of pp.110-111: Karekare Surf Club archives, courtesy Jim Ferguson, except badge, Bob Harvey. p.114: montage from top: *8 o'clock*; Karekare Surf Club archives; Liddle family. Small photograph top right: Harry Liddle collection; small lower right: Jim Ferguson. p.115: *New Zealand Herald*; belt: Vinod Patel; Shanahan family collection; surf club boat: Karekare Surf Club archives. p.116: all Glen Jowitt. p.117: Casey family collection. p.118: all Ted Scott Fotofile. p.119: Ted Scott Fotofile; rest are Antoine Millett. p.120: drinking pics: Bob Harvey; Ted Scott Fotofile; Bob Harvey. p.122: Marge Wales; Ted Scott Fotofile. p.123: Ted Scott Fotofile; *New Zealand Observer*. pp.124-125: CPL, *New Zealand Surfing*. p.126: CPL, *New Zealand Surfing*; courtesy Bishop Museum, Honolulu. p.127 & following, surfboard manufacturer logos: courtesy Tony Reid, The Longboard Shop. p.127: Auckland City Libraries (NZ). p.128: Bob Harvey (board); *New Zealand Herald;* Liddle family. p.129: Kelvin Lane. p.130-131: adv and surfing magazine covers: courtesy Mark Thomson. p.131: CPL, *New Zealand Surfing*. p.132: courtesy Mark Thomson; Glen Jowitt. p.133: courtesy Tony Reid, The Longboard Shop; Jocelyn Carlin. p.134-135: CPL, *New Zealand Surfing*. p.135: logos: Tony Reid, The Longboard Shop. p.136: Ted Scott Fotofile. p.138, 139, 140: from glass slides, Bruce Mai. p.141: cartoon and badge, courtesy Karekare Surf Club archives. Jantzen adv, Robert Newton. p.142: Ted Scott Fotofile; Bob Harvey. p.143: Bob Harvey; Antoine Millett; Bob Harvey; Gribble family album. p.144: Bob Harvey; Walker family album, courtesy Derek Littlewood; Ted Scott Fotofile. p.145: Mrs J. McShane; Ted Scott Fotofile. p.146: Marti Friedlander; Marti Friedlander. p.147: Antoine Millett. p.148: Martin Hill. p.149: Derek Henderson. p.150: Phil Morton. p.151: Phil Morton; Ted Scott Fotofile. p.152: Phil Morton; Phil Morton.

p.153: Bernard Schofield; Phil Morton; Phil Morton. p.154: all Bernard Schofield except lower left, Ted Scott Fotofile. p.155: courtesy Milford Galleries; Paddy Ryan, Ryan Photographic; Paddy Ryan, Ryan Photographic. pp.156-159: Dr Peter Madison found meiofauna; Hort Research electron microscope photographs.

**PEOPLE OF THE VALLEY**
pp.160-161: Gribble album, courtesy Robyn Agnew. p.162: Glen Jowitt. p.163: Leah Mulgrew. p.164: Antoine Millett. p.165: Bob Harvey; Antoine Millett. p.166-167: Liddle family album. p.168-169: Browne family album, courtesy Margaret Clarke. p.170: top right courtesy Dorothy Butler; others are Browne family album. p.171: *New Zealand Herald*; Walker family album, courtesy Kerry Littlewood. p.172: Miles G. Hargest. architectural drawing, courtesy Richard Priest. p.173: Bob Harvey. p.174-175 courtesy Justin Summerton. Summerton portrait: Nerissa Sowerby. p.176: Antoine Millett; Ted Scott Fotofile, courtesy Tony Ogle. p.177: Bob Harvey; Bob Harvey; Antoine Millett. p.179: Jane Ussher, *The Listener*. p.180: Antoine Millett; drawings, courtesy Richard Priest. p.181: Patrick Reynolds, *NZ House & Garden*. p.182: *NZ House & Garden*. p.183: both Tim Chamberlain. p.184: courtesy Olivia Sheehan. p.185: Antoine Millet; Miles G. Hargest. p.186: courtesy Niki Caro. p.187: Becky Nunes. p.188: John Madden painting: Chris Hoult, courtesy the artist; Ellen La Trobe: courtesy Susan Smith; Martin Hill. p.190: Martin Hill. pp.190-191: all Martin Hill. pp.192-193: courtesy Peter Siddell. p.194: Bob Harvey; p.195: Bob Harvey; Antoine Millett. p.196: Ted Scott Fotofile. pp.197-199: courtesy Dean Buchanan, thanks to Helga Strewe. p.200: Antoine Millett. p.201: Antoine Millett. p.202: Antoine Millett. pp.202-203, glass bowls: Haru Sameshima, La Gonda Studio, from *Ann Robinson, Casting Light: A Survey of Glass Castings 1981-1997*, published by Dowse Art Museum 1998; courtesy Ann Robinson. p.204-205: *Greenstone* stills: Chris Bayley, courtesy Communicado; p.204: He Taonga Films for *Feathers of Peace*; p.206-207: courtesy Grant Matthews. p.207: trailer shots courtesy Barry Everard. Waka prop: Ted Scott Fotofile. pp.208 & 209: *Greenstone* stills: Chris Bayley, courtesy Communicado. p.209: John Miller; courtesy Don Selwyn, He Taonga Films. p.210: courtesy Tourism New Zealand. p.211: courtesy Dale Spencer, The Media Edge. p.210 & 211, Molenberg: courtesy Colenso BBDO. p.212: Craig Owen, *Pavement*. p.213: p.212: Derek Henderson, *Pavement*. p.214: Ted Scott Fotofile. p.215: courtesy Capitol Records; Bob Harvey (house & pig). p.216: Ted Scott Fotofile; thanks to Te Vaka and Spirit of Play Productions. p.217: *Pavement*; John Gow, John Leech Gallery; Murray Thom marketing. p.218: Kirsty Russell; Iain Anderson; p.219: Iain Anderson; Photoshop blend by Heather Ball. p.220: Ted Scott Fotofile; Ted Scott Fotofile; Glen Jowitt. p.221: all Jocelyn Carlin. p.222: both Ted Scott Fotofile. p.223: both Jocelyn Carlin, with thanks to Virginia King. pp.224-225: courtesy Gretchen Albrecht.

**INTO THE NIGHT**
pp.226-229: Antoine Millett. p.230-231: Arne Loot, courtesy Richard McWhannell. p.232: Chris Hoult (Madden and kiln); Antoine Millett (Madden). p.233: Jenny Scown Photography, from *Filling The Frame*, Wendyl Nissen and Jenny Scown, Reed Publishing, 1992. p.234: Ted Scott Fotofile. Signpost: Tim Chamberlain. p.235: Michael Bradley. p.236-237: Julien Senamaud. p.238: Ted Scott Fotofile; Tim Chamberlain. p.239: all Ted Scott Fotofile. p.240: Glen Jowitt. Thanks to all those who generously provided photographs that unfortunately did not make final selection.